Microsoft®
PROJECT 98
Step by Step

Other titles in the *Step by Step* series:

*Microsoft Access 97 Step by Step

*Microsoft Excel 97 Step by Step

*Microsoft Excel 97 Step by Step, Advanced Topics

*Microsoft FrontPage 97 Step by Step

 Microsoft Internet Explorer 3.0 Step by Step

 Microsoft Office 97 Integration Step by Step

*Microsoft Outlook 97 Step by Step

*Microsoft PowerPoint 97 Step by Step

 Microsoft Team Manager 97 Step by Step

 Microsoft Windows 95 Step by Step

 Microsoft Windows NT Workstation version 4.0 Step by Step

*Microsoft Word 97 Step by Step

*Microsoft Word 97 Step by Step, Advanced Topics

Step by Step books are also available for the Microsoft Office 95 programs.

*These books are approved couseware for Microsoft Office
User Specialist (MSOUS) exams. For more details about the
MSOUS program, see page xix.

Microsoft®

PROJECT 98

Step by Step

Microsoft Press

PUBLISHED BY
Microsoft Press
A Division of Microsoft Corporation
One Microsoft Way
Redmond, Washington 98052-6399

Library of Congress Cataloging-in-Publication Data
Microsoft Software Package 1 Step-by-Step / Catapult, Inc.
    p.   cm.
    Includes index.
    ISBN 1-57231-605-5
1. Microsoft Project for Windows   2. Industrial project management--Computer
programs   I. Catapult, Inc. II. Series: Step b6 step (Redmond, Wash.)
HD69.P75M5336   1997
658.4'04'02855369--dc21   97-27389
                                                      CIP

Printed and bound in the United States of America.

1 2 3 4 5 6 7 8 9 WCWC 2 1 0 9 8 7

Distributed to the book trade in Canada by Macmillan of Canada, a division of Canada
Publishing Corporation.

A CIP catalogue record for this book is available from the British Library.

Microsoft Press books are available through booksellers and distributors worldwide. For further
information about international editions, contact your local Microsoft Corporation office. Or
contact Microsoft Press International directly at fax (425) 936-7329. Visit our Web site at
mspress.microsoft.com.

For Catapult, Inc.
Managing Editor: Cynthia Slotvig
Writer: Michele Gordon
Project Editor: Holly Knobler
Production Manager: Lori Kenyon
Technical Editor: Jan Gray
Copy Editor: Debbie Wall
Production/Layout: Carolyn Thornley, Editor;
David R. Neeley
Indexer: Julie Kawabata

For Microsoft Press
Acquisitions Editor: Susanne M. Freet
Project Editor: Laura Sackerman

Catapult, Inc. & Microsoft Press

Microsoft Project 98 Step by Step has been created by the professional trainers and writers at Catapult, Inc., to the exacting standards you've come to expect from Microsoft Press. Together, we are pleased to present this self-paced training guide, which you can use individually or as part of a class.

Catapult, Inc. is a software training company with years of experience in PC and Macintosh instruction. Catapult's exclusive Performance-Based Training system is available in Catapult training centers across North America and at customer sites. Based on the principles of adult learning, Performance-Based Training ensures that students leave the classroom with confidence and the ability to apply skills to real-world scenarios. *Microsoft Project 98 for Windows Step by Step* incorporates Catapult's training expertise to ensure that you'll receive the maximum return on your training time. You'll focus on the skills that can increase your productivity the most while working at your own pace and convenience.

Microsoft Press is the book publishing division of Microsoft Corporation. The leading publisher of information about Microsoft products and services, Microsoft Press is dedicated to providing the highest quality computer books and multimedia training and reference tools that make using Microsoft software easier, more enjoyable, and more productive.

Table of Contents

Table of Contents

Part 4   Managing a Project

Part 5   Using Advanced Project Features

Table of Contents

QuickLook Guide

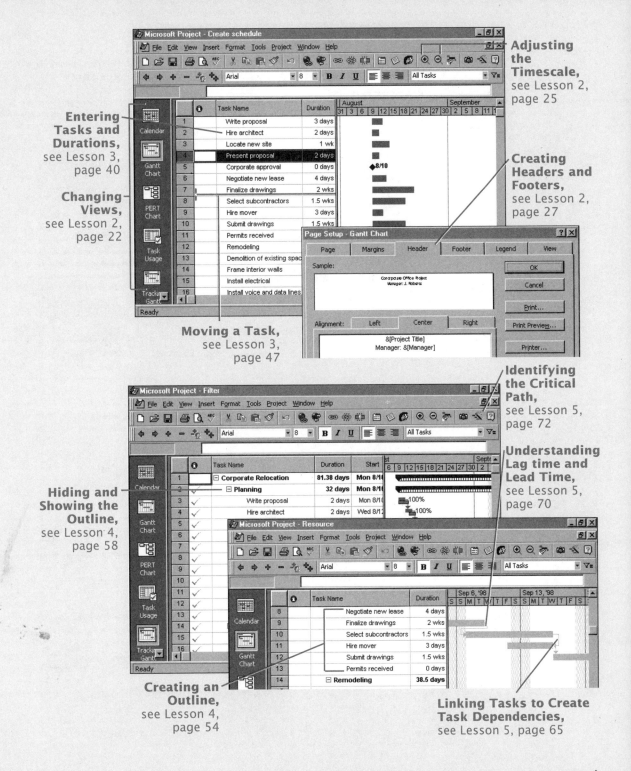

Entering Tasks and Durations, see Lesson 3, page 40

Changing Views, see Lesson 2, page 22

Adjusting the Timescale, see Lesson 2, page 25

Creating Headers and Footers, see Lesson 2, page 27

Moving a Task, see Lesson 3, page 47

Hiding and Showing the Outline, see Lesson 4, page 58

Identifying the Critical Path, see Lesson 5, page 72

Understanding Lag time and Lead Time, see Lesson 5, page 70

Creating an Outline, see Lesson 4, page 54

Linking Tasks to Create Task Dependencies, see Lesson 5, page 65

*Quick*Look Guide

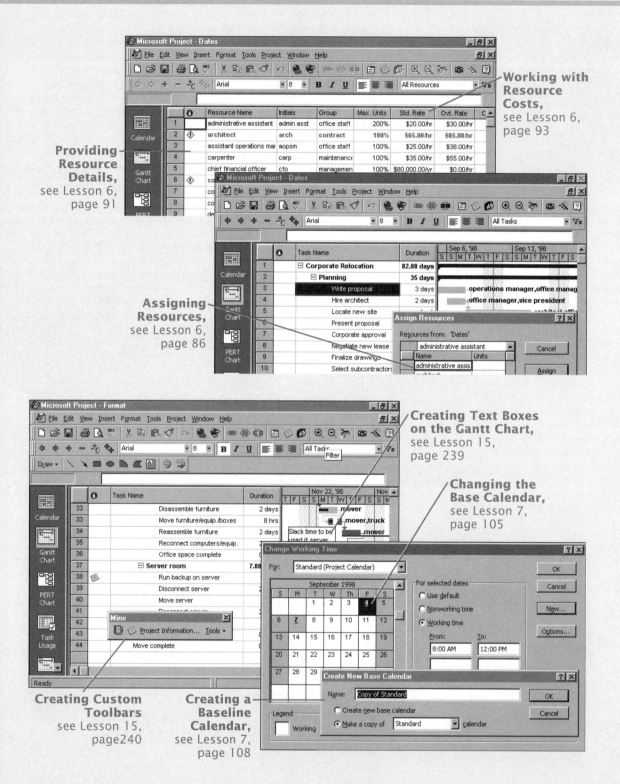

Providing Resource Details, see Lesson 6, page 91

Working with Resource Costs, see Lesson 6, page 93

Assigning Resources, see Lesson 6, page 86

Creating Text Boxes on the Gantt Chart, see Lesson 15, page 239

Changing the Base Calendar, see Lesson 7, page 105

Creating Custom Toolbars see Lesson 15, page240

Creating a Baseline Calendar, see Lesson 7, page 108

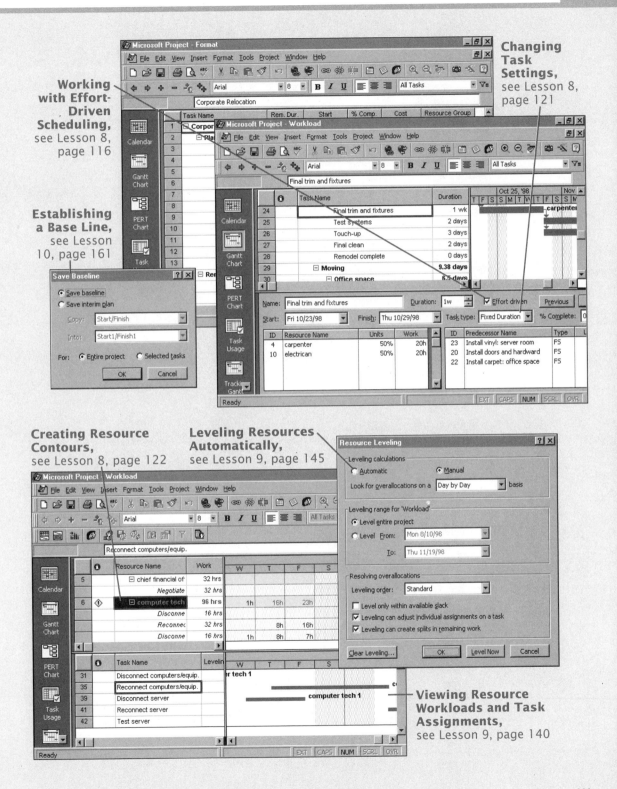

Working with Effort-Driven Scheduling, see Lesson 8, page 116

Changing Task Settings, see Lesson 8, page 121

Establishing a Base Line, see Lesson 10, page 161

Creating Resource Contours, see Lesson 8, page 122

Leveling Resources Automatically, see Lesson 9, page 145

Viewing Resource Workloads and Task Assignments, see Lesson 9, page 140

*Quick*Look Guide

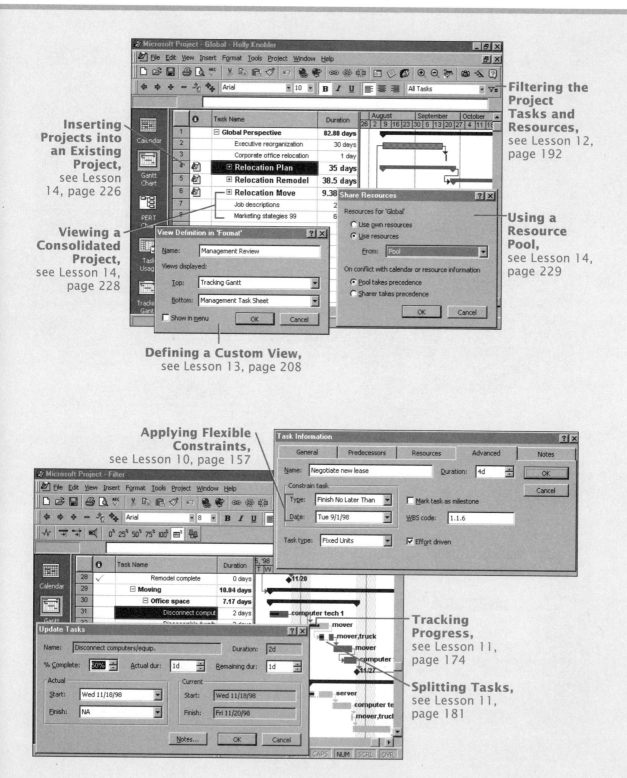

Inserting Projects into an Existing Project, see Lesson 14, page 226

Viewing a Consolidated Project, see Lesson 14, page 228

Filtering the Project Tasks and Resources, see Lesson 12, page 192

Using a Resource Pool, see Lesson 14, page 229

Defining a Custom View, see Lesson 13, page 208

Applying Flexible Constraints, see Lesson 10, page 157

Tracking Progress, see Lesson 11, page 174

Splitting Tasks, see Lesson 11, page 181

Finding Your Best Starting Point

Microsoft Project 98 is a powerful project management program that you can use to efficiently plan, manage, and communicate a project schedule and information. With *Microsoft Project 98 Step by Step*, you'll quickly and easily learn how to use Project to get your work done.

 IMPORTANT This book is designed for use with Microsoft Project 98 for the Windows 95 and Windows NT version 4.0 operating systems. To find out what software you're running, you can check the product package or you can start the software, click the Help menu at the top of the screen, and then click About Microsoft Project. If your software is not compatible with this book, a Step by Step book for your software is probably available. Many of the Step by Step titles are listed on the second page of this book. If the book you want isn't listed, please visit our World Wide Web site at http://mspress.microsoft.com/ or call 1-800-MSPRESS for more information.

Finding Your Best Starting Point in This Book

This book is designed for readers learning Microsoft Project 98 for the first time and for more experienced readers who want to learn and use the new features in Project 98. Use the following table to find your best starting point in this book.

If you are	Follow these steps
New... to computers to graphical (as opposed to text-only) computer programs to Windows 95 or Windows NT	**1** Install the practice files as described in "Using the Microsoft Project 98 Step by Step CD-ROM." **2** Become acquainted with the Windows 95 or Windows NT operating system and how to use the online Help system by working through Appendix A, "If You Are New to Windows 95, Windows NT, or Microsoft Project 98." **3** Learn basic skills for using Microsoft Project 98 by working sequentially through Lessons 1 through 11. Then, you can work through Lessons 12 through 15 in any order.
Switching... from Sure Track from On Target from Time Line	**1** Install the practice files as described in "Using the Microsoft Project 98 Step by Step CD-ROM." **2** Learn basic skills for using Microsoft Project 98 by working sequentially through Lessons 1 through 11. Then, you can work through Lessons 12 through 15 in any order.
Upgrading... from Project for Windows 95	**1** Learn about the new features in this version of the program that are covered in this book by reading through the following section, "New Features in Project 98." **2** Install the practice files as described in "Using the Microsoft Project 98 Step by Step CD-ROM." **3** Complete the lessons that cover the topics you need. You can use the table of contents and the QuickLook Guide to locate information about general topics. You can use the index to find information about a specific topic or a feature from the previous version of Project.
Referencing... this book after working through the lessons	**1** Use the index to locate information about specific topics, and use the table of contents and the QuickLook Guide to locate information about general topics. **2** Read the Lesson Summary at the end of each lesson for a brief review of the major tasks in the lesson. The Lesson Summary topics are listed in the same order as they are presented in the lesson.

Microsoft Office User Specialist Program

About 90 percent of the Fortune 500 companies use Microsoft Office products—so chances are very good that you are one of the many people using Office to get your work done. You might even know more about how to use Office products than most people. Now you can prove it—and give yourself and your organization a competitive edge.

The Microsoft Office User Specialist (MOUS) program provides a benchmark to certify users' skills in using Office. Customers requested a program like this to measure their Office skills and to prove their ability to get the most out of Office. Certification is available for the following Office programs at both Proficient and Expert User levels:

Software	Proficient level	Expert level
Microsoft Word 97	✔	✔
Microsoft Excel 97	✔	✔
Microsoft Access 97		✔
Microsoft PowerPoint 97		✔
Microsoft Outlook 97		✔
Microsoft FrontPage 98	✔	✔
Microsoft Project 98		✔

In addition, a **Microsoft Office Expert** level certification is available. This level indicates that you have attained Expert User status in each of the five core Office 97 programs and have passed the Office 97 Integration exam, demonstrating your ability to integrate these programs. This is the highest level of certification available.

Microsoft Press offers the following books in the *Step by Step* series as approved courseware for the MSOUS exams:

Proficient level:

Microsoft Word 97 Step by Step, ISBN: 1-57231-313-7

Microsoft Excel 97 Step by Step, ISBN: 1-57231-314-5

Microsoft FrontPage 98 Step by Step, ISBN: 1-57231-636-5

Expert level:

Microsoft Word 97 Step by Step, Complete Course, ISBN: 1-57231-579-2

Microsoft Excel 97 Step by Step, Complete Course, ISBN: 1-57231-580-6

Microsoft Access 97 Step by Step, ISBN: 1-57231-316-1

Microsoft PowerPoint 97 Step by Step, ISBN: 1-57231-315-3

Microsoft Outlook 97 Step by Step, ISBN: 1-57231-382-X

Microsoft FrontPage 98 Step by Step, ISBN: 1-57231-636-5

Microsoft Project 98 Step by Step, ISBN: 1-57231-605-5

Tests are conducted at Authorized Certification Testing (ACT) Centers throughout the United States. The U.S. estimated retail price is $50. Ask your ACT Center for details. To find the one nearest you, call (800) 933-4493 in the U.S.

For more information, visit the MSOUS World Wide Web site at http://www.microsoft.com/office/train_cert/

New Features in Project 98

For additional information on new features in Project, type What's New in the Help Index.

The following table lists the major new features in Microsoft Project 98 that are covered in this book. The table shows the lesson in which you can learn how to use each feature. You can also use the index to find specific information about a feature or a task you want to do.

To learn how to use	See
Web capabilities	Lesson 2 and Lesson 3
Multiple critical paths	Lesson 5
Task Usage and Resource Usage views	Lesson 6, Lesson 8, and Lesson 9
Variable pay rates	Lesson 6
Cost rate tables	Lesson 6
Effort-driven scheduling	Lesson 8
Task type settings	Lesson 8
Resource contouring	Lesson 8
Improved resource leveling	Lesson 9
Multiple baselines (interim plans)	Lesson 10
Task splitting	Lesson 11
Status date	Lesson 11
Enhanced earned value analysis	Lesson 11
Progress lines	Lesson 11
AutoFilters	Lesson 12
Inserting projects	Lesson 14
Outline consolidated projects	Lesson 14
Improved resource pooling	Lesson 14

To learn how to use	See
Cross-project linking	Lesson 14
Improved workgroup features	Appendix B
View Bar	Throughout
Indicators	Throughout

Corrections, Comments, and Help

Every effort has been made to ensure the accuracy of this book and the contents of the practice files CD-ROM. Microsoft Press provides corrections and additional content for its books through the World Wide Web at

http://mspress.microsoft.com/mspress/support/

If you have comments, questions, or ideas regarding this book or the practice files CD-ROM, please send them to us.

Send e-mail to:

mspinput@microsoft.com

Or, send postal mail to:

Microsoft Press
Attn: Step by Step Series Editor
One Microsoft Way
Redmond, WA 98052-6399

Please note that support for the Project 98 software product itself is not offered through the above addresses. For help using Project 98, you can call Microsoft Project 98 Technical Support at (425) 635-7155 on weekdays between 6 AM and 6 PM Pacific time.

Visiting Our World Wide Web Site

We invite you to visit the Microsoft Press World Wide Web site. You can visit us at the following location:

http://mspress.microsoft.com/

You'll find descriptions for all of our books, information about ordering titles, notice of special features and events, additional content for Microsoft Press books, and much more.

You can also find out the latest in software developments and news from Microsoft Corporation by visiting the following World Wide Web site:

http://www.microsoft.com/

We look forward to your visit on the Web!

Installing and Using the Practice Files

The CD-ROM inside the back cover of this book contains practice files that you'll use as you perform the exercises in the book. For example, when you're learning how to assign resources to tasks, you'll open one of the practice files—a project file with tasks and dependencies—and then use the Assign Resources dialog box and Resource Sheet. By using the practice files, you won't waste time creating the samples used in the lessons—instead, you can concentrate on learning how to use Project. With the files and the step-by-step instructions in the lessons, you'll also learn by doing, which is an easy and effective way to acquire and remember new skills.

The CD-ROM also contains audiovisual files that demonstrate how to perform some of the more complicated tasks in this book. With the audiovisual files, you can see how the task is completed before you try it.

IMPORTANT Before you break the seal on the practice CD-ROM package, be sure that this book matches your version of the software. This book is designed for use with Microsoft Project 98 for the Windows 95 and Windows NT version 4.0 operating systems. To find out what software you're running, you can check the product package or you can start the software, and then on the Help menu at the top of the screen, click About Microsoft Project. If your program is not compatible with this book, a Step by Step book matching your software is probably available. Many of the Step by Step titles are listed on the second page of this book. If the book you want isn't listed, please visit our World Wide Web site at http://mspress.microsoft.com/ or call 1-800-MSPRESS for more information.

Install the practice files on your computer

Follow these steps to install the practice files on your computer's hard disk so that you can use them with the exercises in this book.

> **NOTE** If you are new to Windows 95 or Windows NT, you might want to work through Appendix A, "If You Are New to Windows 95, Windows NT, or Microsoft Project 98," before installing the practice files.

In Windows 95, you will also be prompted for a username and password when starting Windows 95 if your computer is configured for user profiles.

Close

1 If your computer isn't on, turn it on now.

2 If you're using Windows NT, press CTRL+ALT+DEL to display a dialog box asking for your username and password. If you are using Windows 95, you will see this dialog box if your computer is connected to a network. If you don't know your username or password, contact your system administrator for assistance.

3 Type your username and password in the appropriate boxes, and click OK. If you see the Welcome dialog box, click the Close button.

4 Remove the CD-ROM from the package inside the back cover of this book.

5 Insert the CD-ROM in your CD-ROM drive.

6 On the taskbar at the bottom of your screen, click the Start button.

The Start menu is displayed.

7 On the Start menu, click Run.

The Run dialog box appears.

8 In the Open box, type **d:setup** (or replace the letter "d" with the appropriate CD-ROM drive letter). Don't add spaces as you type.

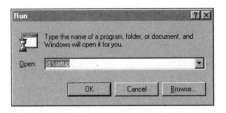

9 Click OK, and then follow the directions on the screen.

The Setup program window opens with recommended options preselected for you. For best results in using the practice files with this book, accept these preselected settings.

10 When the files have been installed, remove the CD from your drive and replace it in the package inside the back cover of the book.

A folder called Project SBS Practice has been created on your hard disk, and the practice files have been put in that folder.

Microsoft
Press
Welcome

NOTE In addition to installing the practice files, the Setup program has created a shortcut on your Desktop. If your computer is set up to connect to the Internet, you can double-click the Microsoft Press Welcome shortcut to visit the Microsoft Press Web site. You can also connect to this Web site directly at http://mspress.microsoft.com/

Install the Microsoft Network

The companion CD also contains the client software for The Microsoft Network (MSN), Microsoft's Internet online service. Install MSN now to get *one month free* unlimited access to MSN and the Internet. To try MSN, follow these steps:

1 On the taskbar at the bottom of your screen, click the Start button, and then click Run.

2 Type **d:\MSN\Msnstart.exe** (or, if your CD-ROM drive uses a drive letter other than "d," substitute the correct drive letter).

3 Click OK, and then follow the directions on the screen to install MSN.

4 When prompted for a registration number, type **9126**

For help with MSN, call Technical Support at (425) 635-7019 (English) or (425) 635-7020 (French) in the U.S. or Canada.

Using the Practice Files

Each lesson in this book explains when and how to use any practice files for that lesson. When it's time to use a practice file, the book will list instructions on how to open the file. The lessons are built around scenarios that simulate a real work environment, so you can easily apply the skills you learn to your own work. For the scenarios in this book, imagine that you're the Project Manager and scheduler for the corporate office relocation project and the annual shareholders meeting project. As the Project Manager, you are in charge of the planning, coordination, and management of all tasks and resources using Project as your management tool. As the scheduler for both projects, you will also input all information into Project.

The screen illustrations in this book might look different from what you see on your computer, depending on how your computer is set up. To help make your screen match the illustrations in this book, please follow the instructions in Appendix D, "Matching the Exercises," located on the CD-ROM.

For those of you who like to know all the details, here's a list of the files included on the practice CD-ROM:

File name	Description
Lesson 1	
None	
Lesson 2	
Meeting	A project file for the Annual Shareholders Meeting held in 1997.
Lesson 3	
None	
Lesson 4	
Outline	A project file with only a task list for the corporate office relocation project.
Lesson 5	
Linking	A project file with an outlined task list for the corporate office relocation project.
Review & Practice 1	
Review1	A project file containing a partial task list for the shareholders meeting project.
Lesson 6	
Resource	A project file with an outlined task list, and task dependencies for the corporate office relocation project.

File name	Description
Costs	A project file with an outlined task list, task dependencies, and resource assignments for the corporate office relocation project.

Lesson 7

Dates	A project file with an outlined task list, task dependencies, resource assignments, and costs for the corporate office relocation project.

Lesson 8

Schedule	A project file with an outlined task list, task dependencies, resource assignments, costs, and calendars for the corporate office relocation project.

Review & Practice 2

Review2	A project file with an outlined task list, and task dependencies for the shareholders meeting project.

Lesson 9

Workload	A project file with an outlined task list, task dependencies, resource assignments, costs, calendars, and task setting adjustments for the corporate office relocation project.

Lesson 10

Restricts	A project file with an outlined task list, task dependencies, resource assignments, costs, calendars, and task setting adjustments. All resource overallocations have been resolved for the corporate office relocation project.

Review & Practice 3

Review3	A project file with an outlined task list, task dependencies, resource assignments, costs, calendars, and task setting adjustments for the shareholders meeting project.

Lesson 11

Track	A project file with an outlined task list, task dependencies, resource assignments, costs, calendars, and task setting adjustments. All resource overallocations have been resolved, task constraints have been applied, and a baseline has been set for the corporate office relocation project.

File name	Description
Lines	A project file with a set baseline. Tracking progress has been entered through a status date for the corporate office relocation project.
Lesson 12	
Filter	A project file with a set baseline, and tracked progress for the corporate office relocation project.
Lesson 13	
Custom	A project file with a set baseline, tracked progress, and custom filters for the corporate office relocation project.
Review & Practice 4	
Review4	A project file with a set baseline for the share holders meeting project.
Lesson 14	
Global	A project file with several tasks, and no re-source assignments to use as a consolidated project.
Move	A project file of the tasks for the moving phase of the corporate office relocation. The task list has been outlined and dependencies have been established.
Plan	A project file of the tasks for the planning phase of the corporate office relocation. The task list has been outlined and dependencies have been established.
Pool	A project file containing only resource information to use as a resource pool for the corporate office relocation project.
Remodel	A project file of the tasks for the remodeling phase of the corporate office relocation. The task list has been outlined and dependencies have been established.
Lesson 15	
Format	A project file with a set baseline, tracked progress, and custom filters, tables, views, and reports for the corporate office relocation project.

File name	Description
Review & Practice 5	
Details	A project file of the tasks for the meeting details phase of the shareholders meeting. The task list has been outlined and dependencies have been established.
Letter	A project file of the tasks for the notification letter phase of the shareholders meeting. The task list has been outlined and dependencies have been established.
Meetpool	A project file containing only resource information to use as a resource pool for the shareholders meeting project.
Planning	A project file of the tasks for the preliminary planning phase of the shareholders meeting. The task list has been outlined and dependencies have been established.
Review5	A project file with several tasks and no resource assignments to use as a project consolidation.
Audiovisual Files	Files that demonstrate how to perform some of the more complicated tasks in this book.
MSN	Files to install an online service that can be used with Windows 95. An icon for The Microsoft Network is located on the Desktop. You double-click the icon to sign up for The Microsoft Network service.
Appendix D	
"Matching the Exercises"	Instructions to help you make your screen match the illustrations in this book.
Glossary.txt	Definitions of the important terms used in this book.

Using the Audiovisual Files

Throughout the book, you will see icons for audiovisual files for a particular exercise. Use the following steps to run the audiovisual files.

1   Insert the CD-ROM in your CD-ROM drive.

2   On the taskbar, click Start, point to Programs, and then click Windows Explorer.

    If you are using Windows NT, click Windows NT Explorer.

3   In the All Folders area, click on drive D (or the appropriate CD-ROM drive letter).

    The contents of the CD-ROM are displayed.

4   In the Contents of 'D:\' area, double-click the AVI Files folder.

    The contents of the AVI Files folder are displayed.

5   Double-click the audiovisual file you need.

    Camcorder runs the video of the exercise. After the video is finished, Camcorder closes, and you return to Windows Explorer.

6   Close Windows Explorer, and return to the exercise in the book.

Deleting the Practice Files

Use the following steps when you want to delete the shortcuts added to your Desktop and the practice files added to your hard drive by the Step by Step Setup program.

1   Click Start, point to Programs, and then click Windows Explorer.

    If you are using Windows NT, click Windows NT Explorer.

2   In the All Folders, scroll up, and click Desktop.

    The contents of your Desktop are displayed.

3   Click the Microsoft Press Welcome shortcut icon, and press DELETE.

    If you are prompted to confirm the deletion, click Yes. The Microsoft Press Welcome shortcut icon is removed from your computer.

4   In the All Folders area, click drive C.

    The contents of your hard drive are displayed. If you installed your practice files on another drive, view the contents of that drive.

5   Click the Project SBS Practice folder, and then press DELETE.

    If you are prompted to confirm the deletion, click Yes. The practice files are removed from you computer.

6 In the Contents area, double-click the Windows folder, and then double-click the Favorites folder.

7 Click the Project SBS Practice shortcut icon, and then press DELETE.

If you are prompted to confirm the deletion, click Yes. All practice files installed on your computer are now deleted.

Need Help with the Practice Files?

Every effort has been made to ensure the accuracy of this book and the contents of the CD-ROM. If you do run into a problem, Microsoft Press provides corrections for its books through the World Wide Web at

http://mspress.microsoft.com/mspress/support/

We also invite you to visit our main Web page at

http://mspress.microsoft.com/

You'll find descriptions for all of our books, information about ordering titles, notices of special features and events, additional content for Microsoft Press books, and much more.

Conventions Used in This Book

You can save time when you use this book by understanding, before you start the lessons, how instructions, keys to press, and so on are shown in the book. Please take a moment to read the following list, which also points out helpful features of the book that you might want to use.

 NOTE   If you are unfamiliar with Windows, Windows NT, or mouse terminology, see Appendix A, "If You Are New to Windows 95, Windows NT, or Microsoft Project 98."

Conventions

- Hands-on exercises for you to follow are given in numbered lists of steps (1, 2, and so on). An arrowhead bullet (➤) indicates an exercise that has only one step.
- Text that you are to type appears in **bold**.
- A plus sign (+) between two key names means that you must press those keys at the same. For example, "Press ALT+TAB" means that you hold down the ALT key while you press TAB.
- The following icons identify the different types of supplementary material:

	Notes labeled	Alert you to
	Note	Additional information for a step.
	Tip	Suggested additional methods for a step or helpful hints.
	Important	Essential information that you should check before continuing with the lesson.
	Troubleshooting	Possible error messages or computer difficulties and their solutions.
	Warning	Possible data loss and tells you how to proceed safely.
	Demonstration	Skills that are demonstrated in audiovisual files available on the Microsoft Project 98 Step by Step CD-ROM.

Other Features of This Book

- You can learn about techniques that build on what you learned in a lesson by trying the optional One Step Further exercise at the end of the lesson.

- You can get a quick reminder of how to perform the tasks you learned by reading the Lesson Summary at the end of a lesson.

- You can quickly determine what online Help topics are available for additional information by referring to the Help topics listed at the end of each lesson. The Help system provides a complete online reference to Microsoft Project 98. To learn more about online Help, see Appendix A, "If You Are New to Windows 95, Windows NT, or Microsoft Project 98."

- You can practice the major skills presented in the lessons by working through the Review & Practice sections at the end of each part.

- You can view audiovisual demonstrations of some of the more complicated tasks in Project from the CD-ROM that came with this book. To learn how to access these demonstrations see "Installing and Using the Practice Files."

Part

1

Learning the Basics of Project Scheduling

Understanding Project Scheduling

Estimated time

25 min.

In this lesson you will learn how to:

- Define project goals.
- Identify the parts of a project.
- Understand project management terms and concepts.

Before you begin a *project*, you need to define the project goal and then determine what *tasks* you need to complete in order to meet the goal. Once you have defined the project goal and determined each task, the next step is to identify who will perform each task, when each task will begin, and how long each task will take to complete. In addition, during the planning phase you should determine how much the project will cost . Once the project is underway, it's a good idea to track the progress of each task. For example, keep track of when the task actually begins, when it is completed, and when there are problems. As each task occurs, adjustments might need to be made for unexpected events, such as a worker's illness or materials not delivered on time. Then, the schedule needs to be adjusted and the information communicated to everyone involved.

As you can see, managing a project requires the use of many different management and coordination skills. It can be a challenge to keep track of all aspects of the project and still keep everything moving toward the project goal. Using Microsoft Project 98, you can efficiently plan, manage, and coordinate a project from conception to completion. You not only can store and display your project information, you can also keep the information up to date, and even create what-if scenarios to anticipate the effects of events on your project. With Project as your project management tool, you can manage your projects with confidence.

What is a Project?

A project is a well-defined sequence of events with an identifiable beginning and ending. A project's focus is to achieve an identified goal, and it's the project manager's responsibility to guide the project toward the goal based upon established parameters, such as time, cost, and resources, while maintaining a specified standard of quality. A project is different from a *process* in that there is always a point when the project is complete and the goal has been met. A process, on the other hand, is a sequence of events with no identifiable ending. For example, if your job is to train employees on a spreadsheet program, the process requires you to perform little project management because the activities are familiar to you and are repeated in the same manner. However, you would probably need to extensively plan and manage the development of a course for a new financial reporting system, which would be a project. You can use Project to organize and manage any project; for example, you can use Project to build a house, move to a new location, organize a marathon, develop a new toy, or write a book.

Setting Project Goals

Before you begin a project, start by determining the goal of the project. Be as specific as you can by including information such as dates, numbers, and items. For example, "Write a 300-page reference manual on company benefits for the company's 150+ employees" is a very specific project goal in comparison to "Write a benefits manual." A specific goal clarifies the extent of the project, the people affected, and the time frame. This makes the planning of the project easier because you have more guidelines on which to base your decisions.

The following table provides more examples of how to make general goals more specific.

General	Specific
Move company to new location	Move office and warehouse to new downtown location by December 15.
Coordinate a retirement party for Julia Martinez	Host company-wide retirement party for company CEO on October 21. Approximately 500 attendees.
Install new financial reporting system	Convert finance department and department heads to new financial reporting system by second quarter for pilot phase. Convert entire organization by year-end.

Assess your project and define a goal

A little planning now, with old-fashioned pencil and paper, will help you when it comes time to use Project for your own project. Complete the following steps for a project you are currently managing or preparing to manage. If you don't have a current project in mind, you can use "planning a vacation" as an example of a project.

1   Consider the complexity of your project. Will your project require a great deal of planning? Will many people be needed to complete the project? Are new procedures or technologies required? Is the budget tight? Do some tasks depend on the completion of other tasks, or are there several phases that need to be coordinated?

   Or, will your project require less planning because it is relatively small? Do you need the assistance of only one or two people to complete the project? Are the procedures familiar? Is the budget flexible? Does your project consist of a simple sequence of events?

2   Write down the parameters or constraints within which you must work for your project to succeed.

   Be sure to identify costs, deadlines or other time constraints, and individuals whose approval is required.

3   Define a goal for your project.

   Be sure that your goal includes the scope, who or how many resources are affected, and the time frame. Identify criteria that will signal the end of the project.

Understanding the Role of the Project Manager

Even though your current job title might not be project manager, you might still need to use project management techniques to successfully meet your goals. A project manager uses project management techniques to define a path to a specified goal and then supervises the project's implementation.

The project manager stands at the hub of a large information network, coordinating, supervising, assessing, planning, and evaluating the project. The project manager's task is to guide the project to a successful conclusion.

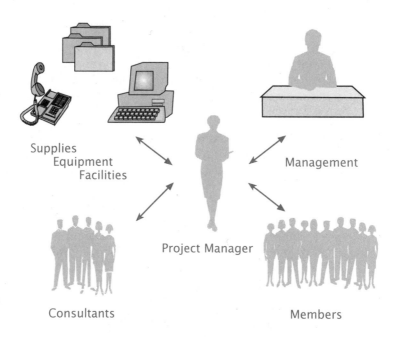

Supplies
Equipment
Facilities

Management

Project Manager

Consultants

Members

The project manager's primary responsibilities are the coordination, collation, and dissemination of project information. During the early stages of a project, the project manager works with the staff and management to define the goals and priorities of the project, and then he or she defines a path to that goal. Once the project is underway, the project manager supervises the progress, assesses the impact of *schedule* variations, and maintains a viable project plan. After the goal is achieved, the project manager completes a project evaluation so that the organization can continue to plan effective projects in the future.

Developing the Parts of a Project

After defining your project, your next job is to decide how and when you will reach your goal. A typical project is composed of these parts, or building blocks:

- Tasks
- Milestones
- Resources

Every sizable project can be broken down into a series of well-defined tasks. Each task takes a certain amount of time to complete. Some tasks can be done simultaneously, while other tasks must be carried out in a specific sequence. You might also want to define certain *milestones*, or interim goals, that can be used to mark the progress of your project before it is finished. Each task also requires the availability of appropriate *resources*, such as people, tools, or facilities.

Defining Project Tasks

The tasks, also called steps, required to complete a project define the *scope* of the project goal. Identifying the tasks is an important step in planning a project. With the project goal in mind, you begin to identify the main elements or phases of the project. Once those are identified, you then begin to expand on each element or phase. For example, if you are planning a retirement party, the main elements could be food, facility, and invitations. You could then
expand the food elements by identifying tasks, such as identify local caterers, interview caterers, or sample each caterer's specialties.

As you identify the tasks, you should also organize them in a hierarchy or outline, also called the *Work Breakdown Structure* (WBS). The WBS lists the tasks to be performed in a sequence determined by the nature of the project. Some tasks occur sequentially, while other tasks can occur concurrently. For example, pouring a concrete foundation for a building must occur before the walls are built, so the concrete task is listed before the walls task. On the other hand, the rough-in of the plumbing and electrical can most likely occur at the same time, so it doesn't matter which task is listed first.

The amount of time it takes to complete a task is its *duration*. When creating the task list, the durations should also be identified. Task duration estimates usually start with one of four sources: (1) historical, (2) participative, (3) intuitive, or (4) unknown. The most reliable duration is historical data that has been collected by the company or some knowledgeable agency. The next most reliable duration is participative data, which comes from someone who has done the same task in the past but not in these circumstances. Intuitive data comes from someone who has done a similar task in the past, and unknown data is an estimate because no other information exists. In Project, a duration can be specified in weeks, days, hours, or minutes.

The project schedule is the list of tasks and the timetable for each task's completion. The schedule indicates when each task is scheduled to begin and end and how long it will take to complete.

Identifying Project Milestones

A milestone represents an event or condition that marks the completion of a group of related tasks or a phase of the project. Milestones help you organize tasks into logical groups or sequences. You can also use them to note the progress of the project. When you complete a group of related tasks, you achieve a project milestone. When you achieve all the milestones in a project, the project is complete. Examples of milestones on a publishing project could be outline completed, copy editing completed, and camera-ready copy completed. In Project, milestones usually have a duration of zero because it marks a specific point in the schedule when a phase of the project is completed.

Define project tasks and milestones in your own project

Identifying tasks in your own project is an important part of the planning process. It is a good idea to identify key tasks and milestones even before you begin entering information. To make it easier to rearrange tasks as the details of your project become clearer, consider writing each task on a separate sheet of paper, individual index cards, or adhesive-backed sticky notes.

1 List several important tasks for your project.

2 Determine which tasks, if any, depend on others. Can any tasks occur simultaneously? Are any tasks repeated throughout the project? Are there any constraints, such as specific dates when a task must begin or end?

3 Consider whether or not tasks are related. Do they represent parts of the same process, or do they complete a phase in the project?

4 Identify points in the project that represent milestones.

Assessing Project Resources

To accomplish a task, you need resources. Resources can include people, equipment, or special facilities necessary to perform the task. The following table provides examples of different kinds of resources you might need to manage during the course of a project.

Resource type	Examples of resources
people	carpenters
	programmers
	names of specific individuals
equipment	computers
	copiers
	moving trucks
facilities	conference rooms
	warehouses

Because resources are seldom available 24 hours a day, 7 days a week, you often need to consider resource availability. Be sure to take into account variables, such as vacation schedules, length of the workday, and access to buildings or equipment.

Identify resources in your own project

As you continue thinking about your own project, consider the resources you need to accomplish the tasks that you've identified.

1   Identify the individuals or groups you need to perform specific tasks.

    To give you the most flexibility when planning your project, use general titles, such as writer, analyst, carpenter, or supervisor, rather than specific names, such as Mark, Maria, or Smith.

2   Identify the equipment you need to accomplish each task.

    Consider only equipment for which you must make special arrangements or which is in limited supply. For example, if everyone on your project team has a computer at his or her desk, you don't need to specify "computers" as an equipment resource. However, if your team members share computer equipment with others in your company, you should include "computers" in your project planning.

3   Identify any rooms or facilities that are required for you to complete the tasks.

    Be sure to consider space requirements for numbers of people or materials involved. Again, you only need to plan for facilities that are not continuously available or that require special arrangements.

Refining the Project Plan

Now that you have identified tasks, milestones, and resources, you should refine your plan and fill in any missing information. Other information about project resources and tasks, such as the availability and cost of resources or scheduling constraints for tasks, notes, and background information, are also part of the project plan.

So far, you've answered the following questions about your project:

■ What is the goal of your project?

■ What steps are needed to accomplish your goal?

■ Who or what is needed to perform each step?

The following are some additional questions you should consider:

■ How much will the project cost?

■ What adjustments can be made to achieve the plan?

■ How can project progress be presented to inform others?

■ How will changes affect the plan?

Identify additional planning issues for your project

Now that you have gathered basic information about your project, think about other issues for which you are responsible. Review the notes you made earlier on your initial project assessment while going through this exercise.

1   Does your project have a budget or other cost constraints that must be monitored?

    For example, when producing a users manual, are there specific costs, such as payment for freelance writers, that you cannot exceed?

2   Who needs to know about the status of your project? Would members of the project team benefit from to-do lists?

    For instance, does a company vice president need to know which tasks are on time and which are late for a software development project? Would the programmers on the development team better understand expectations if you provided them with a to-do list for programming tasks for the month?

3   How flexible are your deadlines? What are the consequences of missing a deadline?

    For example, are your schedules allowed to slip without any negative consequences to the project or your company? Are there penalties for delays or rewards for being early?

How Microsoft Project Can Help

With Project, it is easy to create and modify a set of tasks to meet your goals. Project management software is an invaluable tool for establishing an initial project plan. In addition, Project quickly recalculates schedules and lets you see how changes in one part of the project will affect the overall plan. New tasks, obsolete tasks, interim dates that affect other tasks, or the irregular availability of a resource might otherwise slip by unnoticed, but with Project, you can keep it all under control.

In addition, keeping everyone informed by presenting only the information each person needs could be a lot of work without the aid of Project. Workers need to know what they are expected to do and when they are scheduled to do it. Management needs to be kept informed about the progress of the project. With Project, you can quickly produce the reports and information you need to keep both workers and management informed.

Identifying Project Phases

A project is managed in phases that progress as the project moves along. A project schedule is created before the first task in the project begins. Once the project is underway, you can manage the tasks as they occur and make adjustments to the schedule. As adjustments are made, results and changes need to be communicated to those involved with the project. When the project is completed, you evaluate the project and make suggestions for future projects. The following list identifies the project phases and discusses how Project can be used in their implementation.

- Create a realistic project schedule.

  When you first establish the tasks and schedules and identify the resources for a project, Project provides Planning Wizards that keep track of the
  decisions you make. Then, based on how you use Project, the Planning Wizards offer suggestions and shortcuts to improve your effectiveness.

  Project also facilitates the "brainstorming" process that usually accompanies the design of the project schedule. Features such as drag-and-drop editing make it easy to move tasks and enter new information quickly. For example, if after entering tasks you discover that you need to add time for another site inspection, you can add the new task in the correct sequence in the project.

- Manage the project and adjust to changes.

  Managing a project involves tracking the status of tasks and determining whether tasks are proceeding as planned. If tasks fall behind schedule, you need to determine whether you will still be able to meet your goals, and then adjust the plan if necessary. In addition, you can always count on the unexpected in a project, such as an unavailable resource, a trimmed budget, the purchase of faster equipment, or an additional worker. Because of the interdependent nature of project tasks, such changes often affect the entire project.

  Your project schedule is automatically adjusted, based on changes that you make. You are also notified when resources are overcommitted or when a task cannot be completed in time for subsequent tasks to stay on schedule. With a variety of views and reports, you can quickly identify tasks that are late or overbudgeted.

- Communicate results and progress.

  A project typically involves more than one person. So that everyone can work together effectively, it is important to communicate project schedules and expectations. By using a variety of reports that you can customize, you can coordinate the project effectively. In addition, when management requires information about the progress of the project, you want to be sure to present the project information concisely.

  You can use the reports available in Project to present only the information you require. You can also tailor each report to meet your communication needs or develop your own reports.

■ Evaluate the project performance upon completion.

As a project progresses, Project collects and stores all the information relating to tasks, resources, and costs. At the end of the project, this information can be used to assess the effectiveness of the original plan and make recommendations on how to improve planning and implementation in future projects.

The following illustration shows the different phases of a project and when they occur.

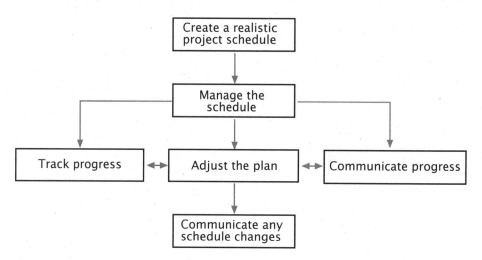

Using Project Management Tools

Two basic tools help you get the answers you need throughout the project. The *Gantt Chart* tells you when tasks are scheduled. The *PERT Chart* helps you understand the relationship between tasks. As your information requirements change in the course of a project, the tools you use will probably change also.

Using the Gantt Chart

One of the most familiar tools for visualizing progress in a project is the Gantt Chart. Each task is represented in the Gantt Chart as a single horizontal bar. The Gantt bars, also known as task bars, are positioned across a period of time called a *timescale*, which is displayed at the top of the Gantt Chart. The length of an individual Gantt bar represents a task's duration, or the length of time it takes to complete a task. A basic fixture in project management, the Gantt

Chart is an excellent tool for quickly assessing the status of individual tasks over time. Link lines connecting individual bars in a Gantt Chart reflect relationships between tasks, for example, if one task cannot start until another task is finished. The name of the resource assigned to a task also appears in the Gantt Chart.

The following illustration shows a typical Gantt Chart.

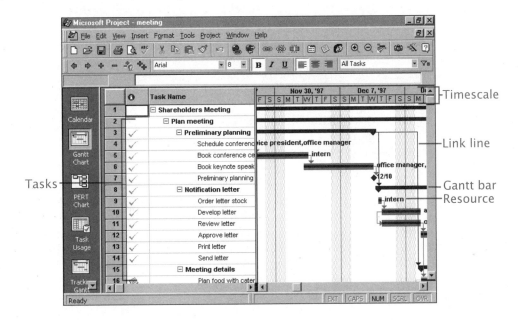

Using the PERT Chart

When it is more important to focus on the relationships between tasks rather than on the schedule, the PERT Chart, also known as the network chart, can be more illustrative than the Gantt Chart. The PERT Chart displays the interdependencies between tasks. In a PERT Chart, each task is represented by a box, called a node, that contains basic information about the task. Tasks that depend on one another for completion, or simply follow one another in a sequence of events, are connected by link lines. The PERT Chart gives you a graphical representation of how tasks are linked to each other in the project. In this book, the focus is on the Gantt Chart, with detailed step-by-step exercises on using PERT Charts in Appendix C.

Understanding Critical Tasks

A *critical task* is one that, if delayed, would also cause the completion of the project to be delayed. The *critical path* is composed of all the critical tasks. Changes to tasks on the critical path can have a significant impact on the completion of a project. With Project, you can quickly identify the critical path so that you can focus on the tasks that require the closest management. Knowing which tasks are critical also helps you assess priorities, effectively assign resources, and determine the effect of changes on the project.

The *Critical Path Method* (CPM) is a standard project management technique for determining which tasks are critical. It is based on a mathematical model that takes into account the relationships between tasks, their duration, and any constraints regarding the availability of resources. CPM is also used to schedule the start and finish dates for individual tasks. Historically, determining the critical path in a large or complicated project was a significant challenge for the project manager. Today, Project brings the power of CPM to your project planning by recalculating the critical path each time a change is made to the project schedule.

One Step Further: Running the Quick Preview

To review project management concepts and to begin getting acquainted with the capabilities of Project, you can use the Microsoft Project Quick Preview. This overview shows you how Project can be a valuable aid in project planning.

Start Quick Preview

If the Office Assistant appears, click the close button.

1   Click Start, point to Programs, and then click Microsoft Project.

2   If the Welcome dialog box appears when you start Project, click Watch A Quick Preview, or, on the Help menu, click Getting Started, and then click Quick Preview.

3   Follow the instructions on the screen to get an overview of Microsoft Project 98.

As you read the information in the Quick Preview, think about which features will be most helpful to you in the planning and implementation of your project.

Finish the lesson

1   To continue to the next lesson, on the File menu, click Close.

2   If you are finished using Microsoft Project for now, on the File menu, click Exit.

Lesson Summary

To	Do this
Assess your project and set a project goal	Assess the complexity of your project and identify any constraints you must work within. Formulate a goal that is specific: Identify the project scope, who is affected, and the time frame.
Identify project tasks, milestones, and resources	List key tasks and durations. Note the relationship between tasks: Which tasks depend on each other? Which occur regularly? Which are part of a larger category? Identify milestones and resources.
Refine the project plan	Review the requirements of the project: which people are needed or new procedures used. Identify project constraints: Are there fixed deadlines and costs or anticipated changes? Who needs to know about the project and how the information is best presented?

For online information about	On the Help menu, click Contents And Index, click the Index tab, and then type
Project management	**project management basics** *or* **project management body of knowledge**

Learning Microsoft Project Basics

In this lesson you will learn how to:

Estimated time
30 min.

- Open and save a project file.
- Change views and move around within a project schedule.
- Adjust the Gantt Chart timescale.
- Create headers and footers for printing.
- Preview and print views and reports.

In this lesson, you will become familiar with the Microsoft Project 98 environment before you create your first project schedule. After opening an existing project file, you will explore the project data in various views and discover the flexibility with which you can present the data. You will then learn how to move within the Gantt Chart view and use the timescale to change a view to smaller or larger units of time. In addition, you will learn how to create headers and footers that will be displayed when printing and how to preview and print a view or report.

Start the lesson

1   On the taskbar, click Start.

     The Start menu is displayed.

2   On the Start menu, point to Programs, and then click Microsoft Project.

3 If the Welcome To Microsoft Project dialog box appears, click the Close button.

A blank project file is opened in the Project program window.

Opening a Project File

Later in this lesson, views and tables will be discussed further.

When you first start Project, a blank project file is displayed in Gantt Chart view. The Gantt Chart is the default view for Project. If you have an existing file you would like to work with, even from an earlier version of Project, you can open that file. To open an existing file, click the Open button on the Standard toolbar or click the Open command from the File menu.

Open an existing file

In this exercise, you open an existing project file that was created while working on the company's shareholders meeting last year.

Open

1 On the Standard toolbar, click the Open button.

The File Open dialog box appears.

Look In box   Look In Favorites button

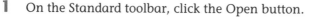

Look In Favorites

2 Click the Look In Favorites button.

The names of all folders and files contained within the Favorites folder are displayed.

3 Double-click the Project SBS Practice folder.

The files contained in the Project SBS Practice folder are displayed.

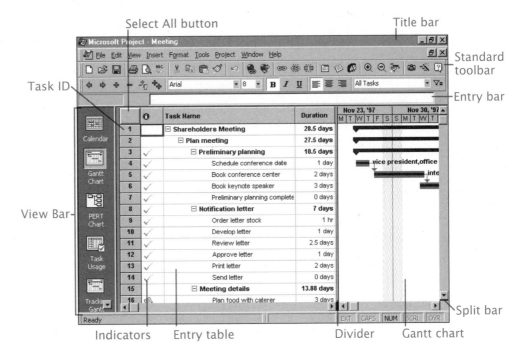

You can also select a file name, and click Open.

4 Double-click the Meeting file.

The Meeting project file is displayed in Gantt Chart view. Your screen should look similar to the following illustration.

Saving a Project File

It's a good idea to save your work when you've made important changes to the file. Saving your work ensures that the changes you've made will not be lost if an accident, such as a power outage, should occur. To save a file using the existing name, click the Save button on the Standard toolbar or click the Save command on the File menu.

Baselines will be discussed further in Lesson 10, "Scheduling Task Constraints."

When you save a file in Project, the *Planning Wizard* appears and asks whether you want to save the file with a *baseline*. A baseline is a record, or "snapshot," taken at a specific time in the project. A baseline is useful for comparing your current schedule with later versions of the schedule to see what changes have occurred. Once a baseline is saved with a file, the Planning Wizard will not appear again. You can overwrite the existing baseline or save another baseline. A baseline is generally saved when you finish planning the project schedule and are ready to begin the first task.

Save an existing file with a new name

In this exercise, you save the Meeting file with a new name so that the original copy of the data is not changed.

Each practice file used in this book is saved with a new name to keep the original files intact.

1 On the File menu, click Save As.

The Save As dialog box appears.

2 Be sure that Project SBS Practice is displayed in the Save In box.

3 Be sure that the text is selected in the File Name box, and then type **Shareholders Meeting**

4 Click Save.

The Save As dialog box closes, and a new copy of the project file is saved as Shareholders Meeting.

If the Project SBS Practice folder is not displayed in the Save In box, click the Look In Favorites button, and double-click the Project SBS Practice folder.

You can also press ENTER to save the file.

Save a Project File as HTML

Data from a project file can be exported to HTML (Hypertext Markup Language) format and used in a Web page on the World Wide Web and intranets. Project data is saved to HTML based on import/export maps used to determine which fields of project data are to be exported. Individual fields of data can be exported, but an entire project cannot be exported.

To export project data to HTML format, perform the following steps.

1 On the File menu, click Save As HTML.

   The File Save dialog box appears.

2 Select a folder where the HTML file is to be saved, and name the file.

3 Click Save.

   The Export Format dialog box appears.

4 In the Import/Export Map To Use For Exporting list, select the name of the map to be used for exporting data.

   You can also define a new map or edit an existing map.

5 Click Save.

   The data is saved as HTML based on the selected map.

Displaying Project Information in Views

You can also create your own custom views, which are discussed further in Lesson 13, "Customizing Tables, Views, and Reports."

A *view* is a format in which you can enter and display information in Project. The Gantt Chart view is the default view. It is made up of the Entry table on the left, used to enter task information, and the Gantt Chart on the right, which graphically represents the task information on a timescale. The timescale is a time period indicator at the top of a view, such as the Gantt Chart.

Views in Project fall into three categories: *sheet views*, *chart and graph views*, and *form views*. Each view displays combinations of project information in different ways. Views are displayed in a single or combination format. A single view is a single sheet, chart, graph, or form. A combination view displays any two single views together. For example, the Gantt Chart view combines the Entry table, sheet view, and the Gantt Chart.

Sheet views display task or resource information in a row and column format. Use a sheet view when you want to enter or view a lot of information at one time. Chart and graph views provide a graphical representation of task or resource information. Use a chart or graph view when you need to visually present information without all the details. Form views display task or resource information in a format that displays a single task or a single resource at a time. Use a form view when you want to focus on detailed information about a specific task or resource.

Changing Views

Project comes with 26 predefined views. Each view can be displayed using the View menu or the View Bar located on the left side of the Project program window. The View Bar displays eight of the most commonly used views as icons, plus an icon to display additional views. The following table shows each view icon on the View Bar and gives a brief description of the view it represents.

Icon	View name	View description
	Calendar	A monthly calendar showing tasks and their durations. Use this view to show the tasks scheduled in a specific week or range of weeks.
	Gantt Chart	A list of tasks and related information, and a chart showing tasks and their durations over time. Use this view to enter and schedule a list of tasks.
	PERT Chart	A network diagram showing all tasks and task dependencies. Use this task view to create and fine-tune your schedule in a flowchart format.
	Task Usage	A list of tasks showing assigned resources grouped under each task. Use this view to see which resources are assigned to specific tasks and to view resource work contours.
	Tracking Gantt	A list of tasks and related information, and a chart showing baseline and scheduled Gantt bars for each task. Use this view to compare the baseline schedule with the actual schedule.

Icon	View name	View description
	Resource Graph	A graph showing resource allocation, cost, or work. Use this view to display information about a single resource or group of resources over time.
	Resource Sheet	A list of resources and related information. Use this view to enter and edit resource information in a spreadsheet-like format.
	Resource Usage	A list of resources showing task assignments grouped under each resource. Use this view to show cost or work allocation information over time for each resource per assignment and to set resource work contours.
	More Views	Opens the More Views dialog box. The More Views dialog box displays a list of every view available.

Use the View Bar

In this exercise, you use the View Bar to display the Calendar, Resource Sheet, and Task Usage views and to return to the Gantt Chart view.

1 On the View Bar, click the Calendar icon.

The view changes to the Calendar view.

2 On the View Bar, click the Task Usage icon.

The view changes to the Task Usage view.

3 On the View Bar, click the Gantt Chart icon.

The view returns to the Gantt Chart view.

Hide and display the View Bar

In this exercise, you use the View menu to hide and display the View Bar.

1 On the View menu, click View Bar.

The View Bar is hidden. The blue, active view bar on the left side of the screen displays the name of the current view. Your screen should look similar to the following illustration.

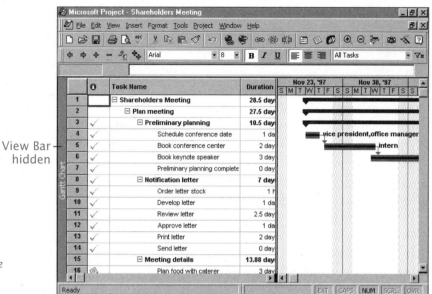

View Bar — hidden

You can use the More Views dialog box to add and remove views from the View Bar and View menu.

2   On the View menu, click View Bar.

The View Bar is displayed. The Gantt Chart icon is selected.

Moving Around in a View

When looking at project information, there is often more information to view than is displayed on the screen. To view all of the information, you need to know how to move around in the views by using scroll bars, buttons, and arrows keys.

You can scroll both vertically and horizontally within a view by using scroll bars. For example, the Gantt Chart view displays two horizontal scroll bars and one vertical scroll bar. You can use the horizontal scroll bar on the left side of the screen, below the Entry table, to scroll through additional columns of information. With the horizontal scroll bar on the right side of the screen, below the Gantt Chart, you can scroll through the timescale of the Gantt Chart. The vertical scroll bar moves you up and down the task list, moving the Entry table and Gantt Chart together.

The Previous and Next buttons, available on forms such as the Task Form, are used to move through either the task list or resource list one task or resource at a time. Sometimes, there are also vertical scroll bars to move through additional information about the task or resource within the form.

The arrow keys and the TAB key on your keyboard can be used to move between fields and boxes within a view. From the Edit menu, you can use the Go To dialog box to locate a specific task based on its *task ID number* or a date in the project schedule. You can also use your mouse to move around the screen.

Move within the Gantt Chart view

In this exercise, you move within the Gantt Chart view using several methods of navigation.

1 At the bottom of the right horizontal scroll bar, click the arrow three times.

The timescale moves approximately three days farther into the project.

You can use SHIFT+TAB to move the cursor selection to the left.

2 In the Task Name column, click the task 8, Notification Letter task name.

The task name is selected.

3 Press TAB.

The duration field for the Notification Letter summary task is selected.

4 On the Edit menu, click Go To.

The Go To dialog box appears.

5 Type **3**, and click OK.

The Indicators field for task 3 is selected, and the Gantt Chart is scrolled to the Gantt bar for task 3.

6 At the bottom of the vertical scroll bar, click the arrow until task 20, Print Agenda, is visible.

7 Click the Print Agenda task name.

8 On the Standard toolbar, click the Go To Selected Task button.

Go To Selected Task

The timescale scrolls to the start of the Gantt bar for task 20, Print Agenda.

9 Press CTRL+HOME.

The view is scrolled to the top of the task list.

Adjusting the Timescale

In addition to moving within a view to display additional project information, you can also adjust the timescale in a chart view to display additional graphical information. The timescale is located across the top of the Gantt Chart and represents the time when the project tasks take place. The timescale includes the major timescale and the minor timescale. The major timescale, located at the top of the timescale, displays larger units of time, and the minor timescale, located below the major timescale, displays smaller units of time. For example, if the major timescale displays the start date for a week, the minor timescale would display the days of the week.

The following illustration shows the major and minor timescales.

To adjust the timescale, you can use the Zoom In and Zoom Out buttons on the Standard toolbar. The Zoom In button changes the timescale to smaller units of time, giving you a more detailed view. The Zoom Out button changes the timescale to larger units of time, giving you a broader view. You can also use the Timescale dialog box on the Format menu to adjust the timescale.

Change the units on the timescale

In this exercise, you use the Zoom In and Zoom Out buttons on the Standard toolbar to change the units of time on the timescale.

Zoom In

The timescale can be zoomed in to units of an hour over 15-minute increments.

1   On the Standard toolbar, click the Zoom In button.

    The major timescale changes to a day, and the minor timescale changes to six-hour increments.

2   On the Standard toolbar, click the Zoom Out button.

    The major timescale returns to a week, and the minor timescale returns to one-day increments.

3   On the Standard toolbar, click the Zoom Out button.

    The major timescale changes to a month, and the minor timescale changes to three-day increments.

Zoom Out

The timescale can be zoomed out to units of a year over six-month increments.

4   On the Standard toolbar, click the Zoom In button.

    The major timescale returns to a week, and the minor timescale returns to one-day increments.

Printing Schedule Information

To manage a project effectively, you need to communicate project information to a variety of people, such as management, the project team, and other individuals who have an interest in the project. To communicate the project information, you can print views and reports that meet the needs of a specific person or group. For example, you can print only the tasks starting during the current month or a report showing the tasks assigned to a specific person.

Project comes with 26 predefined views and 25 predefined reports that can be printed. Before you print a view or report, it can be previewed to determine the number of pages that will be printed and if any additional information needs to be added. Using the Page Setup dialog box, you can select the page orientation, adjust scaling, change margins, and add or change the headers and footers. You can also add page breaks to views and tables to control the flow of information from one page to another.

Creating Headers and Footers

Headers and *footers* are used to display additional information when you print a view or a report. A header is text displayed at the top of every page, and a footer is text displayed at the bottom of every page. Using the Page Setup dialog box, you can specify the information that should be displayed in the header and footer on each printed page. You can also specify the alignment of the information as well as the font and font size of the text. In addition to entering your own text, you can also include the following items, which are drawn from the information you have entered about the project.

Page Number *	Project Current Date	System Date *
Total Page Count *	Project Status Date	System Time *
Project Title	View Name	Subject
Company Name	Report Name	Author
Manager Name	Filter Name	Keyword
Project Start Date	File Name *	
Project Finish Date	Last Saved Date	

* Indicates you can also use a button on the Header tab in the Page Setup dialog box to insert this information.

At the bottom of a Gantt Chart, you also have the option of printing a *legend*. The legend is a graphical key to the symbols and shading in the Gantt bars.

Create a header

In this exercise, you open the Page Setup dialog box and create a header that will be printed when the Shareholders Meeting Gantt Chart view is printed.

1 On the File menu, click Page Setup.

   The Page Setup dialog box appears.

2 Click the Header tab.

3 Be sure that the Center tab is selected, and then click in the Text box.

4 Next to the box displaying the text "Page Number," click the down arrow, and then click Project Title.

   The text "Project Title" is displayed in the Project Information List box.

The Properties dialog box, on the File menu, is discussed further in Lesson 3, "Working with Project Tasks."

5 Click Add.

The project title is displayed in the Preview box. The project title is automatically inserted from the Summary tab in the Properties dialog box.

6 Press ENTER.

A new line is started in the text box.

7 Type **Project:**, and press the SPACEBAR.

The text "Project:" is displayed in the Preview box.

8 Click the Page Information List down arrow, click Subject, and then click Add.

The subject of the project is displayed in the Preview box.

Preview box —
Alignment tabs
Text box
Buttons —
Page Information List box

Create a footer

In this exercise, you create a footer to display the date and time the view is printed.

Date

The system date and time are the date and time your computer is currently programmed to display.

1 Be sure that the Page Setup dialog box is active, and then click the Footer tab.

2 In the Alignment area, click the Right tab.

3 Click the Date button.

The date is displayed as code in the text box. The actual system date is displayed in the Preview box.

Time

4   Click the Time button.

The time is displayed as code in the text box. The actual system time is displayed in the Preview box.

5   Click OK.

The header and footer information is stored. The header and footer information is visible only when previewing and printing.

Save the file

In this exercise, you save the changes that you've made to the file.

Save

➤   On the Standard toolbar, click the Save button.

Because this is a project file where the baseline has already been saved, the Planning Wizard will not appear.

Previewing and Printing Views and Reports

Although you can use the Print button to print a view or report, it is a good idea to preview what you want to print to make sure it prints the way you anticipate. By previewing your view or report, you can make any necessary adjustments so that you only have to print once. When you are satisfied with the appearance of the preview, you can print from the Print Preview window or go back to the program window and use the Print button.

Print Preview displays each page of the active view or report as it will look when printed. The status bar at the bottom of the screen shows the current page number and the total number of pages for the current view or report. If the view consists of more than one page, you can use the buttons in Print Preview to view the additional pages. By clicking the Multiple Pages button or clicking in the gray area outside the preview page, all pages in the view or report are displayed at one time in Print Preview. You can also zoom in to view details of a page by clicking on the page.

In the following exercises, you preview the Gantt Chart view and several reports from the shareholders meeting project. You also print the Gantt Chart view and the Costs report.

Preview and print a view

In this exercise, you preview and print a project schedule in Gantt Chart view.

Print Preview

1   On the Standard toolbar, click the Print Preview button.

The preview window opens to display the Gantt Chart as it would look if printed. Your screen should look similar to the following illustration.

Multiple Pages button

Navigation
buttons

Screen capture of Microsoft Project - Shareholders Meeting print preview window, with Page Setup, Print, Close, and Help buttons, showing a Gantt chart preview. Status bar reads "Page: 1 of 4 Size: 2 rows by 2 columns".

2 Place the mouse pointer over the preview page.

The pointer changes to a magnifying glass.

3 Click the lower-right corner of the preview page.

The view is zoomed in so you can see the footer you created.

Multiple Pages

4 Click the Multiple Pages button.

The view zooms out so that four pages are displayed.

5 If your computer is connected to a printer, click Print, and click OK. If you are not connected to a printer, click Close.

Preview reports

In this exercise, you preview a predefined report in Project.

1 On the View menu, click Reports.

The Reports dialog box appears.

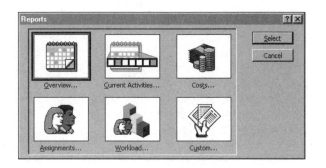

You can also select the Assignments box, and then click Select.

2 Double-click the Assignments box.

The Assignment Reports dialog box appears.

3 Double-click the Who Does What box.

The Who Does What report is displayed in Print Preview.

4 Click the Report Preview button.

The view zooms in to show detailed information about which tasks are assigned to each resource.

5 Click Close.

The Reports dialog box appears.

Print a report

In this exercise, you print the Cash Flow report.

1 Double-click the Costs box.

The Cost Reports dialog box appears.

2 Double-click the Cash Flow box.

The Cash Flow report is displayed, showing the weekly cash flow for the project by task.

3 If you are connected to a printer, click Print, and click OK. If you are not connected to a printer, click Close.

4 Click Cancel.

5 On the Standard toolbar, click the Save button.

The changes made to the file are saved.

Setting Up a Printer

In Project, your views can be printed using either a printer or a plotter. In either case, the printing device you want to use must have been set up through Windows 95 or Windows NT. If the printer is already set up, use the steps under "Change the default printer" to use a different printer. If the printer is not already set up, use the steps under "Set up a new printer or plotter" before changing the printer.

Set up a new printer or plotter

To set up a new printing device to use with Project, perform the following steps.

1   Click Start on the taskbar, point to Settings, and then click Printers.

    The Printers window opens.

2   Double-click the Add Printer icon.

    The Add Printer Wizard appears.

3   Follow the instructions in the Add Printer Wizard dialog boxes to add the printer you want to use.

Change the default printer

To change the default printer before printing, perform the following steps.

1   On the File menu, click Page Setup.

    The Page Setup dialog box appears. Be sure that the Page tab is selected.

2   Click Printer.

    The Print Setup dialog box appears.

3   Select the printer you want to use in the Printer box, and click OK.

4   If you are ready to print, click Print. If you are not ready to print, click OK.

TIP   If you want to use a shared network printer, you can double-click the Network Neighborhood icon on the Windows 95 or Windows NT desktop to set up the printer. Double-click the computer connected to the shared printer. Click the printer icon, and then click Install on the File menu.

One Step Further: Adding a Task Note

Notes regarding project tasks can help to refresh your memory about how the schedule was constructed. Task notes might contain information, such as assumptions, about task durations or task dependencies.

When a note has been included with a task, a note indicator is displayed in the Indicators field for the task. By placing the mouse pointer over a note indicator, you can quickly view all or a portion of the task note, depending on its length.

In the following exercises, you add a task note to document the name of the keynote speaker at last year's shareholders meeting. You also format the task note to highlight the speaker's name within the note.

Create a task note

In this exercise, you create a task note and then view the note in the Indicators field.

1   Be sure the Gantt Chart view is displayed.

Task notes are only available in a task view.

You can select a task by clicking on the task ID number or selecting a field in the task row.

Task Notes

2   Select task 6, Book Keynote Speaker.

3   On the Standard toolbar, click the Task Notes button.

The Task Information dialog box appears. The Notes tab is selected.

4   Click in the Notes box, and then type **The keynote speaker was Frances Smith.**

5   Click OK.

The Task Information dialog box closes. A notes indicator is displayed in the Indicators field for the task. Your screen should look similar to the following illustration.

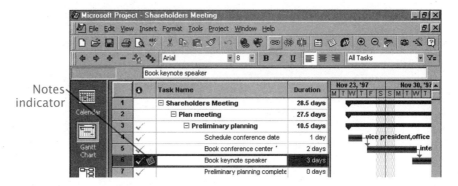

33

6 Place the mouse pointer over the notes indicator for task 6, Book Keynote Speaker.

A ScreenTip with the note text is displayed.

Format a task note

In this exercise, you format text in a task note.

1 Be sure that task 6, Book Keynote Speaker, is selected, and then, on the Standard toolbar, click the Task Notes button.

The Task Information dialog box appears. The Note tab is selected.

2 Select the text "Frances Smith."

3 Above the Notes box, click the Font button.

The Font dialog box appears.

Font button

4 In the Font Style box, select Italic, and click OK.

The selected text in the Notes box is changed to italic.

Although the ScreenTip text format has not changed, the format change is displayed if the note is printed.

5 Click OK.

The note text format is changed.

6 Place the mouse pointer over the notes indicator for task 6, Book Keynote Speaker.

The text in the indicator ScreenTip has not changed.

7 On the Standard toolbar, click the Save button.

The note is saved.

Save button

Finish the lesson

1 To continue to the next lesson, on the File menu, click Close.

2 If you are finished using Project for now, on the File menu, click Exit.

Lesson Summary

To	Do this	Button
Open a file	On the Standard toolbar, click the Open button. Click the Look In Favorites button. In the File list box, double-click the folder where the file is located. In the File list box, double-click the file name.	
Save an existing file with a new name	On the File menu, click Save As. Select the location for the new file in the Look In box. Select the text in the File Name box, type the new file name, and then click Save.	
Change views	On the View Bar, click one of the view icons.	
Move in a view	On the Edit menu, click Go To. Type a task ID number in the ID box, or type a date in the Date box. Click OK. *or* Select a task. On the Standard toolbar, click the Go To Selected Task button.	
Adjust the timescale	On the Standard toolbar, click the Zoom In button to change to smaller units of time. *or* On the Standard toolbar, click the Zoom Out button to change to larger units of time.	
Create a header	On the File menu, click Page Setup. Click the Header tab. Click an alignment tab, and then click inside the text box. Type the text to be displayed in the header or select an item from the Project Information List, and then click Add.	

To	Do this	Button
Create a footer	On the File menu, click Page Setup. Click the Footer tab. Click an alignment tab, and then click inside the text box. Type the text to be displayed in the header or select an item from the Project Information List, and then click Add.	
Preview a view	On the Standard toolbar, click the Print Preview button.	
Print a report	From the program window, on the Standard toolbar, click the Print button. or On the View menu, click Report. Double-click a group box. Double-click a report. From Print Preview, click Print, and click OK.	

For online information about	On the Help menu, click Contents And Index, click the Index tab, and then type
Opening a file	**open a file**
Saving a file	**save a file**
Changing views	**views**
Moving in a view	**views**
Adjusting the timescale	**timescale**
Creating headers and footers	**page setup**
Previewing	**preview printing**
Printing	**printing**

Working with Project Tasks

Estimated time
30 min.

In this lesson you will learn how to:

- Enter initial project information.
- Enter tasks and durations.
- Insert tasks in the task list.
- Move tasks within the task list.

Before a project can begin and a project schedule can be created, the project goal must first be defined. Once the project goal is defined, you can begin the process of creating the project schedule by identifying the tasks necessary to reach the project goal. The project task list, or scope of work, can be assembled by one person, by brainstorming with a project team, by using historical data from past projects of a similar nature, or a combination of all three. You might assemble the task list by writing the tasks on pieces of paper, sticky notes on a wall, or index cards. While these methods of assembling the task list have been used in the past and are probably still used by some, a great deal of additional work is needed if a task is forgotten, placed in the wrong location on the list, or needs to be broken down into several other tasks. For example, a new task that should occur toward the beginning of the project is identified. If you are writing the list on a piece of paper, the list would have to be rewritten to place the new task in its proper location. If the project is already in progress, even more work is required to add the new task.

A more efficient way of creating the project task list is to use a project management program, such as Microsoft Project 98, to collect, organize, and

37

distribute your project schedule information. Using Project, you can begin listing the tasks and durations for a project in one convenient location. As you identify new tasks or find tasks that are out of place, you can quickly insert or move tasks within the list.

In this lesson, you are ready to begin creating a schedule for the relocation of the corporate office. You will create the project task list by entering some of the primary tasks and duration estimates for the project. With a partial list created, you edit the task list by inserting new tasks, moving tasks within the task list, and deleting tasks that will be performed outside your scheduling control.

If the Welcome dialog box appears, click the Close button.

Start the lesson

➤ Start Microsoft Project.

Starting a Project Schedule

Creating a project file is the first step in using Project as your project management scheduling program. A blank project file is opened when you start Project, and you can begin entering information about the project.

The current date, status date, and calendar boxes on the Project Information dialog box arebe discussed in later lessons.

The Project Information dialog box is used to enter information that is critical to the scheduling of tasks and resources. This information includes the start date, finish date, schedule-from date, current date, status date, and calendar. You must first determine whether the schedule will be created from a known project start date or project finish date. If the project has a known start date, Project will calculate the finish date for you based on the information you provide about tasks and resources. You can also schedule a project based on a known finish date, which is called *backwards scheduling*. With the known finish date, Project calculates the date on which the project should start so that it can be completed by the known finish date. All of the information entered in the Project Information dialog box affects when tasks and resources will be scheduled for work on the project. If you do not enter a project start date or finish date, Project automatically uses the current date as the start date for the schedule you are creating.

The Project Properties dialog box contains several tabs of information. The Summary tab is used to enter information about the project title and subject, the schedule author, the project manager, and the company. You can also enter a project category, a keyword for search capabilities, and general comments about the project. The fields of information on the Summary tab can be used in printing views and reports as linked data.

The first project team meeting for the corporate office relocation project will be held this afternoon. In the following exercises, you create a project file and begin entering basic project information in the file.

Enter project information

In this exercise, you create the project file by entering the project start date.

You can also click the New button on the Standard toolbar. A new project file opens, and the Project Information dialog box appears.

1 On the Project menu, click Project Information.

The Project Information dialog box appears.

2 Click the Start Date down arrow.

The date selection calendar is displayed.

3 Click the right arrow until August 1998 is displayed on the calendar.

4 Click the 10th on the calendar.

The calendar closes, and the date is displayed in the Start Date box.

Project Information for 'Project1'	? X
Start date: Mon 8/10/98	OK
Finish date: Tue 8/19/97	Cancel
Schedule from: Project Start Date	Statistics...
All tasks begin as soon as possible.	
Current date: Tue 8/19/97	
Status date: NA	
Calendar: Standard	

5 Click OK.

The Project Information dialog box closes.

> **NOTE** The practice project used in this book will be scheduled to start in August 1998. The project start date is already specified in practice files used later in this book.

Enter properties information

In this exercise, you add project details, such as the subject and project manager, to the project file.

1 On the File menu, click Properties.

The Project Properties dialog box appears. The Summary tab is selected.

You can also enter information, such as the company name, a keyword, and comments, in the Project1 Properties dialog box.

2 In the Title box, type **Corporate Office Project**

3 In the Subject box, type **Relocation**

4 In the Author box, type **(your name)**

5 In the Managers box, type **(your name)**

Project1 Properties

General | Summary | Statistics | Contents | Custom

Title: Coporate Office Project

Subject: Relocation

Author: J. Roberts

Manager: J. Roberts

Company: ABX Compute Corporation

Category:

Keywords:

Comments:

Hyperlink base:

Template:

☐ Save preview picture

OK   Cancel

6 Click OK.

Save the project

In this exercise, you name and save the project file.

Save

1 On the Standard toolbar, click the Save button.

The File Save dialog box appears.

Look In Favorites

2 Click the Look In Favorites button.

The names of all folders and files contained within the Favorites folder are displayed.

The Planning Wizard asking to save with or without a baseline does not appear until tasks are entered into the schedule.

3 Double-click the Project SBS Practice folder.

The files contained in the Project SBS Practice folder are displayed.

4 In the File Name box, double-click the text "Project1."

5 Type **Create Schedule**

6 Click Save.

The project file is saved as Create Schedule in the Project SBS Practice folder. The project file name is displayed on the Project title bar.

Entering Tasks and Durations

A project file contains a list of tasks, or steps, necessary to complete the project goal. When you enter tasks in the task list, you can be either detailed or general in the scope of the tasks, but you need to be sure to include all steps that require planning, measurable time, or special arrangements or accommodations. In Project, each task is entered in the Task Name column of the Entry table in Gantt Chart view (tasks can also be entered in other views that have a Task Name column).

Each task in the task list is associated with a task ID number. The task ID number is assigned as the task is entered and is indicated by the gray row headings to the right of the Gantt Chart view. As the task list is edited, the task ID numbers are automatically renumbered to keep the list in numerical order.

With each task, you also enter a *duration* estimate, or the amount of time it will take to accomplish the task. Durations can be specified in values of minutes, hours, days, or weeks as *working time* or *elapsed time*. A unit of working time is confined by the hours of the day and the number of days that resources are working. A unit of elapsed time includes working and nonworking time based on a 24-hour day and a 7-day week. As tasks are entered, a default duration of 1 and a time unit of a day of working time are automatically entered in the Duration column as 1 day. The default duration can be changed by entering a new value and unit of time in the Duration field for the task. The following table lists the duration abbreviations.

Project also has a duration of a year, but it can only be used for resource salaries.

Durations can be modified by using the spin controls that appear when a Duration field is selected.

Abbreviation	Duration display	Description
m	min	minute
h	hr	hour
d	day	day
w	wk	week
em	emin	elapsed minutes
eh	ehr	elapsed hours
ed	eday	elapsed days
ew	ewk	elapsed week

Tasks with a duration of zero (0) are called milestones. Milestone tasks represent the completion of an event, phase, or other measurable goal within the project. A milestone is created by entering a duration of zero (0) for a task. When a task becomes a milestone, the Gantt bar changes to a diamond-shaped marker with the date the milestone occurs to the left of the marker. Each project should have at least one milestone.

Task information can be entered by selecting a field in the Entry table or by selecting the task ID heading. By default, the cursor moves one row down when you press ENTER in a field. Pressing TAB moves the cursor one field to the right. You can also use SHIFT+TAB to move one field to the left. If the task ID heading is selected, the cursor moves one field to the right when you press ENTER or TAB. The cursor continues to cycle through the selected row as long as the row remains selected. You can also use the mouse or the keyboard arrows to move from field to field in the Entry table.

In the following exercises, you add several tasks and durations to the task list to start the brainstorming process during the afternoon project meeting.

Add a task and task duration

In this exercise, you enter the first task and a duration estimate to the task list.

Typing errors can be corrected by pressing BACKSPACE or DELETE.

You can also click in a different field or click the Enter button on the Entry bar.

1 Click in the first field in the Task Name column.

2 Type **Hire architect**, and then press TAB.

The information is entered, and the selection moves to the Duration column for task 1. A duration of 1d (1 day) is entered by default. The number 1 is displayed on the task ID.

3 Type **2**, and press ENTER.

The duration "days" is entered automatically when an abbreviation is not supplied. The selection moves down one row in the Duration column.

4 On the Standard toolbar, click the Save button.

The Planning Wizard dialog box asking if you want to save a baseline appears.

Baselines are discussed further in Lesson 10, "Scheduling Task Constraints."

5 Be sure that the Save 'Create Schedule' Without A Baseline option is selected, and click OK.

The project file is saved without a baseline. The Planning Wizard dialog box appears every time you save the schedule until a baseline is created.

Add several tasks

In this exercise, you enter several additional tasks to the task list.

➤ Starting below task ID 1, type the following tasks in the Task Name column. Press ENTER after each task.

Hire mover

Finalize drawings

Frame interior walls

Pack boxes

Paint

> **NOTE** If you are using WBS (Work Breakdown Structure) codes or some other task code structure, you can customize a table to enter and view the code. You can also enter codes in the Task Information dialog box. Customizing tables is discussed further in Lesson 13, "Customizing Tables, Views, and Reports."

Add durations

In this exercise, you add duration estimates to the tasks you've entered.

 Starting below task ID 1, type the following durations in the Duration column. Press ENTER after each task.

3	(task ID 2)
1w	(task ID 3)
4	(task ID 4)
2	(task ID 5)
4	(task ID 6)

Enter a milestone

In this exercise, you add a project milestone to the task list.

1   Click in the Task Name column below task 6, Paint.

2   Type **Move complete**, and then press TAB.

3   Type **0**, and press ENTER.

A milestone is represented on the Gantt Chart by a diamond-shaped marker with the date the task is scheduled to occur next to it.

4   Save the file without a baseline.

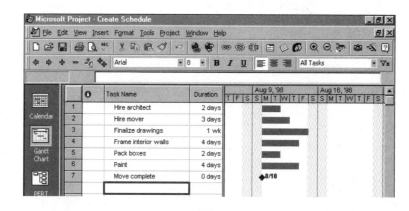

 TIP   You can mark a task with a duration greater than zero (0) as a milestone. Double-click the task. In the Task Information dialog box, click the Advanced tab. Select the Mark Task As Milestone check box, and click OK. The Gantt bar changes to a milestone marker with the date the task is scheduled to be completed. The duration doesn't change to zero (0).

Using Hyperlinks with a Project File

A *hyperlink* can be created for a task, a resource, or an assignment. A hyperlink takes the user to other files on your computer, on a network, or on the *World Wide Web* (also known as the Web). Clicking a hyperlink in a project file launches your Web browser and locates and opens the destination object. The Indicators field displays the hyperlink icon if a hyperlink has been associated with the task, resource, or assignment.

Hyperlink information is stored in the Hyperlink field. You can also add text columns to a sheet view and insert hyperlinks in the column. To use a hyperlink, you click the *hyperlink address* in the Hyperlink field, or click the hyperlink icon in the Indictors field. When you point to the hyperlink icon, it displays a ToolTip with the address of the hyperlink.

To add a hyperlink to a task, resource, or assignment, perform the following steps.

1   Select a task, resource, or assignment.

     The hyperlink will be associated with the selected item.

2   On the Standard toolbar, click the Insert Hyperlink button.

     If a message indicating you should save the file before creating a hyperlink is displayed, click Yes. The Insert Hyperlink dialog box appears.

3   In the Link To File Or URL box, type **www.microsoft.com**

     When using Web sites that start with www, it is not necessary to use http://

4   Click OK.

     A hyperlink icon for the selected item is displayed in the Indicators field.

5   Point to the hyperlink icon.

     The hyperlink address is displayed in a ScreenTip.

Insert Hyperlink

Editing the Task List

With Project, it's easy for you to make changes to a project schedule as it is being developed. You can insert new tasks as they are identified, move tasks within the task list for better sequencing of events, and delete tasks that are not needed.

Inserting a Task

As a project schedule is being developed and as project tasks are being performed, it is common to identify new or additional tasks that need to be added to the schedule. In the past, adding additional tasks to schedules created by hand involved rewriting and redrawing the entire schedule. With Project, you simply insert a new task row and enter the necessary information.

Insert tasks

After entering several tasks, you identify two more tasks that need to be inserted within the task list. In this exercise, you insert two new tasks within the task list.

1 Select task 2, Hire mover.

The new task row will be inserted above the selected task.

You can also use the INSERT key.

2 On the Insert menu, click New Task.

A new task row is inserted above task 2, Hire mover.

If you click the task ID header when inserting, you must click the task name field before typing.

3 Type **Locate new site**, and then press TAB. Type **1w**, and press ENTER.

The new task and duration are entered.

4 Select task 7, Paint, and press INSERT.

5 Type **Disassemble furniture**, and then press TAB. Type **2**, and press ENTER.

Your screen should look similar to the following illustration.

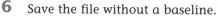

Inserted tasks

6 Save the file without a baseline.

> **TIP** To insert more than one new task row at a time, you can select multiple tasks. The same number of new task rows will be inserted above the selection.

Moving a Task

Drag and drop can be used in Project to move a task from one location to another within the task list. By using drag and drop, you don't need to insert a blank row. Project automatically inserts a row at the new location and deletes the row in the prior location. With drag and drop, you can move a single row or several consecutive rows at the same time. When using drag and drop, you must select task ID heading.

For a demonstration of how to move and delete a task, refer to page xxviii in the Installing and Using the Practice Files section.

NOTE The Cut, Copy, and Paste buttons or commands can also be used to move a task within the task list after a new row is inserted, but can sometimes lead to unexpected results. If you select a field in a row and use Cut or Copy, only the selected field is affected, not the entire row. If you use Cut or Copy, you should select the task ID heading so that the entire row is affected.

Move a task

While looking over the tasks you've entered, you notice a task that is out of order. In this exercise, you move a task in the task list to place it in the proper sequence within the project.

To move a task using drag and drop, the task ID must be selected.

1 Click the task ID for task 3, Hire mover.

The entire task row is selected.

2 With the pointer still positioned on the task ID, drag down until a horizontal gray bar is displayed between task 4, Finalize drawings and task 5, Frame interior walls.

Your screen should look similar to the following illustration.

		Task Name	Duration
1		Hire architect	2 days
2		Locate new site	1 wk
3		Hire mover	3 days
4		Finalize drawings	1 wk
5		Frame interior walls	4 days
6		Pack boxes	2 days
7		Disassemble furniture	2 days
8		Paint	4 days
9		Move complete	0 days

New location

3 Release the mouse button.

The "Hire mover" task is now displayed below the "Finalize drawings" task, and the tasks are renumbered.

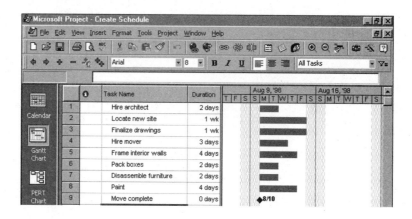

Deleting a Task

After starting a project, you might find that a task is not necessary or is to be performed outside the project schedule. You can then delete this task from the task list.

Delete a task

You decide that the "Pack boxes" task can be scheduled by the individual departments and does not need to be included in the master schedule for the relocation. In this exercise, you delete a task from the schedule.

1 Select task 6, Pack boxes.

You can also press DELETE.

2 On the Edit menu, click Delete Task.

The task is deleted, and the task list is renumbered.

3 Save the file without a baseline.

Using Undo/Redo

If you need to reverse an editing change you've made to the task list, you can use the Undo command to undo your last command or typing action. Unlike many Microsoft programs, Project has just one level of Undo. Therefore, only your last action can be reversed. You can undo your last action by using the Undo button on the Standard toolbar, choosing Undo on the Edit menu, or pressing CTRL+Z. You can also bring back an undo action by using the Redo button or command. After using Undo, the Undo button and command change to Redo. The ToolTip and command name indicate what type of action is available for Undo or Redo.

To use Undo and Redo, perform the following steps.

Undo

Redo

1   On the Standard toolbar, click the Undo button.

     The previous action is reversed.

2   On the Standard toolbar, click the Redo button.

     The original action is repeated.

One Step Further: Entering Recurring Tasks

A task that occurs repeatedly within a project is called a *recurring task*. A recurring task might be a weekly meeting, a status report, or regular inspections. Instead of typing the task and duration many times within a schedule, Project can be used to create a recurring task.

The Recurring Task Information dialog box is used to specify the parameters of the recurring task. A recurring task can be set to occur daily, weekly, monthly, or yearly. You can specify the duration of each occurrence of the task, what day of the week or month it will occur, and how many times or how long it will occur.

Enter a recurring task

The project team will meet every Friday to review how the project is proceeding and make any necessary adjustments to the schedule. In this exercise, you enter a recurring project meeting for the next 20 weeks.

1 Below task 8, Move complete, click in the Task Name column.

2 On the Insert menu, click Recurring Task.

The Recurring Task Information dialog box appears.

3 In the Name box, type **Project meeting**

4 Press TAB, and then type **2h**

The recurring task duration is two hours.

5 In the This Occurs area, be sure that the Weekly option is selected.

6 In the Weekly area, select the Fri check box.

The recurring project meeting will be scheduled every Friday.

7 In the Length area, select the For option.

8 Press TAB, and then type **20**

The project meeting will be scheduled for 20 occurrences.

9 Click OK.

The recurring task is entered. Your screen should look similar to the following illustration.

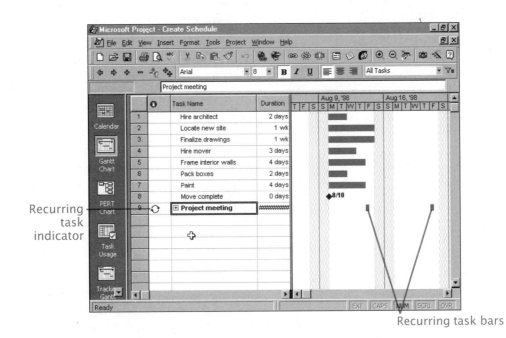

Recurring task indicator

Recurring task bars

10 Save the file without a baseline.

Finish the lesson

1 To continue to the next lesson, on the File menu, click Close.

2 If you are finished using Project for now, on the File menu, click Exit.

Lesson Summary

To	Do this
Enter the project start date	On the Project menu, click Project Information. Click the State Date down arrow. Use the calendar arrows to locate the month and year the project will start. Click the day the project will start. Click OK.
Enter project properties	On the File menu, click Properties. Enter the appropriate information in the boxes.
Enter a task	Click in a blank field in the Task Name column.
Enter a task duration	Click in the Duration field for the task.
Insert a task	Select the Task Name field where the new task is to be inserted. On the Edit menu, click Insert New Task. *or* Press INSERT.
Move a task	Click the task ID of the task to be moved. Drag the selected task until a vertical gray bar is displayed in the location where the task is to be moved. Release the mouse button.
Delete a task	Select the task to be deleted. On the Edit menu, click Delete Task. *or* Press DELETE.

For online information about	On the Help menu, click Contents And Index, click the Index tab, and then type
Entering project information	**start date**
Entering project properties	**properties**
Adding tasks	**enter tasks**
Adding durations	**durations** *or* **entering durations**
Inserting a task	**insert tasks**
Moving a task	**move tasks**
Deleting a task	**delete tasks**

Outlining a Project

Estimated time

25 min.

In this lesson you will learn how to:

- Create a summary task.
- Indent tasks.
- Hide and show subtasks in the outline.

A project task list can be as few as 20 tasks or as many as several hundred tasks. When a project has a large number of tasks, it can become difficult to locate a specific task within the task list. If you are familiar with the project schedule, you might be able to quickly locate a task by its task ID number. But if you are not familiar with the task list, you could spend a great deal of time searching the task list for a particular task.

Using Microsoft Project 98, you can organize the task list by creating a hierarchical structure. The process of structuring the task list is called outlining. You can use outlining to organize common tasks into groups within the task list. The groups created in the task list can represent phases in a project, rooms within a building, or specific buildings in a large construction site. When you outline the task list, the schedule becomes easier to read, and you can locate individual tasks quicker.

In this lesson, you use outlining to group the tasks in the corporate office relocation project into phases. You create a main summary task and several levels of summary tasks below it. You also hide and show the outline structure to display specific phases and tasks within the project.

53

Start the lesson

Open

Look In Favorites

1   Start Microsoft Project.

2   On the Standard toolbar, click the Open button.

    The Open dialog box appears.

3   Click the Look In Favorites button.

4   Double-click the Project SBS Practice folder.

5   Double-click Outline.

    The Outline practice file opens.

6   On the File menu, click Save As.

    The Save As dialog box appears.

7   In the Save In box, be sure that Project SBS Practice is displayed.

8   In the File Name box, be sure that the text is selected, and then type **Relocation outlining**

All exercise files will be saved without a baseline until Lesson 11, "Working with the Critical Path."

9   Click Save.

    The Planning Wizard dialog box appears.

10 Be sure that the Save Relocation Outlining Without A Baseline option is selected, and click OK.

    A copy of the file is saved as Relocation outlining without a baseline.

Creating an Outline

Outlining of multiple projects is discussed further in Lesson 14, "Working with Multiple Projects."

Creating a hierarchical outline organizes the project tasks list into groups of tasks. Each group of tasks is preceded by a *summary task*, which describes the tasks within the group. Each level within the outline provides an additional level of detail for the task below. An outline might be created to make a long list of tasks easier to read, to divide a project into distinct phases, or to create a high-level view of the project for management. An outline can have up to 65,000 levels. Outlining can occur anytime during the scheduling process; however, it is much easier to outline at the beginning.

The outline of a project schedule generally starts with a *main summary task*. The main summary task is a brief description of the project. All tasks are subordinate to the main summary task. A main summary task is useful to quickly identify a project. It can also be useful when using multiple project files in a combined project.

The outline buttons on the Formatting toolbar are used to create and display the outline. These buttons are available only in Gantt Chart, Task Sheet, and Task Usage views. The outlining buttons are described in the following table.

Button	Name	Description
⬅	Outdent	Outdents a task to a higher-level task.
➡	Indent	Indents a task to a lower-level task. Indenting creates a summary task above.
➕	Show Subtasks	Expands the summary task to show the subtasks.
➖	Hide Subtasks	Collapses the summary task to hide subtasks.
➕	Hide Assignments	In Resource Usage and Task Usage views, displays the resource assignments with indentations similar to that of subtasks.
➕➕	Show All Subtasks	Shows all subtasks in the outline.

A task changes to a summary task when a task below it is indented. The indented task then becomes a *subtask* of the summary task. When a task becomes a summary task, the duration, start and finish dates, and cost information change to summarize the information of the subtasks. For example, the start date of a summary task becomes the earliest start date of the subtasks, the finish date becomes the latest finish date of the subtasks, and the cost of a summary task totals the cost of each subtask.

Except for a few important differences, editing the task list after it has been outlined is similar to editing it before it was outlined. If the only subtask of a summary task is deleted or outdented, the summary task becomes a subtask of the summary task one level above. If a summary task is deleted, the subtasks below are also deleted.

The project team has met and developed the task list for the corporate relocation project. The tasks are listed in the approximate order they will occur. While reviewing the task list, you notice that the project is actually taking place in three separate phases: planning, remodeling, and moving. In the following exercises, you use outlining to group the tasks by phase, with a summary task proceeding each group.

Add a main summary task

In this exercise, you insert a new task into the task list and make it the main summary task.

1 Click in the Task Name field for task 1, Write proposal.

The new task will be inserted above the "Write proposal" task.

You can also press INSERT.

2 On the Insert menu, click New Task.

A new blank task row is inserted. The task list is renumbered.

3 Type **Corporate Relocation**, and press ENTER.

The main summary task should describe the project.

4 Drag to select the task ID headings for task 2 through task 42.

5 On the Formatting toolbar, click the Indent button.

The selected tasks are indented one level within the outline.

Indent

6 Press CTRL+HOME.

The cursor moves to the first task in the project. Task 1, Corporate Relocation, is bold, indicating it is a summary task. Your screen should look similar to the following illustration.

Summary task

Subtasks

	❶	Task Name	Duration	Start	
1		⊟ **Corporate Relocation**	**10 days**	**Mon 8/10/98**	
2		Write proposal	3 days	Mon 8/10/98	
3		Hire architect	2 days	Mon 8/10/98	
4		Locate new site	1 wk	Mon 8/10/98	
5		Present proposal	2 days	Mon 8/10/98	
6		Corporate approval	0 days	Mon 8/10/98	◆8/10
7		Negotiate new lease	4 days	Mon 8/10/98	
8		Finalize drawings	2 wks	Mon 8/10/98	
9		Select subcontractors	1.5 wks	Mon 8/10/98	
10		Hire mover	3 days	Mon 8/10/98	
11		Submit drawings	1.5 wks	Mon 8/10/98	
12		Permits received	0 days	Mon 8/10/98	◆8/10
13		Remodeling	1 day	Mon 8/10/98	
14		Demolition of existing :	3 days	Mon 8/10/98	

7 Save the file without a baseline.

> **TIP** You can automatically create a main summary task. On the Tools menu, click Options. Be sure the View tab is selected. In the Outline Options area, select the Project Summary Task check box. The project title is inserted from the Title box on the Summary tab of the Project Properties dialog box. If you have not entered any information in the Project Properties dialog box, on the File menu, click Properties, and then enter the appropriate information on the Summary tab.

Create a summary task

In this exercise, you insert a new task, and then group several tasks together as a phase.

1   Select the Task Name field for task 2, Write proposal.

2   On the Insert menu, click New Task.

    A new row is inserted for task 2.

3   Type **Planning**, and press ENTER.

    The inserted task assumes the same position in the outline structure as the task below.

4   Drag to select the task ID headings for task 3 through task 13.

5   On the Formatting toolbar, click the Indent button.

    Task 3 through task 13 are subtasks of the summary task Planning.

TIP You can also indent tasks using the mouse. To indent a task with the mouse, position the pointer over the first letter of the task name. The pointer changes to a two-way arrow. Drag the task one level to the right.

Create additional summary tasks

In this exercise, you create additional summary tasks within the task list.

The selection of tasks should be cleared if you want to make a new selection within the currently selected tasks. If the selection is not cleared, the selected tasks could accidentally be moved to a different location within the task list.

1   Drag to select the task ID headings for task 15 through task 28.

    Task 14, Remodeling, will become a summary task.

2   On the Formatting toolbar, click the Indent button.

3   Drag to select the task ID headings for task 30 through task 42.

4   On the Formatting toolbar, click the Indent button.

5   Click outside the selected tasks to cancel the selection.

6   Drag to select the task ID headings for task 31 through task 36.

7   On the Formatting toolbar, click the Indent button.

    The "Office space" summary task is now a summary task within the "Moving" summary task.

8   Drag to select the task ID headings for task 38 through task 42.

9   On the Formatting toolbar, click the Indent button.

Note that task 43, Move complete, is only indented one level. This is because it is the last milestone in the project, not part of one of the phases.

10 Press CTRL+HOME.

11 Save the file without a baseline.

> **NOTE** The Outdent button on the Formatting toolbar is used to move a task up in the hierarchy of the outline. If you outdent a subtask that is in the second or lower level of the outline, it becomes a summary task as long as it has one other subtask below it. If you outdent a summary task that has subtasks of another summary task at a higher level of the outline, it becomes a subtask of that summary task. If all subtasks are outdented to the first level, the outline structure is removed.

Hiding and Showing the Outline

By *hiding* and *showing* subtasks in the outline, you can display only the information you need. For example, you are presenting the scheduling information for a single phase within the project. Instead of printing the entire project schedule, you can hide the summary tasks that don't contain the subtasks for the phase being presented. Not only does this cut down on the printing, but it allows you to focus on a specific area without being distracted by divergent information. When you need more information, you can show some or all of the outline.

The outline structure can be hidden or shown using the outline buttons on the Formatting toolbar or the outline symbols next to each summary task. The minus sign (-) outline symbol indicates that all the subtasks of the summary task are shown, while a plus sign (+) outline symbol indicates that the subtasks of the summary task are hidden.

In the following exercises, the corporate relocation schedule has been outlined into three phases. To quickly review the various tasks within each phase, you hide and show various subtasks groups. When you are finished reviewing the phases, you show all subtasks in the outline.

Hide and show subtasks

In this exercise, you hide and show subtasks of summary tasks within the project schedule.

Hide Subtasks

1 Select task 2, Planning.

2 On the Formatting toolbar, click the Hide Subtasks button.

The subtasks to summary task 2, Planning, are hidden. Only the summary task is displayed. Your screen should look similar to the following illustration.

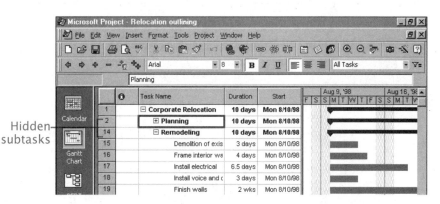

Hidden subtasks

You can also select any subtask of the summary task, and then use the Hide Subtasks button.

3 Click the minus sign (-) outline symbol next to task 14, Remodeling.

The Remodeling phase subtasks are hidden.

4 Click the plus sign (+) outline symbol next to task 2, Planning.

The Planning phase subtasks are displayed.

 TIP Before printing a project schedule, you can hide the subtasks of summary tasks that don't need to be visible to minimize the number of pages printed for the schedule.

Hide and show all subtasks in the outline

In this exercise, you hide all subtasks in the outline so only the main summary task is displayed. You then show all subtasks in the outline.

1   Click the minus sign (-) outline symbol next to task 1, Corporate Relocation.

All subtasks and summary tasks except the main summary task are hidden.

2   On the Formatting toolbar, click the Show All Subtasks button.

All subtasks and summary tasks are displayed.

3   Save the file without a baseline.

Show All Subtasks

> **TROUBLESHOOTING**   If the outline buttons are unavailable while in Gantt Chart, Task Sheet, or Task Usage views, be sure the summary tasks are displayed. On the Tools menu, click Options. On the View tab, be sure the Show Summary Tasks check box is selected. The outline buttons will be unavailable if you have sorted the outline without retaining the structure.

One Step Further: Viewing Outline Numbers

Project automatically assigns an outline number to each task when you outline the schedule. The outline numbers are based on the structure of the outline. Each number indicates the task's position within the outline hierarchy. For example, the first task in the outline is assigned the number 1. The subtask below is then assigned the number 1.1, the next subtask is assigned the number 1.2, and so on. The outline numbers can be useful for reporting purposes.

For more information on outline numbers, see "Outline Number field" in the Help Index.

The outline numbers are similar to a Work Breakdown Structure (*WBS*) code, except that they are created by Project and cannot be changed. The outline number for a task is also entered into the WBS code field by default. Although the outline numbers cannot be changed, the WBS code field can. If you change the WBS code field, it will not affect the outline numbers. The WBS code field can be changed on the Advanced tab in the Task Information dialog box.

Display outline numbers

In this exercise, you display the outline numbers to review the outline hierarchy.

1   On the Tools menu, click Options.

The Options dialog box appears.

2 Be sure the View tab is selected.

3 In the Outline Options area, select the Show Outline Number check box.

4 Click OK.

The outline numbers are displayed in each Task Name field. Your screen should look similar to the following illustration.

Hide outline numbers

In this exercise, you hide the outline numbers.

1 On the Tools menu, click Options.

2 In the Outline Options area, clear the Show Outline Number check box.

3 Click OK.

4 Save file without a baseline.

Finish the lesson

1 To continue to the next lesson, on the File menu, click Close.

2 If you are finished using Project for now, on the File menu, click Exit.

Lesson Summary

To	Do this	Button
Create a summary task	Select one or more tasks below the task that you want to make a summary task. On the Formatting toolbar, click the Indent button.	
Hide the subtasks of a summary task	Select the summary task or one of its subtasks to hide. On the Formatting toolbar, click the Hide Subtasks button. *or* Click the minus sign (-) outline symbol next to the summary task to hide the subtasks.	
Show the subtasks of a summary task	Select the summary task to show. On the Formatting toolbar, click the Show Subtasks button. *or* Click the plus sign (+) outline symbol next to the summary task to show the subtasks.	
Hide all subtasks in the outline	Select the main summary task. On the Formatting toolbar, click the Hide Subtasks button. *or* Click the minus sign (-) outline symbol next to the main summary task.	
Show the entire outline	On the Formatting toolbar, click the Show All Subtasks button. *or* Click the plus sign (+) outline symbol next to the main summary task.	

For online information about	On the Help menu, click Contents And Index, click the Index tab, and then type
Creating a summary task	**outlines**
Hiding and showing subtasks in an outline	**hide subtasks** *or* **show subtasks**

Establishing Task Dependencies

Estimated time
30 min.

In this lesson you will learn how to:

- Link and unlink tasks.
- Change the dependencies between tasks.
- Specify lead and lag time.

When a task list is first developed, the tasks are listed one after another, and the only consideration is the approximate order in which they should occur. Based on that information, each task is scheduled to start at the same time and finish depending on the duration of the individual task. In reality, a project schedule is more than just a list of isolated tasks. Each task is dependent upon one or more tasks to determine when it should start and finish. Some tasks can't start until another task is completed, while other tasks can occur at the same time as other tasks.

With Microsoft Project 98, you can easily create *dependencies* between tasks in a schedule. By *linking* tasks, you create dependencies that identify whether the start or finish of one task depends on the start or finish of another task. You can also create situations where the dependency between tasks is delayed or overlapped. Once links are established between tasks, the project tasks begin to develop into a schedule of events.

In this lesson, the task list for the corporate office relocation project has been completed and outlined into three phases: planning, remodeling, and moving. You begin to identify how the tasks and phases are related by linking them together. You change dependencies between tasks to accurately reflect how the tasks should occur by changing dependency types and creating delay and overlap.

Start the lesson

1   Start Microsoft Project.
2   From the Project SBS Practice folder, open the Linking file.
3   In the Project SBS Practice folder, save the file as Task dependencies without a baseline.

Understanding Dependencies Between Tasks

When a task is initially entered into Project, it is scheduled to begin on the project start date. By linking tasks, you establish a dependency that determines the sequence of tasks. Project then schedules the tasks by setting the start and finish dates of each task. The Gantt bars in the Gantt Chart view are then moved to the appropriate date on the timescale, and *link lines* are drawn to display the dependency.

There are four types of task dependencies: *finish-to-start, finish-to-finish, start-to-start,* and *start-to-finish*. A finish-to-start dependency is the most common, while a start-to-finish dependency is the least common. A description and example of each dependency type is provided in the following table.

Dependency diagram	Description	Example
	Finish-to-start (FS). The finish of one task marks the start of another.	A mailing list is updated before new mailing labels are printed.
	Start-to-start (SS). The two tasks start at the same time.	The electrical and plumbing in a building can be installed during the same time period.
	Finish-to-finish (FF). The two tasks finish at the same time.	The information backup on an old computer should be completed by the time the new computer is installed.
	Start-to-finish (SF). The start of one task marks the finish of another.	Running reports on an old accounting system would not stop until the running of reports on the new system begins.

A task that must start or finish before another task can begin is called a *predecessor* task. A task that depends on the start or finish of a preceding task is called a *successor* task.

Each dependency can either lengthen or shorten the project schedule duration. For example, a finish-to-start dependency extends the duration because one task must finish before the other can start. The start-to-start and finish-to-finish dependencies can shorten the duration because they overlap the duration of the tasks.

Linking Tasks to Create Task Dependencies

Linking tasks creates a default finish-to-start dependency. Because the finish-to-start dependency is the most common dependency type, it is easiest to start by linking all tasks in this relationship. Once all tasks are in the default dependency type, you can begin to identify and address those tasks that are an exception to the common finish-to-start dependency. You can unlink tasks and phases that are not related, and you can link tasks that are not listed consecutively in the task list. Tasks can be linked to a single predecessor and successor or to multiple predecessors and successors.

For a demonstration of how to Link and unlink tasks, refer to page xxviii in the Installing and Using the Practice Files section.

In the following exercises, you are ready to begin linking the tasks within the corporate relocation schedule. You begin by linking a few tasks to see how linking works, and then you continue to link all tasks within the project in a finish-to-start dependency. You then unlink noncontiguous tasks.

Link tasks

In this exercise, you link the subtasks of a summary task and then link all tasks and summary tasks within the schedule.

You can also select any column of fields for the tasks being linked.

1   Drag to select the task ID headings for task 2 through task 13.

2   On the Standard toolbar, click the Link Tasks button.

Each subtask is linked in a finish-to-start dependency. Your screen should look similar to the following illustration.

Link Tasks

When linking tasks, you can link several tasks at a time or all tasks at once.

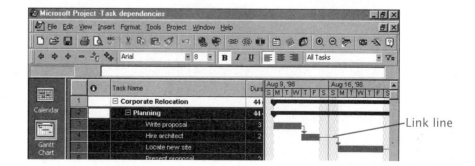

Link Tasks

You can also click Go To on the Edit menu.

3 Click the Task Name column header.

Each task is selected.

4 On the Standard toolbar, click the Link Tasks button.

Each task is linked.

5 Press F5.

The Go To dialog box appears.

6 In the ID box, type **14**, and click OK.

The selection moves to the indicators field for task 14, Remodeling. Your screen should look similar to the following illustration.

Link line between summary task 2, Planning, and summary task 14, Remodeling

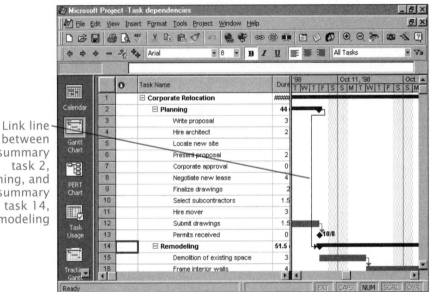

7 Save the file without a baseline.

Unlink tasks

In this exercise, you remove the link between summary tasks.

1 Press F5, type **30**, and click OK.

Task 30, Office space, and task 37, Server room, are displayed.

2 Press CTRL, and then select task 37, Server room.

Both task 30 and task 37 are selected.

3 On the Standard toolbar, click the Unlink Tasks button.

The link between the "Office space" phase and the "Server room" phase is deleted. Your screen should look similar to the following illustration.

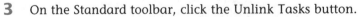

Unlink Tasks

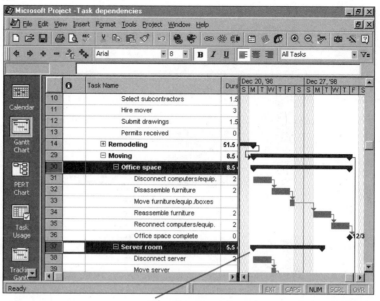

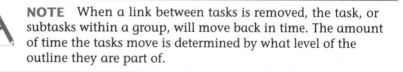

The Server room phase now begins at
the same time as the Office space phase.

4   Save the file without a baseline.

> **NOTE**   When a link between tasks is removed, the task, or
> subtasks within a group, will move back in time. The amount
> of time the tasks move is determined by what level of the
> outline they are part of.

Link noncontiguous tasks

In this exercise, you link a summary task to a subtask within another phase.

*You can also
double-click the
link line and
click Delete in
the Task
Dependency
dialog box. The
button appears
before the OK
and Cancel
buttons. Be
sure not to click
Delete instead
of clicking OK.*

1   Select task 31, Disconnect computers/equip.

2   Press CTRL, and select task 37, Server room.

You can select noncontiguous tasks with CTRL.

3   On the Standard toolbar, click the Link Tasks button.

The start of task 37, Server room, is linked to the finish of task 31,
Disconnect computers/equip. Your screen should look similar to the
following illustration.

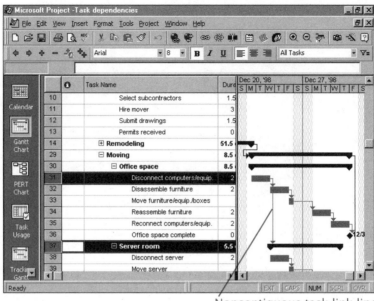

Noncontiguous task link line

4 Save the file without a baseline.

> **TIP** Tasks can also be linked using drag and drop. To use drag and drop to create a link, place the mouse pointer over the center of the Gantt bar for the first task in the link. The pointer changes to a four-headed arrow. Next, drag down to the middle of the Gantt bar for the second task in the link. As you drag over the Gantt bars, the pointer changes to a chain link, and a ScreenTip indicating the link will be established is displayed. When the ScreenTip displays the correct information, release the mouse button.

Changing Task Dependencies

Because not all tasks need to be in a finish-to-start dependency, you can change the dependency type. To change the dependency type, you use the Task Dependency dialog box or any view that displays the Type field. The Task Dependency dialog box is displayed by double-clicking a link line between tasks. The dialog box confirms which tasks the link line is connected to and displays the current dependency. The Type box is used to change the dependency. When a task dependency is changed, the link line on the Gantt Chart is redrawn to reflect the change. Use link lines to quickly identify task dependencies.

In the following exercises, all the tasks in the corporate relocation schedule have been linked in a finish-to-start dependency. You have identified several tasks that do not depend on another task to finish before they can start. You change the dependency between the tasks.

Establish a finish-to-finish dependency

In this exercise, you change the dependency between tasks so they finish at the same time.

1   Press F5, type **10**, and click OK.

2   Double-click the link line between task 10, Select subcontractors, and task 11, Hire mover.

The Task Dependency dialog box appears.

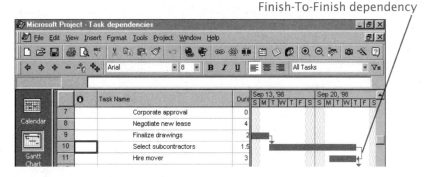

3   Click the Type down arrow.

A list of dependency types is displayed.

4   Select Finish-To-Finish, and click OK.

The two tasks will end simultaneously, and some work will overlap in a finish-to-finish dependency. Your screen should look similar to the following illustration.

Finish-To-Finish dependency

5   Save the file without a baseline.

Establish a start-to-start dependency

In this exercise, you change the dependency between tasks so they start at the same time.

1 Press F5, type **17**, and click OK.

2 Double-click the link line between task 17, Install electrical, and task 18, Install voice and data lines.

The Task Dependency dialog box appears.

3 Click the Type down arrow, select Start-To Start, and click OK.

The two tasks are scheduled to begin on the same date.

4 Save the file without a baseline.

Understanding Lag Time and Lead Time

In addition to changing the dependency type, you can further define the true impact of task relationships using *lead time* and *lag time*. Lead time creates an overlap in a task dependency that can shorten the project duration. For example, if you specify a lead time of one day on a finish-to-start dependency, the two tasks overlap in time by one day. The last day of the first task takes place while the first day of the second task takes place. Lag time creates a delay, or gap, in the task dependency that can lengthen the project duration. For example, if you specify a lag time of one day on a finish-to-start dependency, there is a one-day gap between the tasks. The first task finishes, a day goes by, and the second task starts. Lead time moves the start of the successor task back in time, and lag time moves the start of the successor task forward in time.

In Project, the Lag field is used to specify both lead and lag. In the Lag field, lead is displayed as a negative number and lag is displayed as a positive number. Lead and lag time are entered in the Lag box on the Task Dependency dialog box or in any view that displays the Lag field.

In the following exercises, you've come across some additional information that will affect when tasks occur in the project. To accurately reflect this information, you specify lag and lead time in several task dependencies.

Specify lag time

In this exercise, you specify lag time to delay a dependency.

In Project, lag and lead time are specified as negative and positive numbers in the Lag box in the Task Dependency dialog box.

1   Be sure that task 17, Install electrical, and task 18, Install voice and data lines, are displayed, and then double-click the link line between the two tasks.

The Task Dependency dialog box appears.

2   Press TAB.

The Lag box is selected.

You can also use the spin controls to change the number in the Lag box.

3   Type **1**, and click OK.

The start-to-start dependency is delayed by one day. The start of the second task in the dependency is moved back in time. Your screen should look similar to the following illustration.

You can also specify lag and lead time as a percentage.

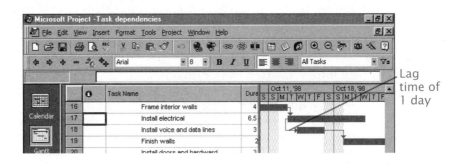

Lag time of 1 day

4   Save the file without a baseline.

Specify lead time

In this exercise, you specify lead time to overlap a dependency.

1   Press F5, type **8**, and click OK.

2   Double-click the link line between task 8, Negotiate new lease, and task 9, Finalize drawings.

You must type the minus sign (-) to create negative lag.

3   Press TAB, type **-2**, and click OK.

The dependency between the two tasks overlaps by two days.

71

🗐 Microsoft Project - Task dependencies				_ 🗗 ✕

File Edit View Insert Format Tools Project Window Help

	❶	Task Name	Dur	3, '98	Aug 30, '98	Sep
				T W T F S	S M T W T F S	S M
7		Corporate approval	0	◆ 8/25		
8		Negotiate new lease	4			
9		Finalize drawings	2			
10		Select subcontractors	1.5			
11		Hire mover	3			

Lead time of 2 days

4 Save the file without a baseline.

Identifying the Critical Path

The *critical path* identifies those tasks that are critical to the duration of the project. A *critical task* cannot have its duration lengthened or its start date delayed without impacting the project finish date. A critical task is a task that has no *slack* time. Critical tasks form a critical path through the project. Once a project schedule is formatted to display the critical path, you can reduce or lengthen the total project duration by changing the duration, dependencies, or resources of the critical tasks.

To format the Gantt Chart to automatically display the critical path, you use the *GanttChartWizard*. The GanttChartWizard contains options you select to format the Gantt Chart. When the Gantt Chart is formatted to display the critical path, critical task Gantt bars are displayed as red, and *noncritical task* Gantt bars are displayed as blue. As you make changes to the project schedule, the critical path will be updated.

Format to view the critical path

In this exercise, you use the GanttChartWizard to format the Gantt bars in the Gantt Chart to display the critical path.

GanttChartWizard

Depending on your selection in each GanttChartWizard dialog box, some steps will be skipped.

1 On the Standard toolbar, click the GanttChartWizard button.

The GanttChartWizard - Step 1 dialog box appears.

2 Click Next.

The GanttChartWizard - Step 2 dialog box appears.

3 Select the Critical Path option, and then click Next.

The GanttChartWizard - Step 9 dialog box appears.

4 Be sure that the Resources And Dates option is selected, and then click Next.

The GanttChartWizard - Step 13 dialog box appears.

5 Be sure that the Yes, Please option is selected, and then click Next.

The GanttChartWizard - Step 14 dialog box appears.

6 Click Format It.

The Gantt Chart is formatted to display critical task Gantt bars as red and noncritical task Gantt bars as blue. The GanttChartWizard - Step 15 dialog box appears.

7 Click Exit Wizard.

The GanttChartWizard closes. The critical path is displayed.

8 Press F5, type **31**, and click OK.

Critical tasks are displayed as red Gantt bars and noncritical tasks are displayed as blue Gantt bars. Your screen should look similar to the following illustration.

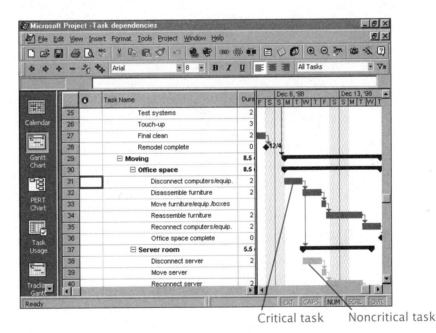

Critical task   Noncritical task

9 Save the file without a baseline.

Displaying Multiple Critical Paths

By default, only one critical path is displayed in Project. However, you can change a calculation option so that Project displays a critical path for each independent network of tasks or summary task groups. When only one critical path is displayed, a task without a successor has its *late finish date* set to the project's finish date, giving the task slack and making it noncritical. When multiple critical paths are displayed, a task without a successor has its late finish date set to the task's *early finish date*, which gives the task zero slack and makes it critical.

To display multiple critical tasks, perform the following steps.

1   On the Tools menu, click Options.

2   Click the Calculation tab.

3   Select the Calculate Multiple Critical Paths check box, and click OK.

One Step Further: Using the Task Form

Information about task dependencies can also be viewed in the Task Form. The Task Form provides details about an individual task, such as start and finish date, predecessor, and dependency type. The Task Form can be viewed as a single view or as a combination view, called the Task Entry view.

In the Task Form, you can view, enter, and edit basic tracking and scheduling information about tasks one at a time. You can use the Task Form when you want to display detailed information about a task or enter and revise task information in one location.

View task dependencies in the Task Form

In this exercise, you change views to the Task Entry combination view and then view several tasks.

1   Press F5, type **9**, and click OK.

You can also click More Views on the View menu to display the More Views dialog box.

2   On the View Bar, click the down arrow, and then click the More Views icon.

The More Views dialog box appears.

3   Scroll within the Views list, select Task Entry, and then click Apply.

The Task Entry view is displayed. The Gantt Chart is displayed in the top pane of the view, and the Task Form is displayed in the bottom pane of the view.

If you cannot see the next button, hide the View Bar.

4   Click Next.

The next task in the task list is displayed in the Task Form.

Change task information in the Task Form

In this exercise, you change the duration estimate for a task from the Task Form.

1 Be sure that task 10, Select Subcontractors, is displayed.

2 On the Duration box, click the up arrow once, and click OK.

   The task duration changes to two weeks in both the Task Form and on the Gantt Chart. Your screen should look similar to the following illustration.

Task dependency details

Duration change

You can also use the split bar to display the Task Entry view.

3 Double-click the split bar.

   The Task Form closes, and the Gantt Chart view is displayed.

4 Save the file without a baseline.

 **TIP** When working in the Task Form, use the OK button instead of pressing ENTER after each change is made. Pressing ENTER does not always accept a change in the Task Form.

Finish the lesson

1 To continue to the next lesson, on the File menu, click Close.

2 If you are finished using Project for now, on the File menu, click Exit.

75

Lesson Summary

To	Do this	Button
Link tasks	Select the tasks to be linked. On the Standard toolbar, click the Link Tasks button.	
Unlink tasks	Select the tasks to be unlinked. On the Standard toolbar, click the Unlink Tasks button.	
Link noncontiguous tasks	Select the first task to be linked. Press CTRL, and select the next task to be linked. On the Standard toolbar, click the Link Tasks button.	
Specify the task dependency	Double-click the link line between the tasks where you want to change the dependency. Click the Type down arrow, select a dependency type, and click OK.	
Specify lead time	Double-click the link line between the tasks where you want to specify the lead time. Press TAB to move to the Lag box. Type a negative number to reflect the amount of lead time. Click OK.	
Specify lag time	Double-click the link line between the tasks where you want to specify the lag time. Press TAB to move to the Lag box. Type a positive number to reflect the amount of lead time. Click OK.	
Format to display the critical path	On the Standard toolbar, click the GanttChartWizard button. Select the Critical Path option in step 2, select the default selection for all other steps, and click Next. Click Format It in step 14, and then click Next. Click Exit Wizard in step 15.	

For online information about	On the Help menu, click Contents And Index, click the Index tab, and then type
Linking tasks	**link tasks**
Specifying task dependencies	**dependencies** *or* **relationship**
Specifying lead and lag time	**lead time** *or* **lag time**
Formatting the critical path	**GanttChartWizard** *or* **critical tasks, determining**

Review & Practice

Estimated time
20 min.

You will review and practice how to:

■ Create a new project file and enter project properties information.

■ Enter tasks and durations to create a task list.

■ Arrange the task list into groups using outlining.

■ Link tasks and specify task dependencies.

■ Format the Gantt Chart to display the critical path.

Before you move on to Part 2, which covers working with resources and calendars, you can practice the skills you learned in Part 1 by working through this Review & Practice section. You will create a new project file, enter and edit tasks, link tasks, and specify dependencies, lead time, and lag time.

Scenario

Because of your success with the schedule for the corporate office relocation project, the Executive department has asked you to create a schedule for the annual shareholders meeting. You begin by setting up a new project file with a start date and project properties information. You then use the project team meeting to begin brainstorming the tasks and durations for the project. You also break the project into three phases, link the tasks, and begin the process of identifying changes in dependencies to further define the way the tasks will be performed.

Step 1: Create a New Project File

The project team has provided you with a start date for the project and basic information such as project title and manager. Before the team meeting, you set up the project file.

1 Create a new project file with a project start date of July 7, 1999.

2 Enter Shareholders Meeting as the project title, 1999 Annual Report, as the project subject, and your name as author and manager.

3 Save the project file as Meeting Tasks in the Project SBS Practice folder.

For more information about	See
Creating a new project file	Lesson 3
Entering project information	Lesson 3
Saving a project file	Lesson 2

Step 2: Enter and Edit Tasks in the Task List

During the project team meeting, you enter the information in Project. You also edit the task list as team members come up with more information.

1 Enter the following tasks and durations to the Shareholders Meeting task list, starting with task 1.

Task Name	Task Duration
Schedule conference date	1 day
Print letter	2 days
Book keynote speaker	2 days
Develop letter	1 day
Plan food with caterer	3 days
Print catering menu	1 day
Meeting occurs	0 days

2 Insert a new task, Book conference center, with a duration of 2 days, before task 2, Print letter.

3 Move task 3, Print letter, after task 5, Develop letter, using drag and drop.

4 Delete task 7, Print catering menu.

5 Save the file without a baseline, and then close the file.

For more information about	See
Entering tasks and durations	Lesson 3
Inserting a task	Lesson 3
Moving a task	Lesson 3
Deleting a task	Lesson 3

Step 3: *Outline the Project Tasks*

The first team meeting was a success, and the task list has been developed. You now use outlining to break up the project into groups of related tasks, called phases. Each phase will be assigned to a group within the project team for further evaluation.

1   In the Project SBS Practice folder, open the Review1 file, and then save the file as Meeting Outline without a baseline.

2   Insert a new task 1, Shareholders Meeting, and then indent task 2 through task 20.

3   Outline the task list into three groups as indicated below:

Indent task 3 through task 6.

Indent task 8 through task 13.

Indent task 15 through task 19.

4   Hide the subtasks of summary task 7, Notification letter, and summary task 14, Meeting details.

5   Show the entire outline.

6   Save the file without a baseline.

For more information about	See
Outlining a task list	Lesson 4
Hiding and showing the outline	Lesson 4

Step 4: *Link Tasks*

Before the phases are handed off to the project team groups, you link all tasks in a finish-to-start dependency. You also make some preliminary dependency changes based on your knowledge of the tasks within the project.

1   Link all tasks in a finish-to-start dependency.

2   Unlink summary task 7, Notification letter, and summary task 14, Meeting details. (Hint: Select the summary tasks only.)

3 Link summary task 2, Preliminary planning, to summary task 14, Meeting details.

4 Link task 11, Approve letter, with summary task 14, Meeting details.

For more information about	See
Linking tasks	Lesson 5

Step 5: Establish Task Dependencies

Each project team group has reviewed its phase of the project. Some groups have submitted changes to the task dependencies. You have been asked to make the requested changes to the schedule based on the information you've received.

1 Change the dependency between task 8, Order letter stock, and task 9, Develop letter, to start-to-start.

2 Change the dependency between task 16, Arrange committee meeting rooms, and task 17, Arrange necessary equipment, to finish-to-finish.

3 Specify lead time of 0.5 day on the dependency between task 4, Book conference center, and task 5, Book keynote speaker.

4 Specify lag time of 2 days between summary task 14, Meeting details, and task 20, Meeting occurs.

5 Save the file without a baseline.

For more information about	See
Changing a task dependency	Lesson 5
Specifying lead time and lag time	Lesson 5

Step 6: Use the GanttChartWizard

Now that the task list and task dependencies are established, you want to view the critical path for the project. You use the GanttChartWizard to format the Gantt Chart to display the critical path.

1 Start the GanttChartWizard.

2 Display the critical path on the Gantt Chart.

3 Display resource names and dates to the right of the Gantt bars.

4 Show link lines between dependent tasks.

5 Format the Gantt Chart, and then exit the GanttChartWizard.

6 Save the file without a baseline.

For more information about	See
Formatting to display the critical path	Lesson 5

Finish the Review & Practice

1 Close the Meeting Outline file.

2 If you are finished using Project for now, on the File menu, click Exit.

Working with Resources

Part 2

Managing Project Resources

In this lesson you will learn how to:

Estimated time
35 min.

- Create a list of resources.
- Assign resources to tasks.
- Enter detailed resource information.
- Assign costs to resources and tasks.
- Assign variable resource pay rates and cost rate tables.

Resources are the people, places, and items necessary to complete a task. A project can be scheduled with or without assigning resources to tasks. If you don't assign resources to tasks, there is less accountability for the completion of tasks and less flexibility in planning. By assigning resources to tasks, you can better track the amount of *work* on a task, the cost of the work, and the progress of the project.

Using Microsoft Project 98, you can quickly assign resources to tasks and accurately track your project costs. You can assign resources with the Assign Resources dialog box. Any information about a resource, from what it costs to when it's available, can be stored in Project. You can also track different rates per resource to reflect varied charges for different types of work. This information can be used to incorporate future rate changes, such as pay increases.

In this lesson, the task list and dependencies have been completed for the corporate office relocation project. You've been assigned the task of creating a resource list and making resource assignments to each task in the project. In addition, you've been provided with cost and detail information regarding each resource.

Start the lesson

1 Start Microsoft Project.

2 From the Project SBS Practice folder, open the Resource file.

3 Save the file as Assigning Resources without a baseline in the Project SBS Practice folder.

Assigning Resources

Each task within a project needs to be assigned all resources necessary to complete the task. A task might only require a single resource to be completed, or it might require several resources. It is important to remember that a resource is not just a person, but any place or item necessary to complete the task. A place resource can be a room, road, or a location, while an item resource can be equipment, such as a projector, or supplies such as books.

Resource names can be generic or specific in their descriptions. For example, a resource that performs administrative duties could be called "administrative assistant," or "J. Robins." How you name your resources depends on the project and the scheduler's preference. Whatever method you choose, make sure you are consistent and accurate in your definition of resources. For example, the resource "Pat" is obviously one person, while the resource "mechanic" could be one person or a team.

When a resource is added to a project, a single *unit*, or 100%, is entered into the *Max. Units* field for the resource by default. This means that only one of that resource is available for the project. Resource units are displayed as percentages by default. You can also display resource units as decimals. The maximum number of units can be increased or decreased. When increasing the maximum units of the resource, be sure that the additional units are actually available so that the schedule is accurate. If you decrease the maximum units to 50%, or 0.5, only half of the resource's time can be used on the project. The same information about resource units can be applied to assigning resources to a task. You can assign a single unit, partial units, or multiple units of a resource to a task. You should not assign more units of a resource to a task than are available to the project.

Resources can be entered into Project in several different locations. The most common locations are the Assign Resources dialog box and the Resource Sheet. In the Assign Resources dialog box, you can enter resource names and assign resources to tasks. On the Resource Sheet, you can enter resource names as well as detail information, such as maximum units and costs.

There are two ways you can assign resources from the Assign Resources dialog box. You can select a task and then select a resource, or you can drag and drop a resource to a task. In both cases, a single unit, or 100%, of the resource is assigned to the task by default. If more than a single unit of a resource is to be assigned to a task, additional units can be indicated in the Units field of the Assign Resources dialog box before the assignment is made. You can also assign parts of a unit. For example, if you assign 25% of a unit, that means a quarter of a resource's available working time is assigned to the task.

In the following exercises, you are ready to begin entering resources for the corporate office relocation project. You begin entering resource names and details using the Assign Resource dialog box and the Resource Sheet. You also begin making resource assignments.

Enter resources in the Assign Resources dialog box

In this exercise, you add resource names to the project using the Assign Resources dialog box.

Assign Resources

You can also click another field in the Name column to enter the resource name.

1 On the Standard toolbar, click the Assign Resources button.

The Assign Resources dialog box appears.

2 Type **administrative assistant**, and press ENTER.

The resource name is entered, and the selection moves to the next row.

Assign Resources	? X
Resources from: 'Assigning Resources'	

Name	Units	
administrative assis		Close
		Assign
		Remove
		Replace...
		Address...

3 Type **operations manager**, and press ENTER.

4 Type **architect**, and press ENTER.

Three resources are displayed in the Assign Resources dialog box.

5 Click Close.

The Assign Resources dialog box closes.

TIP You can also create resources using your e-mail address book. In the Assign Resources dialog box, click Address, and then select a resource from your e-mail list.

Add resources to the Resource Sheet

In this exercise, you add additional resources to the project using the Resource Sheet view.

Resource Sheet

1 On the View Bar, click the down arrow, and then click the Resource Sheet icon.

The resource names entered in the Assign Resources dialog box are displayed on the Resource Sheet. Your screen should look similar to the following illustration.

Resource ID number   Default resource information

Resource name

		Resource Name	Initials	Group	Max. Units	Std. Rate	Ovt. Rate	Co
	1	administrative assistant	a		100%	$0.00/hr	$0.00/hr	
	2	operations manager	o		100%	$0.00/hr	$0.00/hr	
	3	architect	a		100%	$0.00/hr	$0.00/hr	

2 Click in the Resource Name field below the word "architect."

3 Type **demolition contractor**, and press ENTER.

The resource name and default resource information are entered.

4 Type **assistant operations manager**, and press ENTER.

5 Type **conference room**, and press ENTER.

6 Save the file without a baseline.

> **NOTE** To use workgroup features for resources, you must enter resource e-mail addresses. E-mail addresses can be entered in the Resource Information dialog box. Workgroup features are discussed further in Appendix D.

Assign a resource to a task

Gantt Chart

In this exercise, you assign a resource to a task.

1 On the View Bar, click the Gantt Chart icon.

2 Select task 3, Write proposal.

3 On the Standard toolbar, click the Assign Resources button.

The Assign Resources dialog box appears.

Assign Resources

4 In the Name column, select "operations manager," and click Assign.

The resource is assigned to the task. A checkmark appears next to the resource name, and a unit value of 100% is displayed. The resource name is displayed next to the Gantt bar for task 3.

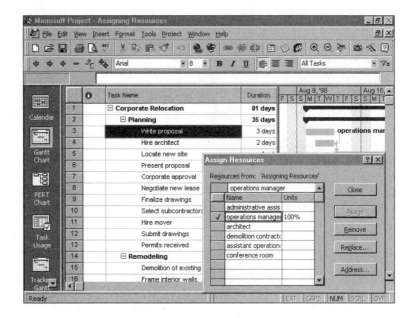

5 Save the file without a baseline.

TIP You can also remove and replace resource assignments on a task using the Assign Resources dialog box.

Assign a resource unit

In this exercise, you assign a resource to a task with a unit other than 100%.

1 Select task 11, Hire mover.

It is not necessary to type %; the default designation is percentage in the Units field.

2 In the Units field for the operations manager, type **50**

The operation manager will be assigned half of his or her available time to the task.

3 Click Assign.

The assignment is made.

4 Save the file without a baseline.

89

Assigning Multiple Resources

As mentioned earlier, a task might require more than one resource to complete the work. Using the Assign Resources dialog box, you can easily assign multiple resources to a single task and multiple tasks to a single resource.

When a task is selected, resource assignments are reflected in the Assign Resources dialog box. A checkmark appears, and the number of units assigned is displayed next to the resource name. If multiple resources are assigned to a task, a checkmark appears next to the name of each resource assigned.

Assign multiple resources to a single task

In this exercise, you assign two resources to the same task.

1   Select task 6, Present proposal.

2   In the Assign Resources dialog box, select "operations manager."

Instead of clicking Assign, you can press ENTER.

3   Hold down CTRL, select "conference room," and then click Assign.

Both the operations manager and the conference room are assigned to the task.

Assign Resources	? X
Resources from: 'Assigning Resources'	
conference room	

	Name	Units	
	administrative assis		Close
✓	operations manager	100%	Assign
	architect		
	demolition contracti		Remove
	assistant operation:		Replace...
✓	conference room	100%	Address...

 NOTE   More than one unit of a resource can be assigned to a task. Using the Assign Resources dialog box, enter a resource unit percentage in the Units field before clicking Assign. Assigning additional units of a resource to a task will be discussed further in Lesson 8, "Scheduling with Resources" and Lesson 9, "Managing Resource Workloads."

Assign a single resource to multiple tasks

In this exercise, you assign a single resource to three tasks.

1   Select task 5, Locate new site.

2   Hold down CTRL, select task 6, Present proposal, and then select task 9, Finalize drawings.

90

3   In the Assign Resources dialog box, select "architect," and then click Assign.

The resource is assigned to each task.

4   Click Close.

5   Scroll the Gantt Chart to view the resource assignments next to the Gantt bars.

6   Save the file without a baseline.

Providing Resource Details

Resource details provide additional information about a resource and can be entered on the Resource Sheet or in the Resource Information dialog box. Information such as resource initials, groups, maximum units, and codes can be kept in Project. The Resource Information dialog box displays additional fields of information not available on the Resource Sheet, such as *e-mail addresses* and availability dates.

Some resource details are used in scheduling tasks and calculating costs. Other resource details can be used for sorting or filtering.

Enter resource information on the Resource Sheet

In this exercise, you enter a resource's initials, group, max. units, standard and overtime rate, and code in Resource Sheet view.

1   On the View Bar, click the down arrow, and then click the Resource Sheet icon.

The Resource Sheet is displayed. The Indicators field for resource ID number 1 is selected.

2   Press TAB twice.

The Initials field is selected.

3   Type **admin assist**, and then press TAB.

The Group field is selected.

To change the resource unit display from percentage to decimal, on the Tools menu, click Options. On the Schedule tab, click the Show Assignment Units As A: down arrow, and select Decimal.

4   Type **office staff**, and then press TAB.

The Max. Units field is selected.

5   Click the up arrow twice to display 200%.

Two units of the resource will be available to the project.

6   Press TAB until the Code field is selected.

7   Type **105-106**, and then press TAB.

The selection moves to the Indicators field for resource ID number 2.

8   Save the file without a baseline.

NOTE The Group and Code fields for resources are user-defined fields. The user determines what kind of information is contained in these fields. For example, in the previous exercise, the Group field contains the resource's employment group, and the Code field contains the accounting code to which the resource's costs are charged.

Use the Resource Information dialog box

In this exercise, you enter a resource's e-mail address and project availability dates in the Resource Information dialog box.

You can also select a resource name, and then click the Resource Information button on the Standard toolbar.

1 Double-click the resource name "administrative assistant."

The Resource Information dialog box appears. Resource details for the administrative assistant are displayed.

2 Click in the E-mail box.

3 Type **jsmith@relocate.com**, and then press TAB.

4 In the Resource Availability area, select the From option.

The From and To boxes are active.

5 Click the From down arrow.

The date selection calendar is displayed.

6 Use the right arrow to scroll to August 1998.

7 Click the 31st on the calendar.

This is the first day the resource will be available for the project.

Resource working and non-working days will be discussed in Lesson 7, "Working with Calendars."

8 Click the To down arrow.

9 Select October 30, 1998, on the calendar.

Resource Information			? X
General	Working Time	Costs	Notes

Name: administrative assistant Initials: admin ass **OK**

Resource availability Group: office staff **Cancel**

○ Available for entire project Code: 105-106 **Details...**

● From: Mon 8/31/98 Email: jsmith@relocate.com

To: Fri 10/30/98 Workgroup: Default

Max units available: 200%

10 Click OK.

The information is saved for the resource.

Save and close the file

In this exercise, you save the file changes and close the file.

You can also click the Close button on the file window.

1 Save the file without a baseline.

2 On the File menu, click Close.

Working with Resource Costs

In Project, there are two types of costs: *resource costs* and *fixed costs*. By entering cost information, you can create project budgets and analyze costs, as well as identify potential cost overruns. Based on the cost information provided, the cost for each task and for the entire project can be calculated.

Each resource or task can have a cost associated with it, such as an hourly wage, yearly salary, or rental on a piece of equipment. Resource costs can be accrued in several ways. In the case of wages, they can be prorated by the hour, or, in the case of a contract, they can be accrued at the end or start of the task. With resource costs, the hourly rate might change during the duration of a project, or a resource might have different rates for each type of work.

The Resource Sheet can be used to enter basic resource costs. To enter additional resource cost information, such as pay rate changes over time or different base rates in cost rate tables, use the Costs tab in the Resource Information dialog box. Basic cost information entered on the Resource Sheet is displayed on the Costs tab.

Fixed costs are used when the task itself has a cost associated with it. Instead of assigning a resource rate–based cost, a fixed cost can be assigned. For example, if a task is being performed by a resource for a fixed price, such as a contract, a fixed cost is entered for the task with no associated resource cost. Unlike resource costs, fixed costs are not dependent on the amount of time it takes to complete a task. A task can also have a resource rate–based cost and a fixed cost. For example, if a task is being performed by a resource and materials are delivered, a fixed cost can be entered for the task materials and a resource cost can be entered for the assigned resource work. The two costs are then combined for the total cost of the task. Fixed costs are entered in the Fixed Cost field on the Cost table.

You can also enter *per-use costs*. Per-use costs are one time costs associated with a resource or a task regardless of the duration of the task or the number of units of a resource assigned to a task. For example, you have a piece of equipment delivered to a construction site. You might be charged a one-time delivery fee for the equipment and an hourly or daily rate. The delivery fee can be entered in the per-use field for the resource.

In the following exercises, you have finished entering the resources for the corporate office relocation project. You have also made the initial resource assignments. You are now ready to begin entering cost information for the project.

Open a new file

In this exercise, you open a new file where all the resources and resource information for the office relocation project have been entered.

1   From the Project SBS Practice folder, open the Costs file.

2   Save the file as **Resource Costs** without a baseline in the Project SBS Practice folder.

Enter a fixed cost for a task

In this exercise, you enter a fixed cost for a resource that is on contract for a specific task.

You can also right-click the Select All button, and then click Cost.

1   On the View menu, point to Table, and then click Cost.

The left side of the Gantt Chart view changes to the Cost table.

2   Click the Fixed Cost field for task 15, Demolition of existing space.

3   Type **4000**, and then press TAB.

A fixed cost of $4,000 is applied to the task. The Fixed Cost Accrual field is selected.

The accrual method determines when the cost for the task or resource is incurred and when actual costs are charged to a project.

4   Click the Fixed Cost Accrual down arrow.

A list of accrual methods is displayed.

5   Select End, and press ENTER.

The cost for task 15 will not be charged to the project until the task is completed.

6   On the View menu, point to Table, and then click Entry.

7   Save the file without a baseline.

Enter resource costs

Red resource text indicates the resource is over-allocated. Resource over-allocations are discussed further in Lesson 9, "Managing Resource Workloads."

In this exercise, you enter the standard and overtime rate for a resource on the Resource Sheet.

1   On the View Bar, click the down arrow, and then click the Resource Sheet icon.

2   Press TAB until the Std. Rate field for the administrative assistant is selected.

3   Type **20**, and then press TAB.

The standard rate of $20 an hour is entered. The Ovt. Rate field is selected.

The default rate abbreviation for the Std. Rate and Ovt. Rate fields is hours. For a resource with a yearly salary, use the rate abbreviation y or yr.

4   Type **30**, and press ENTER.

5   Save the file without a baseline.

> **IMPORTANT**   When a resource works more than the standard work hours in a day, those hours are not necessarily calculated at the overtime rate of pay. Extra work hours must be specified as overtime before the overtime rate of pay is used to calculate the task cost.

Applying Variable Resource Rates

Using *variable resource rates,* you can track resource pay rate changes over time in the project. Variable resource rates are time-stamped so that new rates are applied to the project at the appropriate time. For example, when a project starts, Resource A is being paid $20 an hour. Halfway through the project, the resource receives a pay increase to $22 an hour. By entering the pay rate with an effective date, the resource costs are calculated based on when the task is performed.

The initial cost rate for a resource can be entered on the Resource Sheet or on the Costs tab in the Resource Information dialog box. Any cost rate changes that are to go into effect after the project starts should be entered on the Costs tab. Up to 25 different rate changes can be entered. When the effective date of the new resource cost occurs, the cost information on the Resource Sheet is updated automatically.

Resource rate changes can be entered as a number or as a percentage. Entering a positive percentage in the standard or overtime rate fields automatically calculates the new rate. The new rate is calculated by adding the old rate plus the percentage of the old rate. A negative percentage calculates a decrease from the old rate.

Apply a new resource rate

In this exercise, you enter a new standard and overtime rate for a resource to become effective on a specific day.

For a demonstration of how to apply a new Resource Rate, refer to page xxviii in the Installing and Using the Practice Files section.

1   Select the resource name "computer tech 1."

Resource Information

You can also double-click a task name to open the Resource Information dialog box.

2 On the Standard toolbar, click the Resource Information button.

The Resource Information dialog box appears.

3 Click the Costs tab.

In the Cost Rate Table area, tab A (default) is selected.

4 Click in the second Effective Date field.

A down arrow appears.

5 Click the Effective Date down arrow.

The date selection calendar appears.

6 Select September 1, 1998.

This is the date that the new cost rate for the resource will become effective.

7 Click in the Standard Rate field, type **33**, and press ENTER.

8 Click in the Overtime Rate field, type **10%**, and press ENTER.

The new overtime rate is calculated based on a percentage increase over the previous rate.

9 Click OK.

The current rates are still displayed on the Resource Sheet. The rates displayed on the Resource Sheet will change as of the effective date.

10 Save the file without a baseline.

96

> ⚒ **TROUBLESHOOTING** If you enter resource rate changes on the Resource Sheet instead of on the Costs tab in the Resource Assignment dialog box, the cost change will not be time-stamped. In effect, the cost of all tasks the resource has performed will be recalculated based on the new rate. Enter new rates for a resource only in the Resource Information dialog box.

Assigning Cost Rate Tables

In addition to resource pay rates changing, a resource might also be able to perform several types of work at different rates. In the past, a resource that performed several types of work at different rates might be assigned several different resource names, or an average cost for the resource might be used. This could lead to problems, such as scheduling the same resource to work on two tasks at the same time.

Using *cost rate tables*, each resource can have up to five different cost rates. Each cost rate table can have up to 25 different rate changes. Cost rate tables are created in the Resource Information dialog box on the Costs tab. The default cost table is table A. This is the cost table used when a resource is assigned to a task. Additional tables are labeled B through E. Each additional table is empty until it is used.

The cost table used to calculate resource costs for a task can be changed to one of the five available cost rate tables available for each resource. The assigned cost rate table can be changed in the Assignment Information dialog box, which is available when a usage view, such as the Task Usage view, is displayed. On the General tab in the Assignment Information dialog box, click the Cost Rate Table down arrow, and select a table.

Create a new cost table

In this exercise, you create an additional rate table for a resource that performs more than one type of work.

If the rate is not to take effect until a specific date, enter an effective date. If no effective date is entered, the rate takes effect as of the start of the project.

1 Double-click the resource name "painter."

2 Be sure that the Costs tab is selected. In the Cost Rate Tables area, click tab B.

3 Click in the Standard Rate field, type **55**, and press ENTER.

4 Click in the Overtime Rate field, type **85**, and press ENTER

5 In the Cost Rate Tables area, click tab A (default).

The rates in table B have no effect on the rates in table A.

6 Click OK.

7 Save the file without a baseline.

Apply a resource rate table to a task

In this exercise, you apply a different rate table for the painter on task 19.

Task Usage

If the resource assignments are hidden, click the plus sign (+) outline symbol next to the task to display the resources assigned to the task.

Go To Selected Task

Assignment Information

1 On the View Bar, click the Task Usage icon.

The Task Usage view is displayed.

2 Scroll down to task 19, Finish walls, and then select the resource name "painter."

3 On the Standard toolbar, click the Go To Selected Task button.

The timescale on the right side of the screen scrolls to display the work values for the painter resource on task 19.

4 On the Standard toolbar, click the Assignment Information button.

The Assignment Information dialog box appears. The General tab is selected.

5 Click the Cost Rate Table down arrow, and select B.

All five tables are listed whether they contain rate information or not.

Assignment Information	? x
General	Tracking	Notes

Task:	Finish walls		OK
Resource:	painter		Cancel
Work:	80h	Units:	100%
Work contour:	Flat		
Start:	Thu 10/15/98		
Finish:	Thu 10/29/98		
Cost:	$3,200.00	Cost rate table:	B

6 Click OK.

The new cost rate table is assigned to the task for the painter resource, and the new cost for the task is recalculated.

7 Save the file without a baseline.

TROUBLESHOOTING If costs are not being calculated for a resource assigned to a task, check the resource cost rate table assigned for that task. If a cost rate table is assigned that contains no resource cost information, costs will not be calculated.

One Step Further: Adding a Resource Note

Resource notes are similar to task notes in that you can use them to store additional information about a resource. Resource notes are entered while in a resource view, such as the Resource Sheet. To create a resource note, use the Resource Notes button on the Standard toolbar. When a resource note is created, a note icon is displayed in the Indicators field.

Add a resource note

In this exercise, you add a note to a resource.

Resource Sheet

Resource Notes

1   On the View Bar, click the down arrow, and then click the Resource Sheet icon.

2   Be sure that the "painter" resource is selected.

3   On the Standard toolbar, click the Resource Notes button.

    The Resource Information dialog box appears. The Notes tab is selected.

4   Click in the Notes box.

5   Type **Cost table A is for painting activities. Cost table B is for tape and texture activities.**, and click OK.

6   Place the mouse pointer over the note indicator for the painter.

    The text of the note is displayed in a ScreenTip. The leveling indicator is also displayed.

7   Save the file without a baseline.

TIP   Resource notes and task notes can be printed by creating a new report or customizing an existing report. From the View menu, click Reports. Double-click the Custom box. The Custom Reports dialog box appears. Click New or select a report, and then click Edit. On the Details tab, select the Notes check box. Customizing reports is discussed further in Lesson 13, "Customizing Tables, Views, and Reports."

Finish the lesson

1   To continue to the next lesson, on the File menu, click Close.

2   If you are finished using Project for now, on the File menu, click Exit.

Lesson Summary

To	Do this	Button
Create a resource	On the Standard toolbar, click the Assign Resources button. In the Name field, type the resource name, and press ENTER. *or* On the Resource Sheet, type the resource name in the Resource Name field, and then press TAB or ENTER.	
Assign a resource to a task	Select a task. In the Assign Resources dialog box, select a resource, and then click Assign. *or* Select a task, hold down CTRL, and select additional tasks. In the Assign Resources dialog box, select a resource, and then click Assign. *or* Select a task. In the Assign Resources dialog box, select a resource, hold down CTRL, and select additional resources. Click Assign.	
Add resource details	On the Resource Sheet, enter resource information in the appropriate fields. *or* Select a resource in a resource view. On the Standard toolbar, click the Resource Information button. Click the General tab, and enter resource information in the appropriate boxes.	
Assign a fixed cost to a task	In Gantt Chart view, on the View menu, point to Table, and then click Cost. In the Fixed Cost field for the appropriate task, enter the fixed cost amount.	

To	Do this	Button
Apply a new resource rate	Double-click a resource name in a resource view. Click the Costs tab. Click the first blank Effective Date field. Click the Effective Date down arrow, and then select a date. In the Standard Rate field and Overtime Rate field, enter the new rate or percentage increase or decrease.	
Create a new cost table	Double-click a resource name in a resource view. Click the Costs tab. Click an unused cost rate table tab. Enter an effective date if appropriate. Enter the standard and overtime rate.	
Assign a cost table to a task	Select a task in a task usage view. On the Standard toolbar, click the Assignment Information button. On the General tab, click the Cost Rate Table down arrow. Select the appropriate table letter.	

For online information about	On the Help menu, click Contents And Index, click the Index tab, and then type
Creating and assigning resources	**resource list** *or* **resources**
Adding resource costs	**costs** *or* **resource costs**
Assigning fixed costs	**fixed costs**
Applying new resource rates	**rates** *or* **cost rate tables**
Using cost rate tables	**cost rate tables**

Working with Calendars

Estimated time
30 min.

In this lesson you will learn how to:

- Change the working and nonworking time on the Standard calendar.
- Change the working and nonworking time on a resource calendar.
- Create new base calendars.
- Assign different base calendars to resources.

When scheduling a project, you need to know when resources can perform their tasks. If you do not indicate when resources are available, you might inadvertently schedule tasks when resources are not actually available. This can create problems, especially if the project is under a time constraint or a task is totally dependent on one resource. With *calendars*, you can determine when resources on a project are working and when they are not working. For example, Resource A is assigned to task Z, which is scheduled to take place the first week of August. Resource A will be on vacation that week. By using calendars to indicate working and *nonworking* time, you can reschedule task Z to occur when Resource A returns from vacation.

In Microsoft Project 98, calendars define the working and nonworking time for the project and for each resource assigned to the project. As a change is made to a calendar, Project automatically reschedules all tasks affected by the change. You can easily change an entire day or hours within a day from working to nonworking. You can also create new calendars for resources who work part-time or work different shifts.

In this lesson, the task dependencies and resource assignments have been completed for the corporate office relocation project. You're ready to begin making changes to the working and nonworking time to more accurately reflect when tasks can be scheduled. You define a holiday that will occur during the project, mark a resource that will be on vacation, and create a new calendar for resources working an early evening shift.

Start the lesson

1 Start Microsoft Project.
2 From the Project SBS Practice folder, open the Dates file.
3 Save the file as Calendars without a baseline in the Project SBS Practice folder.

Using Calendars

Tasks and resources are scheduled using calendars. There are two types of calendars in Project: *base calendars* and *resource calendars*. Base calendars define the working days and working hours for a project or a set of resources. Resource calendars define the working days and working hours for a specific resource.

The default base calendar (also known as the Project calendar) is called Standard. When a resource is added to a project, the Standard calendar is assigned as the resource's base calendar. Project comes with two other base calendars, the 24 Hours calendar and the Night Shift calendar, that can be assigned to a project or to resources. You can also create new base calendars for groups of resources.

Project also has calendar options, such as default start time and hours per day. These options are used to assign dates to tasks when no date or time is specifically entered. For example, if the first task is scheduled using the project start date, the task will be scheduled to start at the default start time of 8:00 AM unless specified. If changes are made to the default calendar options, the base calendar should be updated with those changes. If the calendar options and the base calendar do not display the same basic information, tasks and resource assignments might conflict.

 IMPORTANT Resource calendars are updated automatically when the base calendar assigned to the resource changes. However, changes to the default calendar options are not automatically displayed in the base calendar.

In the following exercises, you've been notified of a few changes to the project working time and the working time of several resources. You enter a company and national holiday to the base calendar, and add vacation time to the operations manager's resource calendar.

View the calendar options

In this exercise, you view the default settings for the calendar options.

1   On the Tools menu, click Options.

The Options dialog box appears.

2   Click the Calendar tab.

The default calendar options are displayed.

3   Click Cancel.

> **IMPORTANT**   If you anticipate that your project start time will be earlier than 8:00 AM, you should change the calendar options and the Standard calendar before entering tasks and resource assignments. If these options are not changed prior to entering tasks and resources, the first task will remain scheduled to start at 8:00 AM even if the options and base calendar are changed.

Changing the Base Calendar

The date range of calendars in Project is January 1, 1984, to December 31, 2049.

By default, the Standard calendar has an 8:00 AM to 5:00 PM work day, Monday through Friday, with no holidays. The base calendar for a project must be customized to include any changes in the work hours and work days. Base calendar changes or exceptions might include national holidays, project holidays, and nonstandard working days and hours. Changes made to a base calendar are automatically reflected in any resource calendar with that base calendar assigned to it.

The Change Working Time dialog box is used to make changes to base calendars. You can make changes to a single day, several days, or a month. Changes made in the Change Working Time dialog box are reflected by a pattern or shading. A pattern indicates a date where the working hours have been changed from the default working hours. Shading shows nonworking days. If changes are made to a calendar date, the date changes to bold and underlined.

For a demonstration of how to change the working time, refer to page xxviii in the Installing and Using the Practice Files section.

In the following exercises, the corporate office has decided to give all employees half a day off the Friday before Labor Day. You delete the afternoon working time on the Friday before Labor Day and then change Labor Day to a nonworking day for the project.

Change the working time

In this exercise, you change the working time on a specific date for all resources.

When you click the For down arrow, each base calendar and resource calendar for the project is listed.

1 On the Tools menu, click Change Working Time.

The Change Working Time dialog box appears. The For box displays the Standard calendar.

2 Use the scroll bar to move to September 1998.

3 Select Friday the 4th.

4 Under Working Time, select the text in the second From box.

5 Press DELETE.

The text is deleted.

6 Press TAB to select the text in the second To box. Press DELETE.

The afternoon working hours for the project on September 4, 1998, are deleted.

7 Select Friday the 11th.

The Date box for September 4th is patterned to indicate non-default working hours.

Name of calendar being used — Day titles —

— Working hours of selected date

Set nonworking days

In this exercise, you change a date from working to nonworking.

Only September 7, 1998, is changed to nonworking. All previous and subsequent years for that date remain unchanged.

1 Be sure that the Change Working Time dialog box for the Standard calendar is displayed.

September 1998 should be displayed.

2 Select Monday the 7th.

3 In the For Selected Dates area, select the Nonworking Time option.

4 Select Monday the 14th.

The Date box for September 7th is shaded to indicate it is a nonworking day.

5 Click OK.

The changes to the Standard calendar are saved. Tasks and resources are rescheduled based on the changes.

6 Save the file without a baseline.

Changing a Resource Calendar

Resource calendars are used to track the availability of individual resources. Because a resource calendar begins as a copy of the base calendar assigned to the resource, only exceptions for that resource should be entered in the resource calendar. Changes to a resource calendar might include personal vacation, training, or meetings. A resource calendar for equipment or locations can be used to reflect scheduled maintenance or downtime for cleaning.

Resource calendars are edited in the same way base calendars are edited. Resource calendars are available in the Change Working Time dialog box or on the Working Time tab in the Resource Information dialog box.

Edit a resource calendar

Highlighted resource information indicates that the resource is overallocated. Overallocations are discussed further in Lesson 9, "Managing Resource Workloads."

Resource Information

In this exercise, you make changes to a resource calendar to indicate the time the resource will be away from the project.

1 On the View Bar, click the down arrow, and then click the Resource Sheet icon.

The Resource Sheet view is displayed.

2 Select the "operations manager" resource.

3 On the Standard toolbar, click the Resource Information button.

The Resource Information dialog box for the operations manager appears.

4 Click the Working Time tab.

This information is the same as the information displayed in the Change Working Time dialog box.

5 Use the scroll bar to move to August 1998.

6 Drag to select August 13th and 14th.

7 In the For Selected Dates area, select the Nonworking Time option.

8 Click Friday the 21st.

The dates are shaded to indicate that they are nonworking days for the operations manager resource only.

9 Click OK.

10 Save the file without a baseline.

Creating a New Base Calendar

New base calendars can be created when none of the available base calendars fit the project needs or when a group of resources works different days and hours from the rest of the project resources. A new base calendar should not be created for just one resource.

A new base calendar can be created from the Project calendar defaults or as a copy of an existing base calendar. To minimize the amount of editing on a new base calendar, make a copy of an existing base calendar that already has common work days and holidays specified.

> **NOTE** If you have resources working shifts that span two days, such as 11:00 PM to 7:00 AM, you need to enter the hours before midnight on one day and the hours after midnight on the next day. For example, for the hours before midnight, you would type "11 pm to 12 am"; for the hours after midnight, you would type "12 am to 7 am" on the next day. The first day of the work week has the evening hours only; the last day has the morning hours only.

Create a new base calendar

In this exercise, you create a new base calendar to be used for resources working a late shift.

To make custom calendars easy to distinguish from predefined calendars, type the new calendar name in capital letters.

1 On the Tools menu, click Change Working Time, and then click New.

The Create New Base Calendar dialog box appears.

2 In the Name box, type **LATE SHIFT**

This is the name of the new base calendar.

108

Any existing base calendar can be copied by selecting a different calendar in the Make Copy Of box.

3 Be sure the Make A Copy Of Standard Calendar option is selected, and click OK.

The Change Working Time dialog box displays the Late Shift calendar.

Make changes to a new base calendar

In this exercise, you change the working times to reflect the working hours for the Late Shift calendar.

1 Drag across the day titles to select all days from Monday through Friday.

If you only want to select the same day of the week within a month, click the first day, hold down CTRL, and then select the other dates in that column.

2 Under Working Time, select the text in the first From box.

3 Type **3 pm**, and then press TAB.

This is the starting time for the late shift.

4 Type **7 pm**, and then press TAB.

5 Type **7:30 pm**, and then press TAB.

The late shift only takes a half-hour dinner break.

When you enter an even hour time, you do not have to include the minutes.

6 Type **11:30 pm**, and click OK.

7 On the Tools menu, click Change Working Time.

8 Click the For: down arrow, and choose Late Shift.

Notice the working time for Monday through Friday has changed.

9 Click Cancel.

10 Save the file without a baseline.

NOTE When a new base calendar is created from an existing base calendar, any changes to the default working times are carried over. If the resources that use the new base calendar don't have the same nonworking times as those using the copied base calendar, you need to go back and make those editing changes.

Assigning Resources to Different Base Calendars

Once additional base calendars are available to the project, they can be assigned to the entire project or to specific resources. Base calendars can be assigned to resources on the Resource Sheet, Base Calendar field, or on the Working Time tab in the Resource Information dialog box. If changes have been made to a resource calendar and then a new base calendar is assigned, the resource calendar changes remain in effect.

Assign a new base calendar to a resource

In this exercise, you assign the Late Shift base calendar to the resources that will work those hours on the project.

1 Be sure that the Resource Sheet view is displayed.

You can also change the base calendar assigned to a resource in the Base Calendar field on the Resource Sheet.

2 Double-click "computer tech 2."

The Resource Information dialog box appears.

3 Be sure that the Working Time tab is selected.

The Standard calendar is currently assigned to the "computer tech 2" resource.

4 Click the Base Calendar down arrow, select Late Shift, and click OK.

The working and nonworking time for "computer tech 2" has been set in the Late Shift base calendar.

5 Repeat steps 2 through 4 for the "janitor" resource.

6 Save the file without a baseline.

One Step Further: Using the 24 Hours Calendar

Project comes with a 24 Hours base calendar that can be assigned to an entire project or selected resources. The 24 Hours base calendar schedules tasks and resources to work without interruption in the schedule. A project on the 24 Hours calendar, or a resource assigned to that calendar, works 7 days a week, 24 hours a day. All nonworking time is eliminated in the 24 Hours calendar.

In the following exercises, the task "Run backup on server" has been added to the corporate office relocation project. You assign the 24 Hours base calendar to the server resource so that the backup can occur without interruption.

Change the date format for date fields
to include hours

In this exercise, you change the date format for date fields to include hours and then view the current start and finish dates for a task.

Gantt Chart

1 On the View Bar, click the Gantt Chart icon.

The Gantt Chart view is displayed.

2 On the Tools menu, click Options, and then click the View tab.

3 Click the Date Format down arrow.

The default date format is day and date (Fri 1/31/97).

A list of date format options is displayed.

4 Select Fri 1/31/97 12:33 PM, and click OK.

The display of any date field or box now shows the time.

5 Press F5, type **38**, and click OK.

Task 38, Run backup on server, is selected, and the Gantt bar is displayed.

6 Double-click task 38, Run backup on server.

The Resource Information dialog box appears. The start and finish time format has been changed to hours.

Task Information				? X

General | Predecessors | Resources | Advanced | Notes

Name: Run backup on server   Duration: 15h   OK

Percent complete: 0%   Priority: Medium   Cancel

Dates

Start time —— Start: Wed 11/25/98 8:00 AM   ☐ Hide task bar

Finish time —— Finish: Thu 11/26/98 4:00 PM   ☐ Roll up Gantt bar to summary

7 Click OK.

Assign the 24 Hours calendar to a resource

In this exercise, you assign the 24 Hours base calendar to a resource and then view how the calendar change affects the task.

Assign Resources

1 On the Standard toolbar, click the Assign Resources button.

The Assign Resources dialog box appears.

2 Scroll down in the list, and then double-click server.

The Resource Information dialog box appears. The Working Time tab is selected.

3 Click the Base Calendar down arrow, select 24 Hours, and click OK.

4 Click Cancel.

The length of the Gantt bar for task 38 has decreased.

5 Double-click task 38, Run backup on server.

The Task Information dialog box appears. The task now starts at 5:00 PM and is complete by 8:00 AM the next morning.

6 Click OK.

7 Save the file without a baseline.

Reset view options

In this exercise, you reset the date to the default format.

1 On the Tools menu, click Options.

The View tab is selected.

2 Click the Date Format down arrow.

3 Select Fri 1/31/97, and click OK.

Finish the lesson

1 To continue to the next lesson, on the File menu, click Close.

2 If you are finished using Project for now, on the File menu, click Exit.

Lesson Summary

To	Do this	Button
Edit a base calendar	On the Tools menu, click Change Working Time. In the For box, be sure that the appropriate calendar name is displayed. Scroll to the month and year to edit. Select the day or days to edit. Select the non-working option, or edit the Working Time area. Click OK.	
Edit a resource calendar	Select the appropriate resource name. On the Standard toolbar, click the Resource Information button. Click the Working Time tab. Scroll to the month and year to edit. Select the day or days to edit. Select the nonworking option, or edit the Working Time area. Click OK. *or* On the Tools menu, click Change Working Time. Click the For down arrow, and then select the appropriate resource.	

To	Do this	Button
Create a new base calendar	On the Tools menu, click Change Working Time. Click New. In the Name box, type the new calendar name. Select the Create New Base Calendar option or the Make A Copy Of Standard Calendar option. Scroll to the month and year to edit. Select the day or days to edit. Select the nonworking option, or edit the Working Time area. Click OK.	
Assign a different base calendar to a resource	Select the appropriate resource name. On the Standard toolbar, click the Resource Information button. Click the Working Time tab. Click the Base Calendar down arrow. Select the appropriate base calendar. Click OK.	

For online information about	**On the Help menu, click Contents And Index, click the Index tab, and then type**
Editing a base calendar	**base calendars**
Editing a resource calendar	**resource calendar**
Creating a new base calendar	**base calendars**
Assigning a new base calendar	**calendars**

Scheduling with Resources

Estimated time
35 min.

In this lesson you will learn how to:

- Change the task type settings to control how resources affect task assignments.
- Apply a preset resource contour to change work value distribution.
- Custom contour a resource assignment.

As the planning of a project schedule moves forward, adjustments are made to reflect changes in the project scope, project assignments, and other new information. For many reasons, resource assignments or needs often change. Resources might be added or removed from the project. If a resource is supervising a task, the workload might vary over the duration of the task. There might also be resources who work overtime on a task, start later, or finish earlier than other resources assigned to a task. When any changes are made to the resource assignments, they affect the project schedule. How these changes affect the schedule determines how the changes should be made.

In Microsoft Project 98, when an assignment is changed, the schedule is recalculated to display the changes immediately. You can work with the *scheduling method* and the *task type settings* when making changes to the initial resource assignments. You can also vary the workload of resources to more accurately reflect how resources work on tasks.

In this lesson, the initial resource assignments and calendar changes have been made for the corporate office relocation project. As you review the schedule, you discover some resource assignments that need adjusting.

During the last team meeting, several other resource assignments were also mentioned. Using Project, you make the necessary changes based on the desired result.

Start the lesson

1   Start Microsoft Project.

2   From the Project SBS Practice folder, open the Schedule file.

3   Save the file as Scheduling Methods without a baseline in the Project SBS Practice folder.

Working with Effort-Driven Scheduling

How a task reacts to the addition and removal of resources is defined by the scheduling method and the task type settings. In Project, the default scheduling method is *effort-driven scheduling*. Effort-driven scheduling extends or shortens the duration of a task to accommodate changes to resources, but doesn't change the total work for the task. Work is the amount of effort, or number of hours, resources put into a task.

The total work for a task is determined by the duration estimate for the task and the initial resource assignment. For example, task Z has a duration estimate of one day, or eight hours. If the initial resource assignment is two units of Resource A, the total work for the task will be 16 hours. As resources are added or removed after the initial assignment, the total work is redistributed among the resources. For example, an additional resource assignment of one unit of Resource B is added to task Z, the total work remains 16 hours. The result is that Resource B is scheduled to work 5.33 hours, and each unit of Resource A is scheduled to work 5.335 on the task.

Effort-driven scheduling can be turned off for individual tasks or all new tasks created in a project. When effort-driven scheduling is turned off, total work increases when units of other resources are added to a task. To turn off effort-driven scheduling for a task, clear the Effort Driven check box on the Task Form or the Advanced tab on the Task Information dialog box. To turn off effort-driven scheduling for all new tasks created in a project, on the Tools menu, click Options. Then, on the Schedule tab, clear the New Tasks Are Effort Driven check box.

The task type setting also has an effect on how tasks are scheduled. There are three task types: Fixed Unit, Fixed Duration, and Fixed Work. Using one of these task types, any variable in the standard equation **Work = Duration * Units** can be controlled. The task type setting can be changed on the Task Form or the Advanced tab on the Task Information dialog box.

In the following exercises, you've identified several tasks that should be calculated using different task type settings. The "Finalize drawings" task has a scheduled duration of two weeks. You change the task type, and then add another unit of the architect resource. This reduces the duration by splitting the work between the two resources. The "Final trim and fixture" task work will actually be split with an electrician, but the two resources cannot work at the same time. The total work and duration must remain the same. You change the task type so that each resource will work half-time on the task. And finally, the "Finish walls" task must include the framing contractor. You change the task type, and then add the new resource so that the task duration decreases but each resource is working full-time on the task.

 NOTE In previous versions of Project, effort-driven scheduling is turned off, so adding or removing resource units has a direct impact on the total work.

Modifying a Fixed Unit Task

The task type Fixed Unit is the default task type in Project. When resources are added or removed from a Fixed Unit task, the duration of the task is generally affected. However, designating a task as effort-driven, or adding or removing resources, determines the true effect on the task's duration.

For example, task X has a duration estimate of two weeks, an initial resource assignment of one unit of Resource A, and total work of 80 hours. The following table describes how a Fixed Unit task accommodates resource and scheduling method changes after the initial assignments.

Fixed Unit – effort-driven	Duration	Units	Work
Add one unit of same resource (A)	1 week	200% Resource A	<u>40 hours each</u> 80 hours total
Add one unit of different resource (B)	1 week	100% Resource A 100% Resource B	40 hours <u>40 hours</u> 80 hours total

Fixed Unit – without effort-driven	Duration	Units	Work
Add one unit of same resource (A)	1 week	200% Resource A	<u>40 hours each</u> 80 hours total
Add one unit of different resource (B)	2 weeks	100% Resource A 100% Resource B	80 hours <u>80 hours</u> 160 hours total

NOTE Resource-driven tasks in previous versions of Project are now known as Fixed Unit tasks.

Change to the Task Entry view

You can also double-click the split bar to display the Task Entry view.

In this exercise, you change to the Task Entry view so that you can view resource assignments to tasks.

1 On the View menu, click More Views.

The More Views dialog box appears.

You can type the letter T to scroll to the first view in the list starting with that letter.

2 In the Views box, select Task Entry, and then click Apply.

The Task Entry view is displayed. The Gantt Chart view is displayed in the top pane, and the Task Form is displayed in the bottom pane.

Add an additional resource to a Fixed Unit task

In this exercise, you add another unit of the same resource to a Fixed Unit effort-driven task and view the effect on the resource work and the task duration.

By default, the task type setting is Fixed Unit.

1 In the top pane of the view, select task 9, Finalize drawings.

Task 9 has one unit, 100%, of the "architect" resource assigned with 80 hours of work. The task duration is two weeks.

2 In the bottom pane, click 100% in the Units column for the "architect" resource.

Spin controls are displayed.

3 Click the up arrow twice.

The Units field displays 200%.

Each action in the Task Form should be followed by clicking OK.

4 Click OK.

The units increase to 200%, the duration decreases to one week, and the work remains at 80 hours combined. Your screen should look similar to the following illustration.

Units
increase

Work remains the same   Duration decreases

5 Save the file without a baseline.

Modifying a Fixed Duration Task

If a task has the task type Fixed Duration, the duration of the task remains the same when resources are added or removed. The resource units or the total hours are affected on a Fixed Duration task depending on the scheduling method.

For example, task X has a duration estimate of two weeks, an initial resource assignment of one unit of Resource A, and total work of 80 hours. The following table describes how a Fixed Duration task accommodates resource and scheduling method changes after the initial assignments.

Fixed Duration – effort-driven	Duration	Units	Work
Add one unit of same resource (A)	2 weeks	200% Resource A	80 hours each 160 hours total
Add one unit of different resource (B)	2 weeks	50% Resource A 50% Resource B	40 hours 40 hours 80 hours total

Fixed Duration – without effort-driven	Duration	Units	Work
Add one unit of same resource (A)	2 weeks	200% Resource A	<u>80 hours each</u> 160 hours total
Add one unit of different resource (B)	2 weeks each	100% Resource A 100% Resource B	80 hours <u>80 hours</u> 160 hours total

Change the task type setting

In this exercise, you change the task type setting from the default Fixed Unit to Fixed Duration.

You can also click in the top pane to make it active. Then, press F5, type 24, and click OK.

1 In the top pane, select task 24, Final trim and fixtures.

The Task Form in the bottom pane displays the information for task 24.

2 In the bottom pane, click the Task Type down arrow.

The three task type settings are listed.

3 Click Fixed Duration, and click OK.

At this time, there are no visible changes to the task information.

Assign a unit of a new resource to a Fixed Duration task

In this exercise, you assign a unit of a different resource to a Fixed Duration task and view the effect on the resource units and work.

The bottom pane becomes the active pane when the task type setting is changed. To use the Assign Resources button, the top pane must be the active pane.

1 In the top pane, select task 24, Final trim and fixtures.

Task 24 has one unit, 100%, of the "carpenter" resource assigned with 40 hours of work. The task duration is one week.

2 On the Standard toolbar, click the Assign Resources button.

3 Select electrician, and then click Assign.

One unit of the electrician is also assigned to task 24.

Assign Resources

4 Click Close.

The task duration remains one week. Each resource unit has been changed to 50% with 20 hours of work assigned to each resource. Your screen should look similar to the following illustration.

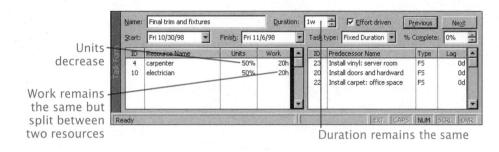

Units decrease

Work remains the same but split between two resources

Duration remains the same

5 Save the file without a baseline.

Modifying a Fixed Work Task

If a task has the task type Fixed Work, the total work for the task remains the same when resources are added or removed. The duration and resource units are affected on a Fixed Work task. A Fixed Work task must be effort-driven.

For example, task X has a duration estimate of two weeks, an initial resource assignment of one unit of Resource A, and total work of 80 hours. The following table describes how a Fixed Work task accommodates resource and scheduling method changes after the initial assignments.

Fixed Work – effort-driven	Duration	Units	Work
Add one unit of same resource (A)	1 week	200% Resource A	40 hours each 80 hours total
Add one unit of different resource (B)	1 week	100% Resource A 100% Resource B	40 hours 40 hours 80 hours total

Change the task type setting

In this exercise, you change the task type setting from the default Fixed Unit to Fixed Work.

1 In the top pane, select task 19, Finish walls.

The Task Form in the bottom pane displays the information for task 19.

2 In the bottom pane, click the Task Type down arrow.

3 Click Fixed Work, and click OK.

The Effort Driven check box is dimmed. A Fixed Work task automatically turns on effort-driven scheduling.

Assign a unit of a new resource to a Fixed Work task

In this exercise, you assign a unit of a different resource to a Fixed Work task and view the effect on the resource units and duration.

**Assign
Resources**

1   In the top pane, select task 19, Finish walls.

Task 19 has one unit, 100%, of the "painter" resource assigned with 80 hours of work. The task duration is two weeks.

2   On the Standard toolbar, click the Assign Resources button.

3   Select framing contractor, and then click Assign.

One unit of the framing contractor is also assigned to task 19.

4   Click Close.

The task duration decreases to one week. The resource units are at 100%, each with 40 hours of work assigned to each resource for a total of 80 hours. Your screen should look similar to the following illustration.

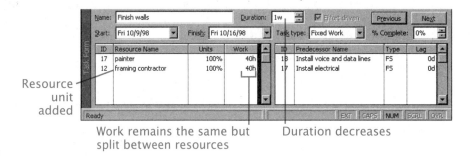

Resource
unit
added

Work remains the same but
split between resources

Duration decreases

5   Save the file without a baseline.

Creating Resource Contours

When a resource is assigned to a task, the total work for the task is evenly applied throughout the duration of the task by default. This is known as a flat *contour*. A contour defines how scheduled work for a resource is distributed over the duration of a task. With Project, how work is assigned can be controlled by applying various preset contours or creating a custom contour for a resource assignment.

Resource workloads can be contoured or edited in the Task Usage view or the Resource Usage view. The Task Usage view displays each task with its assigned resources grouped below it. The Resource Usage view displays each resource with its assigned tasks grouped below it. The right side of each view displays the work values for each resource or task assignment. The right side of the view is used to contour the scheduled work by editing the relevant entries or to view preset contours that have been applied. Preset contours are applied using the Assignment Information dialog box, which is available when an assignment is selected in a usage view.

The resource start and finish dates and work hours can be set for an individual assignment using contouring. Overtime can be assigned as well.

Project comes with eight preset contours that can be applied to a resource's work on a task. The following table describes each of the preset contours.

Contour pattern	Description
Flat	The number of work hours is distributed evenly throughout the duration of the task.
Back loaded	The number of hours per time period start small and are gradually increased to 100% toward the end of the task. The majority of the work is assigned at the end. Also called ramp up.
Front loaded	The number of hours per time period is 100% toward the beginning of the task and gradually decrease to ward the end of the project. Also called ramp down.
Double peak	The number of hours per time period peaks to 100% twice during the duration of the task.
Early peak	The number of hours per time period peaks at 100% in the first quarter of the task duration.
Late peak	The number of hours per time period peaks at 100% in the last quarter of the task duration.
Bell	The number of hours per time period peaks at 100% during the middle of the task duration. The starting and ending work percentages are low.
Turtle	The number of hours per time period peaks at 100% during the middle of the task duration. This differs from Bell in that the percentage is higher at the start and end.

When working with resource contours, keep a few things in mind.

- Once a specific contour has been applied, adding new total work values automatically reapplies the preset contour pattern. The new task work values are first distributed across the affected time period, and then new work values are assigned to the resources for the task.

- If the start date of the task or resource is changed, the contour is reapplied based on the new date. All work values are redistributed.

- If the duration of a task is changed, the contour is stretched to include the added time period.

- If a work value is manually edited, the contour is no longer applied. However, a contour can be reapplied to redistribute the work values.

- If actual work has been entered for a task or resource, any changes to the total work or remaining work are redistributed to the remaining work values, not to the actual work.

 TIP For a percentage breakdown of work distribution in each pre-set contour, see Work Contour field (assignment field) in the online Help Index.

In the last team meeting, you were notified that the work distribution changed on two tasks. In the following exercises, the "Write proposal" task, the operations manager will be in a reviewing position and doesn't need to be assigned to the task full time. To manage the review time, you change the operations manager's ours on the task and then apply a preset contour so the work hours gradually increase toward the end of the task. The "Frame interior walls" task is currently scheduled for a four-day duration, but the task is spread over five days because the first day starts in the afternoon. The framing contractor has requested that the task end on a full day and has agreed to work overtime on day four to finish the task. You apply overtime hours to the fourth day of the task.

Display usage views

When a combination view is displayed, you must remove the split before changing to a single view. Otherwise, only the view in the active pane of the combination view is changed. CTRL+HOME moves the selection to the first task in the Entry table; ALT+HOME scrolls the Gantt Chart to the taskbar for the selected task.

In this exercise, you use the View Bar to display the Resource Usage view, and then display the Task Usage view.

1   Double-click the split bar located on the right side of the screen between the top and bottom panes of the combination view.

   From the Window menu, you can also click Remove Split. The single view, Gantt Chart view, is displayed.

2   Press CTRL+HOME, and then press ALT+HOME.

3   On the View Bar, click the down arrow until the Resource Usage icon is displayed, and then click the Resource Usage icon.

   On the Resource Usage view, the left pane displays each resource with the task assignments grouped and the right pane displays the work values for each assignment over time.

4   On the View Bar, click the Task Usage icon.

   On the Task Usage view, the left pane displays each task with the resource assignments grouped, and the right pane displays the work values over time for each assignment.

Resource Usage

Task Usage

5   Drag the vertical split bar to the left to cover the Start and Finish columns.

   Your screen should look similar to the following illustration.

Work values

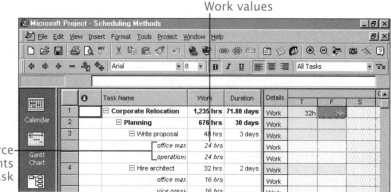

Resource assignments to a task

TIP The timescaled portion of the Resource Usage view and the Task Usage view can be formatted to display other work values. On the Format menu, click Details to display other preformatted values. Also on the Format menu, click Details: Styles to show additional values or change the color, font, and pattern of the timescale cells.

Apply a preset contour

For a demonstration of how to apply a present contour, refer to page xxviii in the Installing and Using the Practice Files section.

In this exercise, you view the current distribution of work values for a task, change the total work a resource will perform on the task, and then apply the back loaded contour to the resource assignment.

1   Under task 3, Write proposal, click the Work field for the "operations manager" resource.

The operations manager is assigned to task 3 for a total of 24 work hours. The work hours are evenly distributed over a three-day period.

Go To Selected Task

The default duration abbreviation in the Work field is hours.

2   On the Standard toolbar, click the Go To Selected Task button.

The timescale on the right side of the screen scrolls to display the first work value for the resource assignment.

3   In the Work field, type **12**, and then press TAB.

The total work performed on the task by the operations manager changes to 12 hours. The total work for the task changes to 36 hours, and the duration remains at three days. The work distribution changes to eight hours the first day and four hours the second day.

Assignment Information

4   On the Standard toolbar, click the Assignment Information button.

The Assignment Information dialog box appears. The "operations manager" resource is displayed in the Resource box on the General tab.

5 Click the Work Contour down arrow, and then click Back Loaded.

The back-loaded contour schedules more of the work toward the end of the task.

6 Click OK.

The work values are now spread over the three-day duration of the task based on the preset back loaded contour. Your screen should look similar to the following illustration.

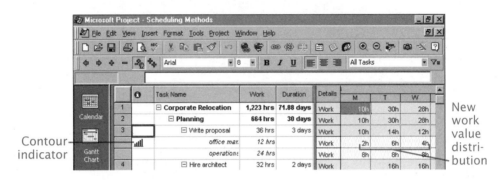

7 Save the file without a baseline.

Create a contour

In this exercise, you customize the contour for a resource to reflect overtime work on a task assignment.

1 Press F5, type **16**, and click OK.

Task 16, Frame interior walls, is selected. Task 16 has a duration of four days and total work of 32 hours. One unit of the framing contractor is assigned to the task.

2 Scroll in the timescale to view the work values for the week of 9/27/98.

3 Click the Work Values field for the framing contractor on Wednesday, 9/30/98, for task 16.

4 Type **12**, and then press TAB.

The total work hours for the assignment change to 36 hours. The Work Values field for 10/1/98 is selected.

5 Type **0**, and press ENTER.

The total work hours for the assignment changes back to 32 hours. The task duration changes to 3.5 days. Your screen should look similar to the following illustration.

4 hours of overtime

Contour indicator for an edited contour

6   On the View Bar, click the Gantt Chart icon.

7   Save the file without a baseline.

One Step Further: Scheduling a Project from the Finish Date

Most project schedules are created based on a project start date. Although it is easiest to create a schedule by basing it on a start date, there are times when it is necessary to base a schedule on the project finish date. For example, a project must be finished on a specific date. By scheduling the project from a known finish date, the date the project must be started in order to be finished on time is calculated for you. Scheduling from the project finish date can also be used to find out what the latest possible dates are for the project tasks even though the project start date is known. This is called backwards scheduling.

Change the Schedule From option

In this exercise, you note the current start and finish date for the project, change the Schedule From option to Project Finish Date, and then view the new project start date.

1   On the Project menu, click Project Information.

The Project Information dialog box appears. The project start date is set at 8/10/98, and the finish date is currently scheduled for 11/19/98.

2   Click the Schedule From down arrow, and click Project Finish Date.

The Start Date box is disabled, and the Finish Date box is enabled.

3   Click the Finish Date down arrow.

The date selection calendar is displayed.

4 Click the 6th on November 1998, and click OK.

The start date is now recalculated.

5 On the Project menu, click Project Information.

The scheduled start date is now 7/28/98.

6 Click Cancel.

7 Save the file without a baseline.

Finish the lesson

1 To continue to the next lesson, on the File menu, click Close.

2 If you are finished using Project for now, on the File menu, click Exit.

Lesson Summary

To	Do this	Button
Change the task type setting	From the Task Entry view, select the desired task in the top pane. In the Task Form, click the Task Type down arrow. Select the appropriate setting, and click OK. *or* Double-click the desired task. On the Advanced tab in the Resource Information dialog box, click the Task Type down arrow. Select the appropriate setting, and click OK.	
Apply a preset contour	In the Task Usage view, select the desired resource under the appropriate task. On the Standard toolbar, click the Assignment Information button. On the General tab, click the Work Contour down arrow. Select the appropriate contour, and click OK.	
Create a custom contour	In the Task Usage view, select the desired resource under the appropriate task. On the right side of the screen, make the appropriate changes to the work values.	

For online information about	On the Help menu, click Contents And Index, click the Index tab, and then type
scheduling methods	**scheduling**
changing task type settings	**task types**
applying contours	**work contours**

Review & Practice

Estimated time
25 min.

You will review and practice how to:

- Assign resources to tasks.
- Apply resource costs.
- Change base calendars and resource calendars.
- Change task settings to affect task effort.

Before you move on to Part 3, which covers resolving resource conflicts and applying task constraints, you can practice the skills you learned in Part 2 by working through this Review & Practice section. You will assign resources to tasks, enter resource details and costs, work with calendars, and change task settings.

Scenario

The task list, outlining, and dependencies have all been completed for the annual shareholders meeting schedule. The project team has identified the resources to be used on the project and provided you with cost and calendar information. You begin entering resource names, details, and costs, and then assign the resources to the appropriate tasks. The project has specific days and times that it will be worked on, so you make calendar adjustments to reflect the project working time. You also work with task settings to further define resource assignments.

Step 1: Create a Resource List

The project team has given you a list of resources for the shareholders meeting project. You enter the resources and the resource details to the schedule.

1 In the Project SBS Practice folder, open the Review2 file, and then save the file as Meeting Resources without a baseline.

2 Using the Assign Resources dialog box, add the intern resource.

3 In the Resource Information dialog box, enter the following resource details for the intern.

Initials	Group	Code
int	office staff	105-303

4 On the Resource Sheet, enter the following resources and resource information.

Resource Name	Initials	Group	Max Units	Code
vice president	vp	management	100%	101-101
office manager	om	management	100%	101-200
administrative assistant	admin	office staff	200%	105-106

5 Save the file without a baseline.

For more information about	See
Entering resources	Lesson 6
Entering resource details	Lesson 6

Step 2: Assign Resources to Tasks

The project team groups have provided you with some preliminary resource assignments. You add the assignments to the schedule.

1   Assign the resources to the following tasks.

Task	Resources
3, Schedule conference date	vice president, office manager
4, Book conference center	intern
5, Book keynote speaker	office manager
8, Order letter stock	intern
9, Develop letter	administrative assistant
10, Review letter	office manager
11, Approve letter	vice president
15, Plan food with caterer	administrative assistant
16, Arrange committee meeting rooms	intern
17, Arrange necessary equipment	administrative assistant

2   Save the file without a baseline.

For more information about	See
Assigning resources to tasks	Lesson 6

Step 3: Apply Resource Costs

The Accounting department has provided you with the necessary cost information for each resource assigned to the shareholders meeting project. You enter the cost information for each resource. You've also been informed that the intern resource will receive a pay raise during the project. Also, the administrative assistant will be paid more for tasks involving any supervisory work. You make the appropriate changes to the schedule.

1   Enter the following costs on the Resource Sheet.

Resource Name	Standard Rate	Overtime Rate
intern	$10 per hour	$15 per hour
vice president	$75,000 a year	NA
office manager	$45,000 a year	NA
administrative assistant	$20 per hour	$30 per hour

2   Effective July 19, 1999, the intern resource will have a pay increase of 10% for standard and overtime hours.

3   The administrative assistant resource has a different rate for supervisory tasks than for other work. Create a new cost table with a standard rate of $25 per hour and an overtime rate of $37.50 per hour.

4   Apply the new cost table for the administrative assistant resource to task 17, Arrange necessary equipment. (Hint: Use the Task Usage view.)

5   Save the file without a baseline.

For more information on	See
Entering resource costs	Lesson 6
Applying variable resource rates	Lesson 6
Creating and assigning cost tables	Lesson 6

Step 4:   Create, Edit, and Assign Calendars

The shareholders meeting project doesn't require a traditional eight-hour day from each resource. Instead, the project tasks will be worked on only in the morning, except for Mondays. You create a new base calendar and assign it to each resource on the project. You've also requested a list of project nonworking days and any special working times for individual resources. You enter those exceptions into the appropriate calendar.

1   From a copy of the Standard base calendar, create a new base calendar called Sharemeet for the shareholders meeting project.

2   Change the working hours to the following.

All Mondays: 1:00 PM to 5:00 PM

All Tuesdays through Fridays: 8:00 AM to 12:00 PM.

3   Add the following nonworking days to the Sharemeet calendar.

July 5, 1999 – 4th of July extended weekend

July 26, 1999 – no afternoon work hours, company picnic (Hint: Because the project only works afternoons on Mondays, the day should be marked as nonworking.)

4   Assign the Sharemeet calendar to all resources assigned to the project.

5   Mark July 6, 1999 as a nonworking day for the office manager on the resource calendar.

6   Save the file without a baseline.

For more information on	See
Creating a new base calendar	Lesson 7
Adding nonworking time to a base calendar	Lesson 7
Assigning a base calendar to resources	Lesson 7
Changing a resource calendar	Lesson 7

Step 5: Work with Task Type Settings

At the most recent shareholders meeting, the schedule was reviewed to see if any resource assignments need to be adjusted. Based on the information you gathered during the meeting, you make the appropriate adjustments to the schedule.

1   Change the task type setting on task 10, Review letter, to Fixed Work, and then add the resource "vice president" to the task. (Hint: Use the Task Entry view.)

2   On task 17, Arrange necessary equipment, assign an additional unit of the administrative assistant to the task.

3   On task 9, Develop letter, remove effort-driven scheduling, and then assign the "office manager" resource to the task.

4   Save the file without a baseline.

For more information on	See
Changing task type settings	Lesson 8
Changing the scheduling method	Lesson 8

Finish the Review & Practice

1   Close the Meeting Resources file.

2   If you are finished using Project for now, on the File menu, click Exit.

Fine-Tuning
the Schedule

Part
3

Managing Resource Workloads

Estimated time
35 min.

In this lesson you will learn how to:

- View resource workloads.
- Locate resource overallocations.
- Use automatic leveling to resolve overallocations.
- Resolve resource overallocations manually.

As resources are assigned to tasks in a project, resource conflicts can occur. A resource conflict occurs when a resource is scheduled to perform more work than the resource can accomplish in the available working time. A resource conflict can occur as a result of a single task assignment or multiple assignments. Once resource conflicts are identified, the schedule must be analyzed and decisions must be made on how to resolve the conflicts.

Using Microsoft Project 98, resource conflicts can be quickly identified using several different views. Usage views display tasks and resources in assignment groups and display a timescale of work values for each assignment. Each resource conflict is identified by highlighting the conflict information in red and displaying a leveling indicator. When resource conflicts arise, Project can be used to automatically make adjustments to the schedule by delaying or splitting resource or task assignments. Resource conflicts can also be resolved manually using scheduling techniques within Project.

In this lesson, the corporate office relocation project is in the final planning stages. Before any further decisions are made, resource conflicts must be identified and resolved. You first use Project to automatically make adjustments to the schedule, and then you manually resolve the resource conflicts that could not be resolved by Project.

Start the lesson

1   Start Microsoft Project.

2   From the Project SBS Practice folder, open the Workload file.

    The file opens in Resource Sheet view. Highlighted resource text indicates that the resource is overallocated.

3   Save the file as resolving overallocations without a baseline in the Project SBS Practice folder.

Viewing Resource Workloads and Task Assignments

Viewing resource workloads helps to identify to what extent a resource is *overallocated* or *underallocated*. The information obtained by viewing workloads helps to resolve resource conflicts within a schedule. A resource is overallocated when it is assigned more work than it can complete in its scheduled working hours.

When a Resource is overallocated, the resource text is highlighted in red, and, in Resource view, a leveling indicator is displayed. Use the Resource Usage view and the Resource Allocation view to identify and resolve resource overalloca-tions. You can also use the Resource Graph, which displays the percentage of resource usage in a bar chart format.

The Resource Management toolbar provides tools for resolving resource over-allocations as well as assigning resources. The following table describes the buttons on the Resource Management toolbar.

Button	Button name	Description
	Resource Allocation View	Displays the Resource Allocation view, which consists of the Resource Usage view in the top pane and the Leveling Gantt view in the bottom pane.
	Task Entry View	Displays the Task Entry view, which consists of the Gantt Chart view in the top pane and the Task Form view in the bottom pane.

Button	Button name	Description
	Go To Next Overallocation	Moves to the next overallocation.
	Assign Resources	Opens the Assign Resources dialog box.
	Share Resources	Displays the Share Resources dialog box, where resources can be made available to other projects.
	Update Resource Pool	Updates the project resource pool.
	Refresh Resource Pool	Refreshes the resource pool.
	Address Book	Displays the e-mail address book for locating resources.
	Resource Details	Displays the Properties dialog box for the selected resource.
	Using Resource	Filters for a resource's tasks with the Using Resource filter.
	Leveling Help	Displays a set of procedures for leveling resources.

View workloads in the Resource Usage view

In this exercise, you change to the Resource Usage view and locate an overallocation.

Resource Usage

1   On the View Bar, click the down arrow until the Resource Usage icon is displayed, and then click the Resource Usage icon.

    The Resource Usage view is displayed.

2   Select the architect resource.

3   On the Standard toolbar, click the Go To Selected Task button.

    The right pane timescale scrolls to the work values for the resource.

Go To Selected Task

4 Press F5.

The Go To dialog box appears.

If you don't know the date, scroll in the timescale until red highlighted work values are displayed.

5 Click the Date down arrow, select August 24, 1998, and click OK.

The timescale scrolls to the date. The red highlighted work values indicate that an overallocation occurs for the architect resource on the Finalize drawings task. Your screen should look similar to the following illustration.

Leveling indicator shows that the architect resource is overallocated.

Locate resource overallocations

In this exercise, you display the Resource Management toolbar, change to the Resource Allocation view, and locate an overallocation.

You can also right-click a toolbar. A shortcut menu of available toolbars is displayed.

1 On the View menu, point to Toolbars, and then click Resource Management.

The Resource Management toolbar is displayed under the Formatting toolbar.

2 On the Resource Management toolbar, click the Resource Allocation View button.

The Resource Allocation view is displayed. The tasks for the selected resource are displayed in the bottom pane, the Leveling Gantt view. Your screen should look similar to the following illustration.

Resource usage view

Leveling Gantt view

	⊕	Resource Name	Work	Aug 23, '98 S	M	T	W	T	F
2	◈	⊟ architect	256 hrs				16h	16h	1
		Locate ne	40 hrs						
		Present p	16 hrs						
		Finalize c	80 hrs				16h	16h	1
		Select su	60 hrs						
		Submit dr	60 hrs						

	⊕	Task Name	Levelin	Aug 23, '98 S	M	T	W	T	F
5		Locate new site		al estate agent					
6		Present proposal		ns manager,conference room,architect,president,vice					
9		Finalize drawings							
10		Select subcontractors							
12		Submit drawings							

The bottom pane must be selected to locate the first overallocation for the resource selected in the top pane.

Go To Next Overallocation

3 Scroll in the top pane, and then select the computer tech 1 resource.

4 Drag the scroll box to the left.

5 Click anywhere in the bottom pane.

6 On the Resource Management toolbar, click the Go To Next Overallocation button.

The first overallocation for the "computer tech 1" resource is displayed. Your screen should look similar to the following illustration.

NOTE The search for an overallocation starts at the currently selected period of time. Dragging the scroll box all the way to the left ensures that the first overallocation for the resource is found. Each time you click the Go To Overallocation button, the next overallocation for the resource is located until no other overallocations exist for that resource. A message indicating that no other overallocations exist is displayed.

Overlapping tasks require 300% units of the resource to do 23 hours of work.

7 Save the file without a baseline.

> **TIP** Before using automatic leveling or manually resolving overallocations, it can be helpful to review all existing overallocations. By identifying each allocation first, you can better understand what changes occur during automatic leveling or how a manual change affects the rest of the project.

Resolving Resource Conflicts

Resource conflicts occur when a resource is overallocated on a task or the project. Before a project begins, all resource overallocations should be resolved so that the schedule accurately reflects the resources and work required to complete all tasks. Overallocations can be resolved automatically or manually. Once the project begins and tasks are completed, the schedule must be continually reviewed for new overallocations.

Ideally, each overallocation should be resolved. However, some overallocations might be unavoidable or might be too insignificant to be resolved. For example, overallocations of less than one hour per day or one day out of a week could be left unresolved. In these cases, the reason for the overallocation and why it was not resolved should be noted.

Leveling Resources Automatically

Leveling is a strategy used to resolve resource overallocations by delaying or splitting tasks. Resource overallocations can be automatically leveled using Project. Project examines overallocations by looking at task dependencies, slack time, dates, *priorities*, and *constraints*, and it determines if a task can be delayed or split to resolve a resource conflict. When Project levels a resource, the resource's selected assignments are distributed and rescheduled according to the resource's work capacity, assignment units, and calendar, as well as the task's duration and constraints.

The Resource Leveling dialog box is used to perform leveling adjustments in Project. There are three setting areas in the Resource Leveling dialog box: leveling calculations, leveling range, and resolving overallocations.

In the Leveling Calculations area, Project can be set to manually or automatically perform leveling and search for overallocations based on a time period. The manual setting performs leveling only when the Level Now button is clicked. The automatic setting performs leveling as changes are made to the schedule. Before performing leveling, you can search for overallocations in specific blocks of time. With this setting, tasks are only considered overallocated if the total assigned work exceeds the total work hours for the specified block of time. The defaults in the Leveling Calculations area are Manual and Day By Day. In the Leveling Range area, you can select either the entire project or only those tasks that occur in a specified date range. The default leveling range is the Entire Project.

In the Resolving Overallocations area, the leveling order, slack, assignments, and split settings are made. The leveling order settings are ID Only, Standard, and Priority Standard. The ID Only order checks the tasks in ascending order by task ID number. Standard order, the default, checks tasks in the order of predecessor dependencies, slack time, dates, priority, and then constraints. Priority Standard order checks the task priority first, and then checks predecessor dependencies, slack time, dates, and constraints. The Level Only Within Available Slack setting levels only those tasks that will not affect the project finish date. The Leveling Can Adjust Individual Assignments On A Task setting levels a resource independent of other resources working on the same task. The Leveling Can Create Splits In Remaining Work setting interrupts tasks by creating splits in the remaining work on tasks or resource assignments. The Assignments and Splitting settings are selected by default; the Slack setting is not.

Leveling changes made by Project can be viewed in the Leveling Gantt view. Bars that represent changes made to tasks and resource assignments during leveling are displayed in the Leveling Gantt view. Green Gantt bars indicate the scheduled start and finish dates for a task before leveling occurred. The blue Gantt bars represent the newly scheduled start and finish dates for tasks after leveling occurred. The olive lines indicate delay, and the aqua lines indicate slack.

When leveling is performed automatically, sometimes the changes made to the schedule are unacceptable due to project restrictions or preferences. When this occurs, you can remove the changes made by the leveling operation. To remove the last leveling operation, click Clear Leveling in the Resource Leveling dialog box. You can also use the Undo button on the Standard toolbar to remove leveling immediately.

In the following exercises, all resource assignments have been made for the corporate office relocation project. The resource sheet indicates that eight resources are overallocated. You use automatic leveling to resolve as many overallocations as possible using the default leveling settings.

Level the entire project

In this exercise, you view the current project finish date and then review the leveling settings.

1 On the Project menu, click Project Information.

The Project Information dialog box appears.

2 View the current project finish date, and then click Cancel.

The current finish date is 11/19/98.

3 Be sure that the bottom pane is the active pane.

4 On the Tools menu, click Resource Leveling.

The Resource Leveling dialog box appears.

5 Be sure that the default options are selected as in the previous screen illustration.

> **TIP** Save the project file before performing automatic leveling. This way, if leveling cannot be removed for some reason, simply close the file without saving the changes. When the file is reopened, only the leveling will be lost.

Review leveling messages

In this exercise, you start the leveling process and examine the leveling messages as leveling progresses.

If the top pane is active, the Level Now dialog box appears. From the dialog box, you can level the entire resource pool or only selected resources.

1 Click Level Now.

A message indicating that the "architect" resource is assigned more than its maximum units in the "Finalize drawings" task on 8/28/98, is displayed.

2 Click Skip five times.

The messages skipped refer to the overallocation of the architect on the same task over several days. A message indicating that Project cannot resolve the overallocation of the administrative assistant on 11/4/98 is displayed.

3 Click Skip.

The leveling process is complete Overallocations remain for the "architect" and "computer tech 1" resources.

Review automatic leveling changes

In this exercise, you view the new project finish date and then review some of the changes made by automatic leveling.

1 On the Project menu, click Project Information.

The newly scheduled project finish date is 12/9/98.

2 Click Cancel.

3 In the top pane, be sure that the computer tech 1 resource is selected.

4 Scroll to the week of 11/29/98 in the bottom pane, the Leveling Gantt view, to view changes to the tasks.

147

5 In the top pane, select the floor-covering contractor.

6 Scroll to the left in the Leveling Gantt view to view changes to the tasks.

On 10/20/98, the original start and finish dates for each task are displayed as green Gantt bars. On 11/3/98, the newly scheduled start and finish date are displayed as blue Gantt bars.

7 Save the file without a baseline.

> **NOTE** When automatic leveling changes the work assignment of a resource on a task, a contour indicator icon is displayed in the Indicators field for the task assignment.

Manually Resolving Resource Overallocations

Using Project to perform leveling operations might not always be enough to completely resolve all the resource conflicts in a project. Automatic leveling might also result in unwanted schedule adjustments or solutions that are not practical for the particular project. When this occurs, other scheduling techniques can be used to manually resolve the overallocations. When deciding which technique to use, consider the following: the reason for the overallocation, the project budget, resource availability, task flexibility, and what adjustments are most acceptable to the project. Some suggestions for manual leveling are as follows.

■ Increase the maximum units of the resource.

Increasing resource units reduces the number of hours a single unit of the resource must work on the task. Before increasing the maximum units of a resource, be sure that the extra units are available to the project and determine the impact on the cost of the project.

148

- Reschedule the task that has created the overallocation.

  The start of a task can be delayed until a resource is available, or a task can be split. Splitting a task interrupts the task, and then it resumes when the resource is available. Both actions will delay successor tasks and can affect the project finish date.

- Add overtime.

  By adding overtime, work is scheduled beyond a resource's regular working hours, but additional work is not added. Assigning overtime shortens the duration of a task. Before assigning overtime work, determine the impact on the cost of the project.

- Adjust task dependencies or constraints.

  Changing the task dependency can remove the overlap between tasks that use the same resource. Removing the overlap between tasks can affect the project finish date.

- Remove the resource if it isn't important to the task.

  Removing a resource from a task might change the task duration. The work assigned to the removed resource is redistributed to the remaining resources assigned to the task.

- Replace the overallocated resource with an underallocated resource.

  Replacing resources can eliminate an overallocation as long as the new resource is available during the overallocation period. Depending on the resource, the cost to the project might increase or decrease.

- Make calendar adjustments to extend the working days and hours for the project or resource.

  By extending the hours and days available to a project, more work can be accomplished. Depending on the changes, extending the hours and days can decrease the need for overtime.

- Decrease the amount of work assigned to the resource.

  The amount of work assigned to a resource can be reduced. If the overallocated resource is the only resource assigned to the task, the duration of the task is affected.

 NOTE Replacing a resource, instead of removing and then assigning a new resource, preserves the work assignment. For example, if you remove a resource that is scheduled to work 6 hours on a 1-day task and then assign a new resource, the new resource will be scheduled for 8 hours instead of the 6 hours of the original resource. If you replace a resource, the new resource is assigned the 6 hours scheduled for the original resource.

In the following exercises, four resources still remain overallocated after using automatic leveling. After further review of the overallocations, you determine that by using various management techniques the remaining overallocations can be resolved without impacting the project's finish date of 12/15/98. You resolve the overallocation of the architect resource by increasing the maximum units on the project. The computer tech 1 overallocation is resolved by changing the work hours on a task. The office manager overallocation is resolved by substituting another resource on the task.

Increase resource maximum units

In this exercise, you increase the number of maximum units for the architect resource.

1   In the top pane, select the architect resource.

2   Drag the scroll box to the left, and then click in the bottom pane.

To view the entire over-allocation, scroll to the right in the Leveling Gantt view.

3   On the Resource Management toolbar, click the Go To Next Overallocation.

The start of the overallocation between task 9, Finalize drawings, and task 10, Select subcontractors, is displayed.

Go To Next Overallocation

4   In the top pane, double-click the architect resource.

The Resource Information dialog box appears. The General tab is selected.

5   In the Resource Availability area, click the Max Units Available up arrow twice.

The maximum units increase to 200%.

6   Click OK.

The overallocation is resolved.

7   Save the file without a baseline.

Change work on a task assignment

In this exercise, you change the work hours for the computer tech 1 on resource task 39, Disconnect server.

1   In the top pane, select the computer tech 1 resource.

2   Drag the scroll box to the left, and then click in the bottom pane.

The work hours on a task should only be changed after analyzing the work necessary to complete the task.

3   On the Resource Management toolbar, click the Go To Next Overallocation.

The overallocation between task 35, Reconnect computers/equip., and task 39, Disconnect server, is displayed.

4   In the timescale portion of the top pane, click the work hours on Tuesday, 12/1 for the Disconnect server task.

5 Type **0**, and press ENTER.

The work on the task for that day is changed to 0 hours. The total work for the computer tech 1 resource on task 39 changes from sixteen to eight hours.

6 Save the file without a baseline.

Check the schedule

In this exercise, you scroll through the top pane, the Resource Usage view, to determine if all overallocations have been resolved. You then check the project finish date to make sure it is still within the project goal.

If any over-allocations still exist, the resource text is highlighted in red.

1 In the top pane, scroll to locate any other overallocations.

All overallocations should be resolved.

2 On the Project menu, click Project Information.

The newly scheduled finish date is 12/9/98.

3 Click Cancel.

4 Save the file without a baseline.

> **NOTE** As you use automatic leveling and manually resolve overallocations, continue to check the project finish date to be sure it is still within the project goal. The same management techniques used to manually resolve overallocations can, in some cases, be used to reduce the total duration of a project. For example, increasing the number of resources assigned to a task reduces the task duration. If the task is on the critical path, the total project duration is also reduced.

One Step Further: Displaying Different Task and Assignment Details

The usage views, such as the Task Usage view, the Resource Graph view, and the Resource Usage view, can be formatted to display additional detail information in the timescale portion of the view. Displaying information such as costs, availability, and actual work can provide needed details quickly. On the Format menu, the Details submenu lists several types of additional information that can be displayed. If information other than what is available through the submenu is needed, the usage detail styles can be changed to include other fields. The font, cell background color, and cell pattern can also be changed.

Add usage details

In this exercise, you remove the split view and then change the view by selecting one of the usage details from the Details submenu.

You can also click Remove Split on the Window menu.

1 Double-click the split bar.

When a split is removed, the top pane becomes a single view. The Resource Usage view fills the screen.

2 On the Format menu, point to Details, and then click Remaining Availability.

A new row, Rem. Avail., is added to the timescale portion of the view.

3 Press F5, type 6, and press ENTER.

The view scrolls to resource ID number 6, computer tech 1. Your screen should look similar to the following illustration.

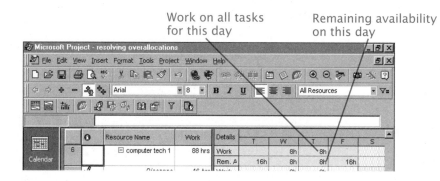

Work on all tasks for this day

Remaining availability on this day

Change detail styles for added detail

In this exercise, you change the cell color in the timescale portion of the view for the remaining availability values.

1 On the Format menu, click Detail Styles.

The Detail Styles dialog box appears.

2 In the Show These Fields box, select Remaining Availability.

3 In the Field Setting For Remaining Availability area, click the Cell Background down arrow.

4 Click the second color, red.

5 Click OK.

The cells in the timescale portion of the view change to red with the default pattern.

6 Save the file without a baseline.

Finish the lesson

1 Right-click a toolbar, and then click Resource Management.

The Resource Management toolbar is hidden.

2 To continue to the next lesson, on the File menu, click Close.

3 If you are finished using Project for now, on the File menu, click Exit.

Lesson Summary

To	Do this	Button
View resource workloads	On the View Bar, click the down arrow until the Resource Usage icon is displayed, and then click the Resource Usage icon. Select a resource. Scroll in the timescale portion of the view to locate the work values for each task assignment.	
	or	
	When in Resource Usage view, select a task assignment for a resource. On the Standard toolbar, click the Go To Selected Task button. The work hours for the selected task are displayed.	
Display the Resource Management toolbar	On the View menu, point to Toolbars, and then click Resource Management.	
	or	
	Right-click a toolbar. From the shortcut menu, click Resource Management.	

To	Do this	Button
Locate resource overallocation	On the Resource Management toolbar, click the Resource Allocation View button. On the top pane, select an overallocated resource. Drag the scroll box to the left, and then click in the bottom pane. On the Resource Management toolbar, click the Go To Next Overallocation button. Keep clicking the Go To Next Overallocation button to view each overallocation for that resource. Eventually, a message indicating that no other overallocations exist for that resource is displayed.	
Use automatic leveling	On the Tools menu, click Resource Leveling. In the Leveling Calculations area, be sure that the Manual option is selected. Select the appropriate additional settings, and then click Level Now. Read each leveling message as it is displayed, and click Skip after each one.	

For online information about	On the Help menu, click Contents And Index, click the Index tab, and then type
Viewing resource workloads	overallocated resources *or* resource usage view *or* resource allocation view
Locating overallocations	overallocated resources *or* leveling
Using automatic leveling	overallocated resources *or* leveling
Manually resolving overallocations	overallocated resources *or* leveling

Scheduling Task Constraints

Estimated time
30 min.

In this lesson you will learn how to:

- Use constraints to set date limitations on tasks.
- Set a project schedule baseline.

During the course of a project, situations might arise where specific tasks need to start or finish on or around a given date. When a start or finish date limitation is imposed on a task, the ability of that task to adjust to changes in the schedule decreases. For example, the first choice in carpet color cannot be delivered until April 1st. If the "install carpeting" task is currently scheduled for March 28th, a date limitation to install the carpet after April 1st would need to be imposed on the schedule. By imposing the date on the task, any time saved on prior tasks could not be to be taken advantage of. However, if the schedule moves the task out past the imposed date, the date limitation has no direct impact on the schedule.

In Microsoft Project 98, all tasks are scheduled to occur as soon as possible based on a given project start date. If it is necessary to impose date limitations on tasks, Project will monitor the proposed limitation and display a message if a possible conflict might arise in the schedule due to the restriction. Once the schedule planning is complete and before the first task in the project begins, you can take a snapshot of the schedule plan for later comparison to the actual dates. This information can be used during the course of the project to analyze the changes between the original plan and the progress of the project.

155

In this lesson, the corporate office relocation project schedule is in the final stage of planning. Several possible date restrictions have been brought to your attention. Before you complete the schedule, you apply several date limitations to tasks that have a time restriction. You then save the schedule as the finalized plan.

Start the lesson

1 Start Microsoft Project.

2 From the Project SBS Practice folder, open the Restrict file.

3 Save the file as task constraints without a baseline in the Project SBS Practice folder.

Restricting Task Start and Finish Dates

When a task is first entered into Project, the task start date is by default the project start date. If a project is being scheduled from the finish date, the task finish date is by default the project finish date. After tasks are linked and re-sources are assigned, Project then sets task start and finish dates based on task dependencies and resource availability. This is the most effective way of scheduling a project because it incorporates flexibility.

Sometimes, however, the schedule needs to reflect real-world time constraints. A constraint is a restriction or limitation imposed on the start or finish date of a task. For example, an order of special light fixtures will not arrive until 10/1. This means that the "install light fixtures" task cannot occur any earlier than 10/1. In Project, a task can be constrained so that it starts or finishes on or near a specific date or starts as late as possible. By default, all tasks in Project are scheduled with the As Soon As Possible constraint.

Flexible constraints are also known as soft constraints. Inflexible constraints are also known as hard constraints.

A constraint is either flexible or inflexible. A flexible constraint is not tied to a specific date. Inflexible constraints are tied to a specific date. Whether a constraint type is flexible or inflexible depends on whether the project is scheduled from the start date or finish date. For example, a Finish No Earlier Than constraint is placed on a task. If the project is scheduled from a given start date, once the constrained task is reached, the project finish date can still be extended. This makes the constraint flexible. If the project is scheduled from a given finish date, once the constrained task is reached, the project finish date cannot be extended. This makes the constraint inflexible.

Task constraints can help create a more accurate schedule by using detailed information to control the start and finish dates of important tasks. However, constraints can also limit a schedule's flexibility. If a scheduling conflict exists between a constraint and a task dependency, the task is scheduled according to the constraint. Constraints should be few and used only when necessary.

At various stages in a project, constraints should be checked to make sure they are necessary, particularly for tasks on the critical path. Any constraint that requires a date should be used carefully because fixed dates prevent the start and finish dates from being recalculated if the schedule changes. It also limits the ability to level resources that are overallocated.

Constraints can be applied to a task using the Advanced tab on the Task Information dialog box. In the Constraint Task area, the constraint type is selected, and a date is entered.

In the following exercises, during the recent team meeting, the facilities department announced two date constraints on the project. The new lease negotiations must be completed by September 1st, the day the current lease must be renewed or canceled. Also, demolition work cannot start until September 21st or later due to summer events in the downtown area. You apply constraints to the two tasks impacted by the facilities announcements.

TROUBLESHOOTING   If a project is being scheduled from a start date, entering a start date for a task or dragging a Gantt bar automatically sets a Start No Earlier Than (SNET) constraint. If a finish date is entered, a Finish No Earlier Than (FNET) constraint is automatically set. If a project is being scheduled from a finish date, entering a start date for a task or dragging a Gantt bar automatically sets a Start No Later Than (SNLT) constraint. If a finish date is entered, a Finish No Later Than (FNLT) constraint is automatically set.

Applying Flexible Constraints

All tasks are assigned a constraint. If a project is scheduled from a start date, a task is entered with a default constraint of As Soon As Possible. The As Soon As Possible constraint is a flexible constraint. Flexible task constraints are not tied to a specific date. For example, if a resource is extremely busy, the As Late As Possible constraint can be applied to less critical tasks, freeing up the resource for more critical tasks. Flexible constraints are the preferred type of constraint because it leaves flexibility in the schedule.

The following table describes the types of constraints and when they are flexible.

Constraint	Description	Is flexible for
As Soon As Possible (ASAP)	Starts the task as soon as possible based on other constraints and dependencies.	All projects
As Late As Possible (ALAP)	Starts the task as late as possible based on other constraints and dependencies.	All projects
Finish No Earlier Than (FNET)	Finishes the task on or after an entered date.	Projects scheduled from a start date
Start No Earlier Than (SNET)	Starts the task on or after an entered date.	Projects scheduled from a start date
Finish No Later Than (FNLT)	Finishes the task on or before an entered date.	Projects scheduled from a finish date
Start No Later Than (SNLT)	Starts the task on or before an entered date.	Projects scheduled from a finish date

The As Soon As Possible constraint is the default constraint for projects that are scheduled from a start date. The As Late As Possible constraint is the default constraint for projects that are scheduled from a finish date. Neither constraint uses a date.

Apply a flexible constraint

In this exercise, you apply a flexible task constraint, Start No Earlier Than, to a task.

1   Press F5, type **15**, and press ENTER.

2   Double-click task 15, Demolition of existing space.

The Task Information dialog box appears.

The currently scheduled start date is 9/28/98, and the finish date is 10/1/98, for task 15.

3   Be sure that the General tab is selected, and view the currently scheduled start and finish dates for task 15.

4   Click the Advanced tab.

5   Click the Type down arrow, and then select Start No Earlier Than.

6   Click the Date down arrow, and then select September 21, 1998.

7   Click OK.

The constraint is set. A flexible constraint indicator icon is displayed in the Indicator field. Your screen should look similar to the following illustration.

Flexible constraint indicator icon

8 Save the file without a baseline.

Applying Inflexible Constraints

Inflexible task constraints are tied to a specific date and should be used less often because they take flexibility away from the schedule. Inflexible constraints are generally applied when outside forces are dictating a task's start or finish date.

The following table describes the types of constraints and when they are inflexible.

Constraint	Description	Is flexible for
Finish No Earlier Than (FNET)	Finishes the task on or after an entered date.	Projects scheduled from a finish date
Start No Earlier Than (SNET)	Starts the task on or after an entered date.	Projects scheduled from a finish date
Finish No Later Than (FNLT)	Finishes the task on or before an entered date.	Projects scheduled from a start date
Start No Later Than (SNLT)	Starts the task on or before an entered date.	Projects scheduled from a start date
Must Finish On (MFO)	Finishes the task on an entered date.	All projects
Must Start On (MSO)	Starts the task on an entered date.	All projects

Apply an inflexible constraint

In this exercise, you apply an inflexible task constraint, Finish No Later Than, to a task.

159

1 Press F5, type **8**, and press ENTER.

2 Double-click task 8, Negotiate new lease.

The Task Information dialog box appears.

The currently scheduled start date is 8/26/98, and the finish date is 8/31/98, for task 8.

3 Click the General tab, and view the currently scheduled start and finish dates for task 8.

4 Click the Advanced tab.

5 Click the Type down arrow, and then select Finish No Later Than.

6 Click the Date down arrow, and then select September 1, 1998.

7 Click OK.

The constraint is set. An inflexible constraint indicator icon is displayed in the Indicator field.

8 Save the file without a baseline.

TIP Project can move the start date of a task beyond its constraint date. On the Tools menu, click Options. Click the Schedule tab, and then clear the Tasks Will Always Honor Their Constraint Dates check box. Task links will now take precedence over constraints. For example, if a constraint is set and there is no way to make the constraint date, you might want to leave the constraint information in the project file for documentation purposes.

Scheduling Constraints that Create Conflicts

When task constraints are set, conflicts can occur that can affect the project finish date or a task dependency. When a conflict occurs, the *Planning Wizard* appears, indicating that a conflict, or a potential conflict, will exist if the constraint is applied. The Planning Wizard is an assistant that monitors scheduling activities and offers suggestions when appropriate.

Apply a constraint that conflicts with the schedule

In this exercise, you apply a Must Start On constraint on task 6, Present proposal.

1 Double-click task 6, Present proposal.

The Task Information dialog box appears.

The currently scheduled start date is 8/24/98, and the finish date is 8/25/98, for task 6.

2 Click the General tab, and view the currently scheduled start and finish dates for task 6.

3 Click the Advanced tab.

4 Click the Type down arrow, and then select Must Start On.

For more information about the Planning Wizard message, click Help in the Planning Wizard dialog box.

The conflict arises because task 8, Negotiate new lease, has a Finish No Later Than constraint prior to 9/7.

5   Click the Date down arrow, and then select September 7, 1998.

6   Click OK.

The Planning Wizard dialog box appears. A scheduling conflict could occur if the constraint is set.

7   Be sure that the Cancel. No Constraint Will Be Set On "Present Proposal" option is selected, and click OK.

You can also click Cancel. The Planning Wizard closes, and the constraint is not set.

8   Save the file without a baseline.

TIP   To turn off the Planning Wizard, on the Tools menu, click Options. Click the General tab. In the Planning Wizard area, clear the Advice From Planning Wizard check box.

Establishing a Baseline

Once a project schedule is created and the resource and task conflicts have been resolved, the current schedule represents the best estimate of how the project should proceed and what resources it will take. Before the first task in the project begins, a baseline should be set. A baseline is a record, or "snapshot," taken at a specific time in the project.

Setting the baseline is a critical step in the scheduling process. As a project progresses, the start times, finish times, and resource assignments can change. A baseline is useful for comparing the planned schedule with later versions of the schedule to see what changes have occurred. When a baseline is set, those dates, times, and other critical pieces of data are stored and do not change. Once a baseline is saved, the Planning Wizard no longer prompts the user when saving a project file. A baseline is saved using the Planning Wizard prompt or the Save Baseline command.

A project baseline should be viewed as a learning tool. The information gathered by comparing the baseline to the actual progress on a project might be used to identify upcoming problems during the project, to prevent problems on future projects, to establish better task duration estimates, or to make more accurate resource assignments.

> **TIP** If a baseline is saved before the schedule planning is finished, a new baseline can be saved over the existing baseline. On the Tools menu, point to Tracking, and then click Save Baseline. This should only be done to reset a baseline that was saved by accident.

Set a baseline

The schedule planning for the corporate office relocation project is complete. In this exercise, you set the baseline.

1 On the Tools menu, point to Tracking, and then click Save Baseline.

   The Save Baseline dialog box appears.

2 Be sure that the Save Baseline option is selected.

3 In the For area, be sure that the Entire Project option is selected.

4 Click OK.

View baseline statistics

In this exercise, you view the summary baseline information in the Project Statistics box.

1 On the Project menu, click Project Information.

   The Project Information dialog box appears.

2 Click Statistics.

   The Project Statistics For Task Constraints dialog box appears. Baseline information is displayed.

3 Click Close.

4 Save the file.

   Once the baseline is saved, the Planning Wizard no longer prompts you.

> **NOTE** There are three types of date data kept for each task in Project: scheduled, actual, and baseline. When a baseline is set, the data in the scheduled fields is copied over to the baseline fields. Dates in Project are discussed further in Lesson 11: "Tracking Project Progress".

Creating Interim Plans

In addition to saving a baseline, *interim plans* can also be saved. An interim plan is generally saved at certain stages in a project. These plans can then be compared to the baseline plan and the current schedule. For example, while a project that involves access to a new facility is underway, you are notified that the new facility will not be available for an additional two weeks. By the time the project is complete, the baseline and actual comparison might be off by at least two weeks. Once adjustments are made to the current schedule for the delay, an interim plan that includes the rescheduled tasks and resources can be set. When the project is finished, it can be compared to the baseline and the interim plan to assess the true impact on the project both before and after the delay.

The data saved in an interim plan includes the start and finish dates and any split dates. No resource or assignment data is saved in an interim plan. Up to 10 interim plans can be set in Project.

To set an interim plan, perform the following steps.

1 On the Tools menu, point to Tracking, and then click Save Baseline.

   The Save Baseline dialog box appears.

2 Select the Save Interim Plan option.

   The Copy and Into boxes are active.

3 Click the Copy down arrow, and select the date fields to be copied.

   Generally, the Start/Finish fields should be copied.

4 Click the Into down arrow, and select the date field to which you wish to copy.

   If this is the first interim plan for the project, select Start1/Finish1. Each interim plan set after that goes to the subsequent Start/Finish number; for example, Start2/Finish2 would be the next interim plan for the project.

5 In the For area, be sure that the Entire Project option is selected.

   You can also set an interim plan for specific tasks.

6 Click OK.

   The interim plan is saved in the designated Start/Finish fields.

One Step Further: Displaying Project Constraints

Task constraint information can be displayed in several ways within Project. If a constraint has been applied to a task, the Indicators field displays a constraint icon. When the mouse is positioned on an indicator icon, a ScreenTip displays details regarding the indicator. An inflexible constraint icon has a red dot, and a flexible constraint indicator has a blue dot. Tasks that are not completed within their constraints have an exclamation sign on the constraints icon. Constraints can also be viewed by applying the Constraint Dates table. The Constraint Dates table displays the Task Name, Duration, Constraint Type, and Constraint Date fields.

View constraint dates

In this exercise, you view constraint information in ScreenTips, and then apply the Constraint Dates table in Sheet view.

1   Position the mouse pointer on the constraint indicator icon for task 8, Negotiate new lease.

A ScreenTip displays the constraint type and date for the task.

2   Position the mouse pointer on the constraint indicator icon for task 15, Demolition of existing space.

More Views

3   On the View Bar, click the down arrow until the More Views icon is displayed, and then click the More Views icon.

The More Views dialog box appears.

4   In the Views box, click Task Sheet, and then click Apply.

5   On the View menu, point to Table, and then click More Tables.

The More Tables dialog box appears.

6   In the More Tables dialog box, double-click Constraint Dates.

The Constraint Dates table is displayed.

	Task Name	Duration	Constraint Type	Constraint Date
8	Negotiate new lea	4 days	Finish No Later Than	Tue 9/1/98
9	Finalize drawings	1 wk	As Soon As Possible	NA
10	Select subcontra	1.5 wks	As Soon As Possible	NA
11	Hire mover	4 days	As Soon As Possible	NA
12	Submit drawings	1.5 wks	As Soon As Possible	NA
13	Permits received	0 days	As Soon As Possible	NA
14	⊟ Remodeling	39.5 days	As Soon As Possible	NA

7   Save the file.

Finish the lesson

1   To continue to the next lesson, on the File menu, click Close.

2   If you are finished using Project for now, on the File menu, click Exit.

Lesson Summary

To	Do this	Button
Apply a task constraint	Double-click the task to which the constraint will be applied. Click the Advanced tab. In the Constrain Task area, click the Constraint Type down arrow. Select the appropriate constraint type. If appropriate, click the Date down arrow. Select the appropriate date, and click OK. *or* Select a task, and then, on the Standard toolbar, click the Task Information button.	
Set a baseline	On the Tools menu, point to Tracking, and then click Save Baseline. Be sure that the Save Baseline option is selected. Be sure that the Entire Project option is selected, and click OK.	

For online information about	**On the Help menu, click Contents And Index, click the Index tab, and then type**
Applying task constraints	**constraint tasks** *or* **constraint types** *or* **constraints**
Setting a baseline	**baseline**

Review & Practice

You will review and practice how to:

- Use automatic leveling to resolve resource conflicts.
- Resolve resource overallocations manually by using management techniques.
- Apply flexible and inflexible task constraints.
- Set a baseline.

Before you move on to Part 4, which covers tracking project progress, filtering and sorting, and creating custom tables, views, and reports, you can practice the skills you learned in Part 3 by working through this Review & Practice section. You will view and resolve resource conflicts, apply task constraints, and set a project baseline.

Scenario

The project schedule for the shareholders meeting is just about ready to finalize. At the last project team meeting, the final resource assignments and working times were completed. You're now ready to resolve any resource overallocations based on parameters set at the meeting. You've also been informed of several date constraints for vital tasks that need to be imposed on the project. Once the project is fine-tuned and before the first task begins, the baseline can be set.

Step 1: View Resource Workloads

The current schedule for the shareholders meeting has been turned over to you with all the resource assignments made. You view the resource workloads to prepare for resolving any resource overallocations.

1 Open the Review3 file in the Project SBS Practice folder, and then save the file as Meeting Leveling without a baseline in the Project SBS Practice folder.

2 Display the Resource Usage view.

3 View the workload for the intern resource.

4 Display the Resource Management toolbar.

5 Display the Resource Allocation view.

6 Find the overallocation for the vice president resource.

For more information about	See
Viewing resource workloads	Lesson 9
Displaying the Resource Management toolbar	Lesson 9
Finding resource overallocations	Lesson 9

Step 2: Use Automatic Leveling

After reviewing the resource workloads, you use automatic leveling to see what overallocations can be resolved within certain leveling settings. Once automatic leveling is done, you view the changes to schedule.

1 Check the current project finish date.

2 Open the Resource Leveling dialog box.

3 Be sure that the following options are set in the Resource Leveling dialog box.

Dialog box area settings	Option, check box, or list
Leveling Calculations	Manual, Day By Day
Leveling Range	Level Entire Project
Resolving Overallocations	Standard, Leveling Can Adjust Individual Assignments On A Task, Leveling Can Create Splits In Remaining Work

4 Level the project. (Hint: Be sure the bottom pane of the Resource Allocation view is selected.)

5　Skip the overallocations for the administrative assistant and intern resources on 8/10/98 and 8/11/98.

6　View the leveling changes to the vice president resource on 7/25/98.

7　Check the project dates to see if automatic leveling extended the scheduled finish date.

8　Save the file without a baseline.

For more information about	See
Using automatic leveling	Lesson 9

Step 3:　*Manually Resolve Resource Overallocations*

You couldn't resolve all the overallocations with automatic leveling. You use management techniques to resolve the remaining overallocations within the acceptable parameters as set by the project team.

1　Locate the overallocation for the administrative assistant resource.

2　Resolve the overallocation by removing the administrative assistant from task 17, Arrange necessary equipment.

3　Locate the overallocation for the intern resource.

4　Resolve the overallocation by increasing the maximum units available to the project to 200%.

5　Scroll through the Resource Usage view to be sure that no other overallocations exist.

6　Save the file without a baseline.

For more information about	See
Manually resolving overallocations	Lesson 9

Step 4:　*Apply Task Constraints*

During the last project team meeting, several tasks were identified as being scheduled. The agenda for the shareholders meeting should be printed right before the meeting in case there are any last minute changes. The letter notifying the shareholders of the meeting needs to be mailed at least a week before the meeting date. Finally, the meeting must occur on August 27th because that is when the conference center is booked.

1　Display the Gantt Chart view in a single pane.

2　Place an As Late As Possible constraint on task 19, Print agenda.

3　Place a Finish No Later Than constraint for 8/18/98, on task 13, Send Letter. Allow the constraint to be placed.

4 Place a Must Start On constraint for 8/27/98 on task 20, Meeting occurs. Allow the constraint to be placed.

5 Save the file without a baseline.

For more information about	See
Applying task constraints	Lesson 10

Step 5: Set a Baseline

The shareholders meeting schedule has been fine-tuned and now resembles the project team's best effort at creating a project plan. To finalize the plan, you set the project baseline for later comparison to the actual progress of the project.

1 Set a baseline for the shareholders meeting project.

2 Save the file.

For more information about	See
Setting a baseline	Lesson 10

Finish the Review & Practice

1 Hide the Resource Management toolbar.

2 Close the Meeting Leveling file.

3 If you are finished using Project for now, on the File menu, click Exit.

Part

4

Managing a Project

Tracking Project Progress

Estimated time
40 min.

In this lesson you will learn how to:

- Track the actual progress of tasks.
- Split tasks to reschedule work on a task.
- Compare baseline data to actual and scheduled data.

Once the first task in a project starts, it's time to begin tracking the actual progress of tasks and resources. Tracking is the process of gathering and entering task information into the schedule, such as actual start and finish dates. By tracking the progress of tasks, you can take advantage of the time saved from tasks that proceed ahead of schedule and make decisions about how to proceed when tasks fall behind schedule.

With Microsoft Project 98, you can update the schedule quickly and easily using several convenient features. You can track progress by entering all or some of the actual information for a task. If partial information is entered, Project updates the remaining information based on the schedule for that task. This information can be used to compare the plan to the actual progress of the project. The plan and the actuals can be compared graphically. Gantt bars reflect the baseline information with one color and reflect the actuals with another color. Tables numerically display the information, and filters quickly locate tasks and resources that might be behind schedule or overbudget.

In this lesson, the corporate office relocation project is underway. Several tasks in the project have progressed, and it's time to begin entering the actual data. You enter actual data based on the information provided for individual tasks. You split a task that work has stopped on, and you update the remainder of the project based on the schedule. After entering the data, you view the project information to identify where the project is behind and ahead of schedule for the upcoming team meeting.

Start the lesson

1   Start Microsoft Project.
2   From the Project SBS Practice folder, open the Track file.
3   Save the file as Tracking Progress in the Project SBS Practice folder.

Tracking Progress

Before the first task in a project can begin, the project schedule should be fully developed and a baseline plan should be set. Once work begins on a project, it is time to start tracking the progress of tasks. The progress should be tracked throughout the project. The frequency of updates depends on the control needed over the project. If progress is tracked more often, it is easier to identify problems and take corrective action.

Tasks that do not occur as scheduled should be tracked manually by entering actual progress information for the individual tasks. These tasks might have start and finish dates that occur later or earlier than scheduled, or durations that run longer or shorter. Even in the best planned schedules, new tasks might be identified after the project begins. All of these situations affect the remaining tasks in a project.

When actual task progress is entered, the project is automatically recalculated, and nonprogressed tasks are rescheduled based on the actual data, task dependencies, resources, and constraints. For this reason, task progress should be entered starting at the top of the task list and continuing down the list. With the correct information, the remainder of the project can be evaluated, and both positive and negative impacts can be dealt with on a proactive basis rather than a reactive basis.

There are three types of dates stored for each task in Project: scheduled (current), actual, and baseline. The following table describes the three types of dates.

Date type	Description
Scheduled (current)	Tasks that haven't started yet or are in progress. These dates change as the project progresses. After the tasks have started, actual information about the tasks is entered.
Actual	Tasks that are in progress or are completed. These dates do not change once a task has been tracked, unless they are edited.

174

Date type	Description
Baseline	Originally planned dates. These dates are used to compare the original plan with the actual dates and scheduled dates. The baseline dates do not change.

When the project schedule is in the planning stage, the only dates that exist are scheduled dates. When a baseline is set, the scheduled dates become the baseline dates. As tasks are completed, the scheduled dates and the actual dates become the same. When the project is completed, the scheduled dates and actual dates are all the same. The scheduled dates for tasks that are in progress or have not occurred change as the schedule is recalculated. Project also stores the same three types of information for costs.

As tasks are tracked, the Gantt Chart begins to reflect the progress information. The Gantt bars contain *progress bars* that indicate the progress of each task. Tasks that are 100% complete are deleted from the critical path because they no longer impact the project finish date. The critical path is automatically recalculated as progress is entered. Completed tasks also have a checkmark in the Indicators field.

For exercise purposes, the first tracking period covers a longer period of time than would usually pass before actual data is entered.

In the following exercises, the corporate office relocation project has begun. You've been asked to maintain the schedule. You've identified when to gather progress information and what information is needed. The first tracking point has been reached, and you're ready to update the schedule using actual task information.

 TIP It is best to decide early in the project when and how progress will be tracked. For example, a weekly team meeting is a good tracking point. Information on task progress can be gathered at the end of the working day prior to the meeting and then entered into the schedule. The revised schedule can then be distributed at the meeting for further updates and discussion.

Entering Actual Progress Information

There are five types of actual data that can be entered in Project: (1)actual start and finish dates, (2)percentage complete, (3)actual duration and remaining duration, (4)actual and remaining work, and (5)actual and remaining costs. Project calculates actual data based on what information is entered for a task. For example, if an actual finish date is entered for a task, Project calculates the actual start date and actual duration. The actual start date is based on the scheduled start date, and the actual duration is based on the difference between the scheduled start date and the actual finish date provided.

When an actual duration is entered, the remaining duration must also be considered. If an actual duration that is less than the scheduled duration is entered, Project calculates the difference between the two, and this difference becomes the remaining duration. If the task was actually accomplished in a shorter time frame than scheduled, a zero needs to be entered as the remaining duration. If an actual duration that is greater than the scheduled duration is entered, Project calculates the remaining duration as zero. If the task is still not complete, a value needs to be entered for the remaining duration. These same principles exist for actual work and cost values.

Actual task data can be entered using several different features: the Update Tasks dialog box, the Task Information dialog box, the Tracking table, and the Tracking toolbar. The individual user decides which values to enter and what feature to use for entering the values.

The Task Usage view and the Resource Usage view can be used to track project progress on a day-to-day basis.

IMPORTANT Progress information should only be entered in table fields and dialog boxes labeled Actual. If actual data is entered into the scheduled (current) fields and boxes, only the scheduled information is changed, and no tracking occurs.

In the following exercises, you enter actual data up to a status date of October 8, 1998, using the different features available in Project. The "write proposal" task finished one day ahead of schedule. The "negotiate new lease" task is ahead of schedule one day. The "finalize drawings task" is 75% complete as scheduled. The "frame interior walls" task is requiring less work than scheduled. The work on the "install electrical" task was interrupted due to a supply delivery that was late. The remainder of the project is progressing as scheduled up to the status date.

Enter an actual finish date for tasks

In this exercise, you enter the actual finish date of a task.

1   Select task 3, Write proposal.

2   On the Tools menu, point to Tracking, and then click Update Tasks.

    The Update Tasks dialog box appears.

Update Tasks		? X
Name: Write proposal		Duration: 3d
% Complete: 0%	Actual dur: 0d	Remaining dur: 3d
Actual		**Current**
Start: NA		Start: Mon 8/10/98
Finish: NA		Finish: Wed 8/12/98
	Notes...	OK Cancel

All successor tasks are rescheduled based on the actual data entered.

3 In the Actual area, click the Finish down arrow.

4 Select August 11, 1998, and click OK.

The actual finish date is entered. A checkmark is displayed in the Indicators field, and a progress bar is displayed on the Gantt bar.

5 On the Tools menu, point to Tracking, and then click Update Tasks.

The actual start date is entered as scheduled. The actual task duration is recalculated at two days. The scheduled and actual data is now the same for task 3, and the percentage complete is 100%.

6 Click Cancel.

7 Position the mouse pointer on the task indicator.

A ScreenTip with the task completion date is displayed.

8 Save the file.

Enter actual and remaining durations

In this exercise, you enter the actual duration complete and the remaining duration on a task.

1 Select task 8, Negotiate new lease.

2 On the Tools menu, point to Tracking, and then click Update Tasks.

3 Click the Actual Dur. up arrow until 2d is displayed.

4 Click the Rem. Dur. down arrow until 1d is displayed, and click OK.

5 On the Tools menu, point to Tracking, and then click Update Tasks.

The actual start date is entered as scheduled. The finish date is re-scheduled. A percentage complete of 67% is calculated.

6 Click Cancel.

7 Save the file.

Enter a percentage complete

In this exercise, you display the Tracking table and the Tracking toolbar, and then enter a percentage complete for a task.

More Views

1 On the View Bar, click the down arrow until the More Views icon is displayed, and then click the More Views icon.

2 In the Views box, select Task Sheet, and then click Apply.

3 On the View menu, point to Table, and then click Tracking.

4 On the View menu, point to Toolbars, and then click Tracking.

5 Select task 9, Finalize drawings.

75% Complete

6 On the Tracking toolbar, click the 75% Complete button.

The actual start date is entered as scheduled. The actual and remaining durations are updated as scheduled.

		Task Name	Act. Start	Act. Finish	% Comp.	Act. Dur.	Rem. Dur.	Act. Cost
	1	⊟ Corporate Relocati	Mon 8/10/98	NA	8%	6.15 days	72.72 days	$1,778.45
	2	⊟ Planning	Mon 8/10/98	NA	20%	6.53 days	25.47 days	$1,778.45
	3	Write propos	Mon 8/10/98	Tue 8/11/98	100%	2 days	0 days	$586.15
	4	Hire architec	NA	NA	0%	0 days	2 days	$0.00
	5	Locate new	NA	NA	0%	0 wks	1 wk	$0.00
	6	Present prop	NA	NA	0%	0 days	2 days	$0.00
	7	Corporate aj	NA	NA	0%	0 days	0 days	$0.00
	8	Negotiate ne	Tue 8/25/98	NA	67%	2 days	1 day	$1,192.30
	9	Finalize drav	Wed 8/26/98	NA	75%	0.75 wks	0.25 wks	$0.00
	10	Select subcc	NA	NA	0%	0 wks	1.5 wks	$0.00
	11	Hire mover	NA	NA	0%	0 days	4 days	$0.00
	12	Submit draw	NA	NA	0%	0 wks	1.5 wks	$0.00
	13	Permits rece	NA	NA	0%	0 days	0 days	$0.00
		⊟ Remodeling	NA	NA	0%	0 days	20.5 days	$0.00

7 Save the file.

> ⚠ **WARNING** Using percentage complete data for tracking tasks can be somewhat subjective and should only be used when everyone involved understands what the percentage means. For example, Resource A reports that task Z is 100% complete. Unless other information is provided, this implies that the task started on time and took the scheduled duration to finish on time. To use percentage complete as an effective means of communicating progress, everyone involved in providing and receiving the information must understand what it implies.

Enter actual work

In this exercise, you enter the actual work hours performed on a task.

Task Usage icon

1   On the View Bar, click the down arrow until the Task Usage icon is displayed, and then click the Task Usage icon.

2   On the Format menu, point to Details, and then click Actual Work.

The Actual Work fields are displayed in the timescale portion of the view.

3   Press F5, type **16**, and click OK.

*Tuesday,
September 29,
1998, is in
the week
beginning on
September 27,
1998.*

4   Scroll in the timescale portion of the Task Usage view until September 29, 1998, is displayed, and then click the Actual Work field for the framing contractor resource on that date.

5   Type 6, and then press TAB.

The actual hours are entered. The scheduled hours for October 2, 1998, are rescheduled from 12 hours to 10 hours.

		🛈	Task Name	Work	Details	T	W	T	F
	16		⊟ Frame interior wa	32 hrs	Work	6h	8h	8h	10h
					Act. W	6h			
		📊	*framing co*	*32 hrs*	Work	6h	8h	8h	10h
					Act. W	6h			
	17		⊟ Install electrical	48 hrs	Work				1.33h
					Act. W				
			electrican	*48 hrs*	Work				1.33h
					Act. W				
	18		⊟ Install voice and c	24 hrs	Work				
					Act. W				

6   Save the file.

Tracking Work and Costs Daily

Both actual work and actual cost values can be tracked in the time-phased fields in the Task Usage and Resource Usage views. By entering information for a particular day, the project is kept up-to-date on a daily basis by resource task assignments. Tracking actual data in this way is helpful when a task assignment has been contoured. It is also useful when a resource is one of multiple resources assigned to a task, and that resource performs less scheduled work on the task than the other resources.

Track actual work on a daily basis

1   On the View Bar, click the down arrow until the Task Usage icon is displayed, and then click the Task Usage icon.

2   On the View menu, point to Table, and then click Work.

3   To enter actual values for a resource, type the work value in the appropriate day field for the resource.

4   To enter actual values for a task assignment, type the work value in the appropriate day field for the task.

Track actual costs on a daily basis

1   On the Tools menu, click Options.

The Options dialog box appears.

2   Click the Calculation tab.

3   In the Calculation Options area, clear the Actual Costs Are Always Calculated By Microsoft Project check box, and click OK.

By default, Project calculates actual costs. This setting must be cleared for the user to enter actual cost values.

4   On the View Bar, click the Task Usage icon.

5   On the View menu, point to Table, and then click Tracking.

6   On the Format menu, point to Details, and then click Actual Cost.

7   To enter actual values for a task, type the cost value in the appropriate day field for the task.

Actual cost information can only be entered after the remaining work for the task is zero.

8   To enter actual values for a resource assignment, type the cost value in the appropriate day field for the resource.

Splitting Tasks

A task can be *split* or *rescheduled* to interrupt the work and then resume the remainder of the work at a later point in the schedule. For example, a resource is assigned to a task that is scheduled to occur on a day that the resource is also scheduled to attend a seminar. Instead of delaying the entire task until after the seminar, the task can be split so that it starts before the seminar date, stops the day of the seminar, and then resumes the day after the seminar.

For a demonstration of how to split a task, refer to page xxviii in the Installing and Using the Practice Files section.

If it is known that a task will be interrupted, the task can be split when it is created. If an interruption occurs after the task has started, it can be split where the work is stopped and the remainder of the task can be rescheduled. A task can be split many times to create gaps in work of any size. When a task is split, the Gantt Chart displays a gap in the Gantt bar for the task. The width of the gap represents the length of the interruption in work.

For tasks that are partially complete, Project automatically splits the task between the completed work and the remaining work. The split is not visible on the Gantt Chart because there is no gap between the actual work and remaining work. If the remaining work is rescheduled, a gap will then be visible to indicate the length of time between the completed portion and the start of the uncompleted portion.

To move all parts of a split task relative to each other, hold down SHIFT while dragging a split portion.

To reschedule a task, use the mouse in Gantt Chart view, the Reschedule Work button on the Tracking toolbar, or the Update Project dialog box. A split can be removed by dragging the split portion of a Gantt bar back to the previous portion, which closes the gap.

NOTE If the resources assigned to the task are at different levels of completion, the task split might not occur at the point on the task bar indicated by the progress line.

Split a task

In this exercise, you split a task on which work will be interrupted and reschedule it to resume a day later.

Gantt Chart

Split Task

1   On the View Bar, click the Gantt Chart icon.

2   Press F5, type **17**, and click OK.

3   On the Standard toolbar, click the Split Task button.

   A ScreenTip is displayed as the action is performed.

4   Position the mouse pointer on the Gantt bar for task 17, Install Electrical.

   The pointer changes to a right-pointing arrow.

5 Position the mouse pointer on the Gantt bar until the start date of October 6, 1998, is displayed on the ScreenTip. Your screen should look similar to the following illustration.

Pointer position indicated in Screentip

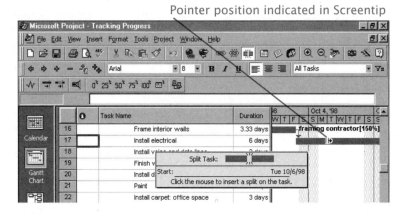

When work is interrupted on a task, create a task note to explain why the work was interrupted.

6 Hold down the left mouse button, and drag the split Gantt bar to the right until the finish date of October 14, 1998, is displayed on the ScreenTip.

The task is split into two sections.

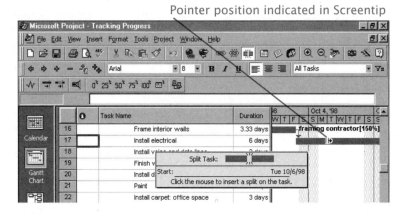

7 Save the file.

⚠ **WARNING** Rescheduling remaining work might remove or reset any task constraint applied to a task. If a constraint exists on a task that needs to be rescheduled, the remaining work should be rescheduled manually to preserve the constraint.

Updating the Remainder of the Project

Tasks that did not occur as scheduled should be updated before updating the remaining schedule. Tasks that occur as scheduled can be updated at the same time based on their scheduled data. Multiple tasks can be updated using the Update Project dialog box or the Update As Scheduled button on the Standard toolbar.

The Update Project dialog box can be set to update tasks from 0% to 100% complete or as either 0% or 100% complete based on an entered date or the current date. When updating using the 0% or 100% complete option, only tasks that are 100% complete are updated. All other tasks remain at 0% whether they have started or not. Tasks can be updated for the entire project or selected tasks.

By default, the current date is the system date.

Using the Update As Scheduled button on the Tracking toolbar, tasks are automatically updated from 0% to 100% complete. The update is based on the current date as set in the Project Information dialog box. If the actual project information that has been entered is based on a date other than the current date, change the current date prior to using the Update As Scheduled button.

Update the project as scheduled

In this exercise, you update the remaining project tasks as scheduled up to a specific date.

1 On the Tools menu, point to Tracking, and then click Update Project.

   The Update Project dialog box appears.

2 Be sure that the Update Work As Complete Through option is selected.

3 Click the down arrow, and then select October 8, 1998.

   The schedule will be updated through Thursday, 10/8/98.

4 Be sure that the Set 0% - 100% Complete option is selected.

5 Be sure that the Entire Project option is selected, and click OK.

   All tasks that are scheduled to start on or before 10/8/98, are updated as scheduled.

6 Save the file.

Comparing the Baseline to Actual Data

The project baseline provides the basis for comparing costs, work, and dates for all tasks and resources. By comparing the project progress to the baseline, the project can be monitored to ensure tasks are on schedule, resources are completing their work, and costs are not exceeding the budget.

Filters are discussed further in Lesson 12, "Applying Filters and Sorting Data."

Project baselines and actual data can be viewed graphically in charts or numerically in tables. The following table describes the tools in Project to analyze and compare baseline, actual, and scheduled data. Additional filters for data comparison are also available.

Tool	Type	Description
Tracking Gantt	Chart	Displays the actual and baseline information for tasks in a graphical format.
Variance	Table	Displays the difference between the actual information and the baseline information.
Work	Table	Displays the actual and baseline work hours and shows the variances.
Cost	Table	Displays the actual and baseline costs and shows the variances.
Cost Overbudget	Task Filter	Displays all tasks with a cost greater than the baseline cost.
Slipping Tasks	Task Filter	Displays all tasks that are behind schedule.
Work Overbudget	Resource Filter	Displays all resources with scheduled work greater than the baseline work.

Display project statistics

In this exercise, you view the Project Statistics dialog box.

1 On the Project menu, click Project Information.

The Project Information dialog box appears.

2 Click Statistics.

The Project Statistics window opens. View the project statistics.

3 Click Close.

View the Tracking Gantt Chart

In this exercise, you apply the Tracking Gantt Chart to graphically display project data.

Tracking Gantt

1   On the View Bar, click the down arrow until the Tracking Gantt icon is displayed, and then click the Tracking Gantt icon.

2   Press F5, type **15**, and press ENTER.

The task that was split, task 16, Frame interior walls, is displayed.

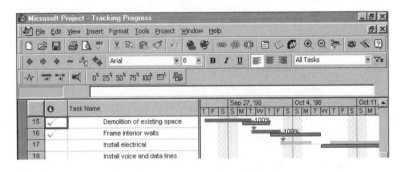

3   Scroll within the Gantt Chart to view the remaining schedule.

Patterned Gantt bars represent the updated schedule for tasks that have not started or are in progress.

Viewing project data in tables

In this exercise, you apply several tables displaying baseline and actual data.

1   On the View Bar, click the down arrow until the More Views icon is displayed, and then click More Views.

2   In the Views box, click Task Sheet, and then click Apply.

The Task Sheet view displays the Entry table.

3   On the View menu, point to Table, and then click Cost.

The Cost table is displayed. All task cost information, including variances, is displayed.

4   Scroll within the table to view the cost information for each task.

The Select All button is located at the intersection of the row and column headings.

5   Right-click the Select All button, and then click Variance.

The Variance table displays start date and finish date information.

6   Save and close the file.

Analyzing Earned Values

Earned values are a measure of the cost of the work performed up to a given date on a project. Earned values are calculated using the baseline costs and the actual work to show whether the actual costs incurred are over- or underbudget. Earned values indicate how much of the budget, or baseline cost, should have been spent based on the work completed. Earned values can also be used to forecast whether a task will finish under- or overbudget.

In Project, the Earned Value table displays time-scaled earned value calculations. These calculations are based on work and costs through and including a status date. The status date is set in the Project Information dialog box. If a status date is not set, the current date is used.

Earned values can be viewed graphically by exporting the values from Project to a Microsoft Excel workbook. In Excel, charts and PivotTable dynamic views can be created to further analyze the data.

Export Earned Values Data to Excel

1   On the File menu, click Save As.

    The Save As dialog box appears.

2   Click the Save As Type down arrow, and select Microsoft Excel Workbook.

3   Type a name for the new file, select the folder location to save the file, and then click Save.

    The Export Format dialog box appears.

4   In the Import/export map to use for exporting, click Earned Value Information.

    Note the other maps that are available. You can also create custom maps.

5   Click Save.

    The earned values data is saved in the Excel workbook format for use in Excel.

One Step Further: Viewing Progress Lines

A *progress line* is a visual representation of a project's progress. For a given date, Project draws a line that connects the progress tasks, creating a line graph. Progress lines can be drawn on the Gantt Chart view and Tracking Gantt view. The progress line creates peaks. Peaks point to the left for work that is behind schedule and point to the right for work that is ahead of schedule. The length of

186

a peak from the vertical portion of the progress line indicates how far behind or ahead of the schedule the task is at that date.

Multiple progress lines can be displayed at different dates to gauge how progress varies over phases within a project. Progress lines can be automatically displayed for the current date, at recurring intervals, and on specific dates. Formatting can also be applied to progress lines to change the line type, color, and style. Progress lines can be displayed in relation to the actual dates or baseline dates for the project.

Progress lines can be created in two ways. On the Tracking toolbar, the Add Progress Line button is used to set progress lines using default settings. The Progress Lines dialog box provides additional settings for creating progress lines.

Apply progress lines

In this exercise, you apply a progress line to the schedule to get a quick view of which tasks are behind schedule and which tasks are ahead of schedule.

Tracking Gantt icon

You can also point to Tracking on the Tools menu, and then click Progress Lines. Select the appropriate progress line options, and click OK.

1   From the Project SBS Practice folder, open the Lines file.

2   Save the file as Progress Lines in the Project SBS Practice folder.

3   On the View Bar, click the down arrow until the Tracking Gantt icon is displayed, and then click the Tracking Gantt icon.

4   Press F5, type **29**, and click OK.

5   On the Tracking toolbar, click the Add Progress Line button.

    The mouse pointer changes to a jagged line with left and right pointing arrows.

6   Position the mouse pointer on the Gantt Chart until the ScreenTip displays a progress date of November 25, 1998, and then click the left mouse button.

    A progress line is displayed on the Gantt Chart.

Remove a progress line

In this exercise, you remove the progress line placed on the date November 25, 1998.

1   Double-click the progress line on the Gantt Chart.

    The Progress Lines dialog box appears. The Dates and Intervals tab is selected.

2   Click Delete.

    The Progress Lines box is cleared.

3   Click OK.

    The progress line is removed from the Gantt Chart.

187

4 Save the file.

Finish the lesson

1 Right-click a toolbar, and then click Tracking.

The Tracking toolbar closes.

2 To continue to the next lesson, on the File menu, click Save.

3 On the File menu, click Close.

4 If you are finished using Project for now, on the File menu, click Exit.

Lesson Summary

To	Do this	Button
Enter actual task progress	Select the task to be updated. On the Tools menu, point to Tracking, and then click Update Task. Enter the appropriate actual data. *or* On the View Bar, click the down arrow until the More Views icon is displayed, and then click the More Views icon. In the Views box, click Task Sheet, and then click Apply. On the View menu, point to Table, and then click Tracking. On the View menu, point to Toobars, and then click Tracking. Select a task, and then use the percentage buttons to update the percentage complete.	
Split a task	On the Standard toolbar, click the Split Task button. Position the mouse pointer on the appropriate Gantt bar until the start date is displayed on the ScreenTip. Drag the split Gantt bar to the right until the appropriate finish date is displayed on the ScreenTip.	

To	Do this	Button
Update the remainder of the project	On the Tools menu, point to Tracking, and then click Update Project. Be sure that the Update Scheduled Work As Completed Through option is selected. Click the down arrow, and then select the appropriate date. Be sure that the Set 0% - 100% Complete option is selected. Be sure that the Entire Project option is selected. Click OK.	
View project statistics	On the Project menu, click Project Information. Click Statistics.	
View the Tracking Gantt chart	On the View Bar, click the Tracking Gantt icon.	
View table data	On the View Bar, click the down arrow until the More Views icon is displayed, and then click the More Views icon. In the Views box, click Task Sheet, and then click Apply. On the View menu, point to Table, and then click a table.	

For online information about	On the Help menu, click Contents And Index, click the Index tab, and then type
Tracking task progress	**track progress** *or* **actuals**
Splitting a task	**split a task**
Comparing baseline and actual data	**track progress** *or* **compare actual task information**

12

Applying Filters and Sorting Data

Estimated time
30 min.

In this lesson you will learn how to:

- Use AutoFilter.
- Apply interactive filters.
- Create custom filters.
- Sort tasks and resources.

During a project, specific information must be viewed within a schedule to evaluate areas of the plan and to monitor progress on the project. Changing to different views and scrolling through all the information for tasks and resources can be overwhelming. But, you can use filtering and sorting to extract information quickly.

In Microsoft Project 98, filtering and sorting is used to display specific information within a project schedule. Project includes many predefined filters to display information, such as tasks in progress, work overbudget, and tasks that are slipping. Custom filters can be created to meet a project's specific requirements. Sorting can also be performed on one or more levels to organize project information.

In this lesson, the corporate office relocation project is progressing. For the upcoming team meeting, you've been asked to provide specific information regarding costs, dates, and tracking. You use filters and sorting to display the requested information.

Start the lesson

1   Start Microsoft Project.
2   From the Project SBS Practice folder, open the Filter file.
3   Save the file as Filtering and Sorting in the Project SBS Practice folder.

Filtering the Project Tasks and Resources

Filters can be used to focus on specific tasks or resources in a project. A filter displays only those tasks or resources that meet the filter *criteria*. All other tasks or resources are temporarily hidden on the screen. Project includes 30 predefined task filters and 21 predefined resource filters. Applying a filter does not change any project data; only the display is affected. Filters can make it easier to manage large project schedules by displaying only those tasks or resources being analyzed or changed at that time.

Applying AutoFilters

Project has a filtering feature called AutoFilter. AutoFilter provides a quick way to find information in a field. When AutoFilter is turned on, arrows appear on each column heading to the right of the column name. These arrows are used to apply a filter to data in the column fields. When an AutoFilter is applied to a column, the arrow and column title turn blue. AutoFilters can be applied to multiple columns in a view.

There are two common filters in AutoFilter: All and Custom. The All filter is used to remove any filter criteria. The Custom filter is used to filter a column by more than one criterion or to apply operators. A predefined filter can be further defined using AutoFilter. AutoFilters cannot be applied to the PERT Chart, Task PERT, or any form view.

TIP   An AutoFilter can be saved as a regular filter. Start by applying the desired AutoFilter to the appropriate columns of information. Click the Column down arrow again, click Custom, and then click Save.

Use AutoFilters

In this exercise, you change to Task Sheet view, apply the AutoFilter feature, and then use AutoFilter to filter the task list.

More Views icon

1   On the View Bar, click the down arrow until the More Views icon is displayed, and then click More Views.
2   In the Views box, select Task Sheet, and then click Apply.
3   On the View menu, point to Table, and then click Cost.

AutoFilter

You can also point to Filtered For on the Project menu, and then click AutoFilter.

Each subtask that meets the criteria is displayed with its summary task and main summary task.

4   On the Formatting toolbar, click the AutoFilter button.

Down arrows appear on each column heading.

Task Name	Fixed Cost	Fixed Cost Accru	Total Cost	Baseline	Variance
1 ⊟ Corporate Relocation	$0.00	Prorated	$51,366.37	$52,403.61	($1,037.24
2 ⊟ Planning	$0.00	Prorated	$28,570.37	$29,799.61	($1,229.24
3 Write proposal	$0.00	Prorated	$586.15	$819.23	($233.08
4 Hire architect	$0.00	Prorated	$923.07	$923.07	$0.0(
5 Locate new site	$0.00	Prorated	$5,465.38	$5,465.38	$0.0(

5   Click the Fixed Cost down arrow, and then click >$0.00.

Task 15, Demolition of existing space, is displayed as the only task with a fixed cost.

6   Click the Fixed Cost down arrow, and then click All.

7   On the View menu, point to Table, and then click Tracking.

AutoFilter remains on even when tables are changed.

8   Click the % Complete down arrow, and then click Within 26% and 50%.

The subtasks that are between 26% and 50% complete are displayed.

When AutoFilter is removed, all tasks are displayed by default.

9   On the Formatting toolbar, click the AutoFilter button.

The AutoFilter button functions as a toggle for on and off. All tasks are displayed.

Specifying Filter Criteria

Filters can be specific or interactive. Interactive filters display a question dialog box during the filtering process and use the information provided to complete the filter criteria. Creating an interactive filter is preferable to duplicating an existing filter. For example, you often filter for tasks assigned to resources.
Instead of having a filter to search for each resource name, a single filter can be used to search for any resource.

Use an interactive filter

In this exercise, you use an interactive filter to display tasks within a date range.

1   On the Project menu, point to Filtered For, and then click Date Range.

The first Date Range dialog box appears.

You can also
press ENTER.

2   Type **11/6/98**, and click OK.

The second Date Range dialog box appears.

3   Type **11/24/98**, and click OK.

The tasks that start or finish between November 6th and November 24th are displayed.

4   On the Formatting toolbar, click the Filter down arrow, and then click All Tasks.

All tasks are displayed.

> **NOTE**   A predefined or custom filter will not filter another predefined or custom filter. When a predefined or custom filter is applied, all tasks are considered.

Filtering Tasks for a Specific Resource

Resource filters are used to either display tasks assigned to a resource or to change resource information. For example, the code for a group of resources has changed. A filter can be applied that displays only those tasks that have the current code. The new code can then be entered without scrolling through the entire resource list.

Filter resources

In this exercise, you filter the resource list for resources in a specific group and then change the group name for the resources.

Resource Sheet

1   On the View Bar, click the down arrow until the Resource Sheet icon is displayed, and then click the Resource Sheet icon.

The Resource Sheet is displayed.

2 On the Formatting toolbar, click the Filter down arrow, and then click Group.

The Group dialog box appears.

3 Type **management**, and click OK.

The five resources with "management" in the Group field are displayed.

4 Click the Resource Name column heading.

5 On the Standard toolbar, click the Resource Information button.

The Multiple Resource Information dialog box appears. The General tab is selected.

6 In the Group box, type **executive**, and click OK.

The text in the Group field for each resource is changed from management to executive.

The filter list automatically displays resource filters in Resource view and task filters in task views.

Resource Information button

			Resource Name	Initials	Group	Max. Units	Std. Rate	Ovt. Rate	C
	5		chief financial officer	cfo	executive	100%	$80,000.00/yr	$0.00/hr	
	15		office manager	om	executive	100%	$45,000.00/yr	$0.00/hr	
	16		operations manager	opsm	executive	100%	$52,000.00/yr	$0.00/hr	
	18		president	pres	executive	100%	$90,000.00/yr	$0.00/hr	
	21		vice president	vp	executive	100%	$75,000.00/yr	$0.00/hr	

7 On the Formatting toolbar, click the Filter down arrow, and then click All Resources.

All resources are displayed.

8 Save the file.

Creating a Custom Filter

If a predefined filter does not meet specific criteria, a custom filter can be created. A custom filter can be created from scratch, an existing filter can be edited, or a new filter can be created from an existing filter. The fastest way to create a filter is to make a copy of a similar filter, and then edit the filter.

The Filter Definition dialog box is used to create a custom filter, which includes naming the filter, selecting the settings, and defining the criteria. The Entry bar is used to fill in required information about the field, test, and value for each criteria line. Using the Entry bar instead of typing the information yourself eliminates possible typing errors and misidentification of field names.

A filter can have a single criterion or multiple criteria. When multiple criteria are used in a filter, they are separated by *operators*, such as the *And* operator and the *Or* operator. Operators are used to specify the relationship between two or more criteria. For example, the focus needs to be on tasks that begin after a specific date using a specific resource. A custom filter can be created using the And operator to display only those tasks that start after a specific date and are performed by a specific resource.

The And operator specifies that both criteria must be met to return a result. The Or operator specifies that either the first or second criterion or both criteria can be met to return a result.

NOTE Custom interactive filters can be created using specific syntax. To create an interactive filter criteria, type a message enclosed in quotation marks followed by a question mark in the Values field. For example, type "Enter a resource name:"? To create an interactive filter requesting a range of information, use Is Within or Is Not Within in the Test field. Then, in the Values field, separate the syntax for each portion of the criteria with a comma.

Create a new filter

In this exercise, you create a new filter for tasks that start after a specific date.

Gantt Chart icon

1   On the View Bar, click the Gantt Chart icon.

2   On the Project menu, point to Filtered For, and then click More Filters.

    The More Filters dialog box appears.

3   Click New.

    The Filter Definition dialog box appears.

4   In the Name box, be sure that the text is selected, and then type **Start on or after 11/15**

TIP To make custom filters easy to distinguish from predefined filters, you can type the new filter name in all caps or initial caps.

For a demonstration of how to enter filter criteria, refer to p.xxviii in the Installing and Using the Practice Files section.

Enter filter criteria

In this exercise, you enter the criteria that creates the filter.

1   Click in the Field Name column in the first row, and then click the down arrow.

2   Scroll in the list, and then click Start.

3 Click in the Test column, click the down arrow, and then click Is Greater Than Or Equal To.

The test is used to determine if the value is met for the named field.

4 Click in the Value(s) column, click in the Entry bar, type **11/15/98**, and press ENTER.

Filter Definition in 'Filtering and Sorting'			? X
Name: START ON OR AFTER 11/15		☐ Show in menu	
Filter			
Cut Row	Copy Row	Paste Row	Insert Row	Delete Row
11/15/98			
And/Or	Field Name	Test	Value(s)
	Start	is greater than or equal to	11/15/98
☐ Show related summary rows		OK	Cancel

5 Click OK.

The filter name can be added to the Filter submenu by selecting the Show In Menu check box.

Go To Selected Task

The new filter name is displayed in the Views box of the More Views dialog box.

6 Be sure that the Start On Or After 11/15 filter is displayed, and then click Apply.

7 On the Standard toolbar, click the Go To Selected Task button.

The tasks that start on or after 11/15/98 are displayed.

8 Save the file.

TIP The * and ? characters can be used as wildcards for the value of a text field name.

Create a new filter from a copy of an existing filter

In this exercise, you make a copy of an existing filter to be edited to create a new filter.

1 On the Project menu, point to Filtered For, and then click More Filters.

2 Be sure that the Start On Or After 11/15 filter is selected, and then click Copy.

A copy of the Start On Or After 11/15 filter is displayed in the Filter Definition dialog box.

197

3   In the Name box, type **Computer Tech 1 on or after 11/15**

Combine filter criteria

In this exercise, you add an operator and a second criterion to a copy of an existing filter.

1   Click in the And/Or column in the second row, click the down arrow, and then click And.

Both criteria need to be met to return the result.

2   Click in the Field Name column, click the down arrow, and then click Resource Names.

3   Click in the Test column, click the down arrow, and then click Contains.

Contains is used so that even if other resources are assigned to a task, the result will be returned.

4   Click in the Values column, click the Entry bar, type **computer tech 1**, and press ENTER.

5   Click OK.

6   In the Filters box, be sure that the Computer Tech 1 On Or After 11/15 filter is selected, and then click Apply.

7   On the Formatting toolbar, click the Filter down arrow, and then click All Tasks.

Grouping Criteria in a Filter

How a filter operates is determined by the listing or grouping of criteria and the operators used. If three or more criteria are entered within one group of expressions, the And operator statements are evaluated before the Or operator statements. Across multiple groups, the And operator statements are evaluated in the order they appear. To group criteria so that they are evaluated together, leave a blank line between the sets of criteria, and then select the operator between the groups in the blank row.

Sorting Tasks and Resources

By default, tasks and resources are displayed in ascending order by ID number, from lowest to highest. Sorting creates an alternate display order of tasks or resources based on a specified field. When information in a sorted field is duplicated, sorting can be performed on multiple keys. Keys are the fields by which information is sorted. For example, you need to sort tasks based on their total scheduled cost. If there are some tasks that have the same cost, the Cost field could be the first key and the Duration field could be the second key. Then, when two or more tasks have the same total cost, they are sorted by their duration.

In addition to selecting multiple keys to sort tasks or resources, sorting can include settings, such as ascending or descending order. You can also sort with or without the outline structure. By default, sorting is performed within the outline structure. All subtasks of summary tasks are sorted first, the summary tasks are sorted second, and the sort progresses up the outline structure. If a sort is performed without the outline structure, the subtasks and summary tasks are sorted independent of one another. By default, ID numbers remain with the associated task or resource. If desired, ID numbers can be restructured based on a sort. For example, you want the resource list to be in alphabetical order. After a descending order sort is performed on the Resource Name field, you can permanently renumber the resources so that they are in alphabetical order. However, if tasks are permanently renumbered in sorting, the dependencies will be destroyed.

 NOTE The Outlining buttons on the Formatting toolbar will not be available if the task list is sorted without the outline structure. Because the outline is not in the original structure, the hierarchy cannot be changed.

Sort the task list

In this exercise, you change to Task Sheet view and then sort the task list by actual duration.

More Views icon

1   On the View Bar, click the down arrow until the More Views icon is displayed, and then click the More Views icon.

2   In the Views box, select Task Sheet, and then click Apply.

3   On the Project menu, point to Sort, and then click Sort By.

The Sort By dialog box appears.

4   Click the Sort By down arrow, and then click Actual Duration.

5   Click the Descending option.

6   Click Sort.

The tasks are sorted in descending order by duration, within the outline structure.

> **NOTE**   Sorting can be performed in any view. However, when sorting tasks in a chart view, the dependency link lines are no longer useful for indicating links between predecessors and successors.

Sort by multiple keys

In this exercise, you sort the task list by actual duration and then by actual cost.

1   On the Project menu, point to Sort, and then click Sort By.

2   In the Sort By area, be sure that the Actual Duration key is selected.

3   Click the first Then By down arrow, and then click Actual Cost.

4   Click the Descending option, and then click Sort.

The tasks are sorted first by actual duration, and then those tasks with the same actual duration are sorted by actual costs.

5   On the Project menu, point to Sort, and then click By ID.

6   Save the file.

One Step Further: Applying a Highlight Filter

By default, when tasks and resources are filtered, the tasks or resources that do not meet the filter criteria are hidden. A highlight filter can be applied so that all tasks and resources are displayed but the tasks and resources that meet the criteria are highlighted. Typically, a highlight filter displays the criteria matches as blue text.

Apply a highlight filter

In this exercise, you apply a highlight to all milestone tasks.

1 On the Project menu, point to Filtered For, and then click More Filters.

2 In the Filters box, click Milestones.

3 Click Highlight.

All tasks are displayed. The milestone tasks are highlighted in blue. Your screen should look similar to the following illustration.

4 Scroll to view other highlighted milestones.

5 On the Formatting toolbar, click the Filter down arrow, and then click All Tasks.

6 Save the file.

Finish the lesson

1 To continue to the next lesson, on the File menu, click Close.

2 If you are finished using Project for now, on the File menu, click Exit.

Lesson Summary

To	Do this	Button
Use AutoFilter	On the Formatting toolbar, click the AutoFilter button. Click a column heading down arrow, and then select a filter value.	
Use a predefined filter	On the Project menu, point to Filter For, and then click More Filters. In the Filters box, click a filter, and then click Apply. If the filter requires a value, type the value, and click OK. *or* On the Formatting toolbar, click the Filter down arrow, and then select a filter. If the filter requires a value, type the value, and click OK.	
Return the display after a filter is applied	On the Formatting toolbar, click the AutoFilter button. *or* On the Formatting toolbar, click the Filter down arrow, and then click All Tasks or All Resources.	
Create a custom filter	On the Project menu, point to Filter For, and then click More Filters. Click New, Edit, or Copy. In the Name box, type the filter name. Click in field, click the down arrow, and then select the appropriate field, test, or value. In the Values field, you can also click in the Entry bar, and then type a value.	
Sort on a single key	On the Project menu, point to Sort, and then click Sort By. Click the Sort By down arrow, and then click the field name to be sorted. Click the Ascending or Descending option. Click Sort.	

To	Do this
Sort on multiple keys	On the Project menu, point to Sort, and then click Sort By. Click the Sort By down arrow, and then click the field name to be sorted. Click the Ascending or Descending option. Click the first Then By down arrow, and then click the field name to be sorted. Click the Ascending or Descending option. Click the second Then By down arrow, and then make the appropriate selections. Click Sort.

For online information about	On the Help menu, click Contents And Index, click the Index tab, and then type
Using AutoFilter	**AutoFilter**
Applying filters	**filters**
Creating custom filters	**filters** *or* **customize filters**
Sorting	**sort tasks** *or* **sort resources**

Lesson

13

Customizing Tables, Views, and Reports

Estimated time

35 min.

In this lesson you will learn how to:

- Create a custom table.
- Create a custom single or combination view.
- Create a custom report.

While working on projects, you determine the information requirements for the projects. Most requirements should be provided by the scheduling software. But, some of these requirements might not be provided. For example, you might want certain columns of schedule information in one table, or you might want to change the sort order for a report. For these special requirements, you can create your own tables, views, and reports and customize those items to meet your project needs.

Microsoft Project 98 has many predefined items that are designed to meet your scheduling information needs. But, if a project requires unique information or information arranged in different ways, Project provides an effective way to create custom items. The definition dialog boxes for tables and views are designed to make the process of creating custom items as easy as possible. With more than 200 fields of information, Project can meet virtually any information requirements. Reports can also be customized to print information formatted in a more formal manner. In Project, these custom items can also be shared between files so that items do not have to be re-created for each project.

205

In this lesson, you've been working with the information in the corporate office relocation project and have determined that creating some custom items will increase the efficiency in reporting information to management. You create a custom table, views, and a report to meet those needs.

Start the lesson

1 Start Microsoft Project.

2 From the Project SBS Practice folder, open the Custom file.

3 Save the file as Customizing Items in the Project SBS Practice folder.

Creating a Custom Table

Custom filters are discussed further in Lesson 12, "Applying Filters and Sorting Data."

Tables are columns and rows of schedule information. Project includes 19 predefined task tables and eight predefined resource tables. If none of the predefined tables provides the needed information, a custom table can be created to display the information required. Custom tables can be combined with predefined or custom filters to further define information requirements.

Custom tables can be created from scratch, an existing table can be edited, or a new table can be based on an existing table. Custom tables are created by defining the field name, alignment, column width, and column title for each required field in the table.

In the following exercises, you create a custom table to display the information requested by management for its biweekly review of the project. You start with a copy of the Summary table, which is similar to what management wants. You then delete unnecessary information, and add necessary information.

Copy an existing table

In this exercise, you copy the Summary table as a starting point for a new table.

An ampersand (&) can be added to the beginning of a table name to designate the first letter as a menu access key. The Show In Menu check box must be selected to add the table to the Table submenu.

1 On the View menu, point to Table, and then click More Tables.

2 In the Tables box, select Summary, and then click Copy.

A copy of the Summary table is displayed in the Table Definition dialog box.

3 In the Name box, type **Management Summary**

Delete columns

In this exercise, you delete unnecessary columns of information from the table definition.

1 In the Field Name column, click Duration.

2 Click Delete Row.

The Duration column information is deleted from the table definition.

3 In the Field Name column, click Finish, and then click Delete Row.

4 In the Field Name column, click Work, and then click Delete Row.

Add new columns

In this exercise, you add new columns of information to the table definition.

1 In the Field Name column, click Start.

2 Click Insert Row.

You can press TAB or ENTER, or click in another field, to enter the changes to a field.

3 Click the down arrow, select Remaining Duration, and then press TAB.

The new column, Remaining Duration, is entered. Criteria for Align Data, Width, and Align Title are added by default.

4 Click in the Title field, type **Rem. Dur.**, and press ENTER.

5 Click in the blank Field Name field below Cost, click the down arrow, click Resource Group, and then press TAB.

6 Click in the Align Data column, click the down arrow, and then click Left.

You can also use the up and down arrow spin controls to adjust the column width.

7 Click in the Width column, type **15**, and then press TAB.

Table Definition in 'Customizing Items'

Name: Management Summary   ☐ Show in menu

Table

[Cut Row] [Copy Row] [Paste Row]   [Insert Row] [Delete Row]

Field Name	Align Data	Width	Title	Align Title
ID	Center	5		Center
Name	Left	24	Task Name	Left
Remaining Duration	Right	10	Rem. Dur.	Center
Start	Right	12		Center
% Complete	Right	9	% Comp.	Center
Cost	Right	11		Center
Resource Group	Left	15		Center

Date format: [Default]   Row height: [1]

☑ Lock first column   [OK] [Cancel]

8 Click OK.

The More Tables dialog box appears.

Apply the custom table

In this exercise, you display the Management Summary table.

1 In the Tables box, be sure that the Management Summary table is selected, and then click Apply.

		Task Name	Rem. Dur.	Start	% Comp.	Cost	Resource Group
	1	⊟ **Corporate Relocation**	**10.92 days**	**8/10/98**	**87%**	**$51,366.37**	
	2	⊟ **Planning**	**0 days**	**8/10/98**	**100%**	**$28,570.37**	
	3	Write proposal	0 days	8/10/98	100%	$586.15	executive
	4	Hire architect	0 days	8/12/98	100%	$923.07	executive
	5	Locate new site	0 wks	8/14/98	100%	$5,465.38	contractor,executi
	6	Present proposal	0 days	8/21/98	100%	$2,709.23	executive,equipme
	7	Corporate approv	0 days	8/24/98	100%	$0.00	
	8	Negotiate new lex	0 days	8/25/98	100%	$2,988.46	executive,contrac
	9	Finalize drawings	0 wks	8/26/98	100%	$5,200.00	contractor

2 Save the file.

TIP Quick edits of existing tables can be made while the table is displayed. Double-click the column heading of the column to be edited. In the Column Definition dialog box, the field name, title, alignment, and column width can be changed. The change is saved when the file is saved.

Defining Custom Views

A view organizes schedule information for display and entry. There are 26 predefined views in Project. If none of the predefined views meet the needs of the project, custom views can be created. There are two types of views in Project: single views and combination views. A single view combines a screen, table, and filter to create a view. A combination view combines two single views into a split-pane window, with one view in the top pane and the other view in the bottom pane. Custom views can include predefined and custom items.

In the following exercises, you create two new views to be used by management to view summary information. You start with a single view displaying the Management Summary table you created and use the Incomplete filter so that only those tasks that aren't completed are displayed. You then create a combination view displaying the Tracking Gantt chart and the new single view for the task selected in the Tracking Gantt chart.

> **IMPORTANT** If a view will include a custom filter or table, the custom items must be created before they can be included in the custom view. If a combination view will include a custom single view, the custom single view must be created first.

Create a single view

In this exercise, you create a new single view.

1 On the View menu, click More Views.

2 Click New.

The Define New View dialog box appears.

3 Be sure that the Single View option is selected, and click OK.

The View Definition dialog box appears.

4 In the Name box, type **Management Task Sheet**

5 Click the Screen down arrow, and then click Task Sheet.

The Task Sheet screen view will be applied to the new view.

6 Click the Table down arrow, and then click Management Summary.

7 Click the Filter down arrow, and then click Incomplete Tasks.

Only those tasks that aren't completed will be displayed in the view.

8 Click OK.

9 In the Views box, be sure that the Management Task Sheet is selected and then click Apply.

You can select the Highlight Filter check box to apply the selected filter as a highlight filter. Highlight filters are discussed further in Lesson 12, "Applying Filters and Sorting Data."

10 Save the file.

TIP To make custom filters easy to distinguish from predefined filters, type the new filter name in all caps or initial caps.

Create a combination view

In this exercise, you create a custom view using the new single view and the Tracking Gantt view.

1 On the View menu, click More Views, and then click New.

2 Click the Combination View option, and click OK.

3 In the Name box, type **Management Review**

4 Click the Top down arrow, and then click Tracking Gantt.

The Tracking Gantt view will be displayed in the top pane.

5 Click the Bottom down arrow, and then click Management Task Sheet.

The Management Task Sheet will be displayed in the bottom pane.

6 Click OK.

7 In the Views box, be sure that the Management Review is selected, and then click Apply.

8 Save the file.

Creating a Custom Report

Reports in Project are used to print project information in different formats or to provide information that isn't displayed in a predefined table or view. For example, the Project Statistics dialog box cannot be printed. Instead, the

Summary report can be printed with the same information. Project provides 25 predefined reports in five report groups. Reports can be created from scratch, an existing report can be edited, or a new report can be based on a report filter within certain parameters. New reports can be created from four report templates: task, resource, monthly calendar, and crosstab.

In the following exercises, you preview a cash flow report to see if it meets the project needs. You then customize a new copy of the report so that it displays cash flow values on a monthly basis.

Preview a predefined report

In this exercise, you preview a predefined report.

1 On the View menu, click Reports.

   The Reports dialog box appears.

2 Double-click the Costs box.

   The Cost Reports dialog box appears.

3 Double-click the Cash Flow box.

   The Cash Flow report is displayed in Print Preview.

4 Click the report preview to zoom in.

   The Cash Flow report details task costs on a weekly basis.

For a demonstration of how to customize a report, refer to page xxviii in the Installing and Using the Practice Files section.

In a Crosstab report, the General tab defines the rows, columns, and data as well as the filter to apply.

The Details tab defines the display and format.

The Sort tab defines the sort order of the displayed information.

5 Click Close.

Customize a report

In this exercise, you customize a copy of a predefined report.

1 Double-click the Custom box.

   The Custom Reports dialog box appears.

2 In the Reports box, click Cash Flow, and then click Copy.

   The Crosstab Report dialog box appears. The Definition tab is selected.

3 In the Name box, select the text, and then type **Monthly Cash Flow**

4 Click the Column down arrow, and then click Months.

5 Click the Details tab.

6 In the Show area, clear the Summary Tasks check box.

7 Select the Show Zero Values check box.

8 Click the Sort tab.

9 Click the Sort By down arrow, and then click Cost.

10 Click the Descending option, and click OK.

   The Custom Reports dialog box appears.

Preview the custom report

In this exercise, you preview the custom report.

1 In the Reports box, be sure that Monthly Cash Flow is selected, and then click Preview.

The Monthly Cash Flow report is displayed in Print Preview.

2 Click below the title of the report.

The report is zoomed in and more detail is shown.

3 Click Close.

The Print Preview window closes.

4 Click Close, and then click Cancel.

5 Save the file.

One Step Further: Using the Organizer to Share Custom Items

All custom items created in Project are stored in the project file where they were created. The predefined items used with a project file, such as the Gantt Chart, are copied into the project file from a global template called GLOBAL.MPT. Any other views are only copied into the project file when they are used. If an item is not used, it can still be made available through the global template.

Custom items can be shared with other project files and the global template using the Organizer. The Organizer is a tabbed dialog box used to copy, delete, and rename items in a project file and in the global template. The Organizer can be used to share views, reports, tables, filters, forms, calendars, toolbars, maps, and modules. When sharing items between files, both files must be open in Project. The Organizer dialog box displays two boxes that show the availability of files. One box is displayed on the left side of the dialog box, and the other box is displayed on the right side. The file containing the items to be shared must be selected on left side, and the file the items are to be shared with on the right side. Each open file, including the GLOBAL.MPT, is displayed when clicking one of the two Available In boxes.

IMPORTANT If a network copy of Project is being used, the network administrator or appropriate individual should be contacted before copying, deleting, or renaming items in the global template.

In the following exercise, you want to use the Management Review table for an upcoming project. Instead of re-creating the table, you use the Organizer to copy the table from the file it was created into the new project file.

Create a new file

In this exercise, you create a new file and copy custom items to the file.

New

1 Be sure that the Customizing items file is open.
2 On the Standard toolbar, click the New button.

   A new file is created, and the Project Information dialog box appears.
3 Click Cancel.
4 Save the file as Share in the Project SBS Practice folder.

Copy a table

For purposes of this exercise, project information is not necessary.

In this exercise, you copy a custom table to the new file.

1 On the View menu, point to Table, and then click More Tables.
2 Click Organizer.

The Organizer dialog box can be opened from the More Views, More Tables, and More Filters dialog boxes. You can also add the Organizer button to a toolbar.

   The Organizer dialog box appears. The Tables tab is selected. The GLOBAL.MPT tables are displayed on the left side of the dialog box. The tables in the Share file are displayed on the right side of the dialog box.
3 On the left side in the Organizer dialog box, click the Tables Available In down arrow.

   A list of all open files is displayed.
4 Click Customizing Items.

   The tables in the Customizing Items file are displayed.
5 On the left side in the Customizing Items box, click Management Summary.

6 Click Copy.

The Management Summary table is displayed on the right side in the Share box.

Organizer			? X
Views	Reports	Modules	
Calendars	Toolbars	Maps	
Forms	Tables	Filters	

⦿ Task   ○ Resource

'Customizing Items':
```
Cost
Delay
Entry
Management Summary
Summary
Tracking
Usage
Variance
```

Copy >>
Close
Rename...
Delete...

'Share':
```
Entry
Management Summary
```

Tables available in:
Customizing Items

Tables available in:
Share

7 Click Close.

IMPORTANT If a custom item is copied to another file that contains other custom items, those items must also be copied. For example, a custom view includes a custom filter. If the custom filter is not copied as well, the view will not work. A message indicating what item is missing is displayed when the view is applied.

Display a shared table

In this exercise, you display the copied table in the new file.

1 Be sure that the More Tables dialog box is displayed.

2 Click Management Summary, and then click Apply.

The table is applied.

3 Drag the vertical split bar to the right to display the other column headings.

4 Save the file.

NOTE Custom toolbars and menus are automatically saved in the global template. If a project file will be used on another computer, copying custom toolbars and menus to the file makes them available on the other system.

Finish the lesson

1   To continue to the next lesson, close all open files.
2   If you are finished using Project for now, on the File menu, click Exit.

Lesson Summary

To	Do this
Create a custom table	On the View menu, point to Table, and then click More Tables. In the More Tables dialog box, click New, or select an existing table, and then click Edit or Copy. In the Name box of the Table Definition dialog box, type a new table name. Click the Field Name field, click the down arrow, and select the appropriate field name. Edit the Align Data, Width, Title, and Align Title fields as appropriate. Continue entering desired fields to create table columns. Click OK.
Create a new single view	On the View menu, click More Views. In the More Views dialog box, click New. In the Define New View dialog box, be sure that the Single View option is selected, and click OK. In the Name box of the View Definition dialog box, type a new view name. Click the Screen down arrow, and then select the appropriate screen. Click the Table down arrow, and then select the appropriate table. Click the Filter down arrow, and then click the appropriate filter. Click OK.

To	Do this
Create a new combination view	On the View menu, click More Views. In the More Views dialog box, click New. In the Define New View dialog box, click the Combination View option, and click OK. In the Name box of the View Definition dialog box, type a new view name. Click the Top down arrow, and then select the appropriate single view. Click the Bottom down arrow, and then select the appropriate single view. Click OK.
Create a custom report from a copy of an existing report	On the View menu, click Reports. Double-click the Custom box. In the Custom Reports dialog box, select an existing report, and then click Copy. In the Name box of the Report type dialog box, type a new name. Change the appropriate settings on the Definition, Details, and Sort tabs. Click OK.

For online information about	On the Help menu, click Contents And Index, click the Index tab, and then type
Creating a custom table	**tables** or **customize tables**
Creating a single view	**views** or **customize views**
Creating a combination view	**views** or **customize views** or **combination views**
Creating a custom report	**reports** or **customize reports**

Review & Practice

You will review and practice how to:

- Track the progress of tasks.
- Update the project as scheduled.
- Split a task to reschedule work.
- Create custom tables, views, and reports.

Before you move on to Part 5, which covers working with multiple projects and customizing the Project environment, you can practice the skills you learned in Part 4 by working through this Review & Practice section. You will track the actual progress of tasks, use filtering and sorting to find and display project information, and create custom tables, views, and reports.

Scenario

The shareholders meeting project has begun, and it's time to begin tracking the progress. The resources have provided you with tracking data, and you enter the information into the schedule. Management has requested specific reports be presented at the next team meeting. You create several custom items to meet those needs.

Step 1: Track the Progress of Individual Tasks

Several tasks have not progressed as scheduled. You enter the actual data for those tasks into the schedule and then update the remaining tasks as of the status date. You have also been informed that the copier has shut down during the printing of the notification letters. A repair technician cannot come out until August 8th. You reschedule the remaining duration on the task to resume the next day.

1 Open the Review4 file in the Project SBS Practice folder, and then save the file as Meeting Tracking in the Project SBS Practice folder.

2 Display the Tracking toolbar.

3 Update Task 3, Schedule conference, to reflect an actual finish date of 7/9/99.

4 Update Task 4, Book conference center, took two days to complete. Hint: Enter actual duration of two days with zero days remaining.

5 Task 5, Book keynote speaker, took two days to complete.

6 The office manager spent a total of three hours working on the draft of the notification letter on 7/22/99. Change the actual working time for task 9, Develop letter, to reflect the actual time spent on the task. (Hint: Use the Task Usage View.)

7 The remainder of the tasks progressed as scheduled through 8/2/99.

8 Split task 12, Print letter and reschedule the remaining work, to resume on 8/9/99.

9 Save the file.

For more information about	See
Entering actual task progress	Lesson 11
Updating the remainder of the project	Lesson 11
Splitting a task	Lesson 11

Step 2: Filter Tasks and Resources

While updating the progress of the shareholders meeting project, you've been asked to provide some preliminary information before the team meeting next week. There is a possibility that the intern resource might be taken from the project. You filter for the intern resource to demonstrate how necessary it is to the project. You also filter for critical tasks and then create a custom filter to find those tasks that start in August.

1 Display the Entry table in Task Sheet view.

2 Use AutoFilter to locate the tasks that have the intern resource assigned.

3   Turn AutoFilter off.

4   Use the Critical filter to locate those tasks that are still on the critical path.

5   Create a custom filter to locate all tasks that start on or after 8/1/99.

6   Apply the custom filter.

7   Display all tasks.

8   Save the file.

For more information about	See
Using AutoFilter	Lesson 12
Creating a custom filter	Lesson 12

Step 3:   *Sort Tasks and Resources*

The Accounting department has requested some cost information for the shareholders meeting project. First, you sort by cost and percentage complete so Accounting knows what tasks have the greatest costs. You also sort the resource sheet by the resource code for verification by the Accounting department.

1   In Task Sheet view, display the Cost table.

2   Sort the tasks by cost in descending order and then by percentage complete in descending order.

3   Display the Resource Sheet.

4   Sort the resources by Code in ascending order.

5   Save the file.

For more information about	See
Sorting tasks and resources	Lesson 12

Step 4:   *Create a Custom Table*

Management is requesting information on variances with dates and costs for the project. You create a custom table based on the Variance table by adding the costing variance information.

1   Display the Gantt Chart view.

2   Create a custom table named Total Variance based on a copy of the Variance table.

3   Delete the Start and Finish fields.

4   Add the Baseline Cost and Cost Variance fields. Use Base. Cost and Cost Var. as the column titles.

5 Apply the custom table.

6 Save the file.

For more information about	See
Creating a custom table	Lesson 13

Step 5: Create Custom Views

Management has requested weekly information about the project. To prepare for presenting this information, you create two new views. You create a single view using the custom table you created with a predefined filter for overbudget costs. You then create a combination view using the new single view and the Tracking Gantt view.

1 Create a single view named Overbudget.

2 Use the Task Sheet view, Total Variance table, and Cost Overbudget filter.

3 Apply the view.

4 Create a combination view called Task Overbudget.

5 Display the Tracking Gantt view in the top pane, and the Overbudget view in the bottom pane.

6 Apply the view.

7 Save the file.

For more information about	See
Creating a single view	Lesson 13
Creating a combination view	Lesson 13

Step 6: Create a Custom Report

The project team would like to have work-related information for each resource at the weekly team meeting. A predefined report is similar to what they are looking for but needs to include baseline information. You customize the predefined report to include baseline information.

1 View the Who Does What report.

2 From a copy of the Who Does What report, create a custom report named Who Does Work.

3 On the Definition tab, use the work table.

4 On the Details tab, display schedule and work assignments.

5 Preview the new report.

6   Save the file.

For more information about	See
Creating a custom report	Lesson 13

Finish the Review & Practice

1   Hide the Tracking toolbar.

2   Close the Meeting Tracking file.

3   If you are finished using Project for now, on the File menu, click Exit.

Using Advanced Project Features

Part 5

Working with Multiple Projects

In this lesson you will learn how to:

- Insert project files into other project files.
- Share resources in a resource pool.

When managing multiple projects, it can be hard to see how the projects relate to each other and how resources are allocated across them. At times, it might be helpful to bring the individual projects together to see how they relate to each other and to see if any resource overallocations exist. With a large, complex project, it can be difficult to locate information or focus on specific areas of the project. In this case, it might be helpful to break down the project into smaller components and then bring them back together when necessary to get an overall view.

In Microsoft Project 98, you can bring projects together to get the big picture. By inserting one project into another project, a global view of all the projects or components of a project can be brought together in one location. In the file containing the inserted files, you can view only as many details as you need. Resources can also be shared among project files from one common source. This source contains all the resource information, including costs and calendars. When any changes occur, the information needs be updated only in the common source. Then, all assignments can be made and allocations can be viewed without switching between files.

In this lesson, the corporate office relocation project has been broken into three phases, which will be managed by separate departments. As the manager for the project, your job is to find a way to keep up-to-date on the tasks and to use the same resources for all phases. You use inserted projects to get a global view of the corporate office relocation project and several other projects in your control. You also use a common set of resources for all departments.

Start the lesson

1   Start Microsoft Project.

2   From the Project SBS Practice folder, open the Global file.

3   Save the file as All Projects without a baseline in the Project SBS Practice folder.

4   From the Project SBS Practice folder, open the Plan file.

5   Save the file as Relocation Plan without a baseline in the Project SBS Practice folder, and then close the file.

6   From the Project SBS Practice folder, open the Remodel file.

7   Save the file as Relocation Remodel without a baseline in the Project SBS Practice folder, and then close the file.

8   From the Project SBS Practice folder, open the Move file.

9   Save the file as Relocation Move without a baseline in the Project SBS Practice folder, and then close the file.

Consolidating Projects

When multiple projects are under your supervision, a project file, called a *consolidated project*, that contains inserted project files can be created. A consolidated project provides a larger view of the projects under your control, providing as much or as little detail as required. Inserted project files are linked to their original project file by default. Any changes to the inserted project within the consolidated project are automatically made in the original file. Likewise, changes made in the original file are automatically made in the inserted file within the consolidated project. If the link is not needed, it can be removed on a file-by-file basis. For example, if a consolidated project is being created for a what-if scenario, the link can be removed so that any changes will not affect an original file.

Inserting Projects into an Existing Project

A project file can be inserted into an existing project file or into a new project file created specifically to view all projects under your supervision. When a project is inserted into another project file, the inserted file is displayed as a task within that project file. An inserted file can be linked to its original file or made read-only so that changes in the inserted file do not affect the original file. The subtasks of an inserted file can be either displayed or hidden.

Insert project files

In this exercise, you insert the relocation project phase files into the All Projects global perspective file.

1 Be sure that the All Projects file is open.

2 Select task 4, Job descriptions.

3 On the Insert menu, click Project.

The Insert Project dialog box appears.

4 In the Look In box, be sure that Project SBS Practice is displayed, click Relocation Move, and then click Insert.

The Relocation Move file has been inserted above the job descriptions task as a summary task.

You can also press ENTER.

5 On the Insert menu, click Project.

6 Click Relocation Remodel, and press ENTER.

The Relocation Remodel is inserted as a summary task above the Relocation Move summary task.

An inserted project file is always added above the selected task.

7 On the Insert menu, click Project.

8 Click Relocation Plan, and press ENTER.

The Relocation Plan is inserted as a summary task above the Relocation Remodel summary task.

The Link To Project check box is selected by default. Clear the check box if you don't want to establish a link between the original file and the inserted file.

The Indicators field for tasks 4 through 6 displays an Inserted Project indicator. Placing the mouse pointer over the indicator displays a ScreenTip with the inserted file location.

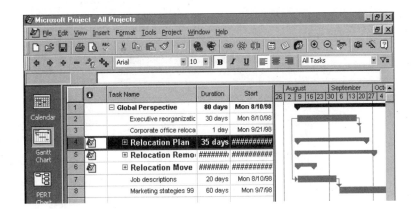

9 Save the file without a baseline.

Create a hierarchy

In this exercise, you indent inserted project files below a descriptive summary task.

Indent

1   Use the task ID numbers to select task 4 through task 6.

2   On the Formatting toolbar, click the Indent button.

The inserted project files are displayed as subtasks of the "Corporate office relocation" task.

3   Save the file without a baseline.

Viewing a Consolidated Project

When a project file is inserted into another project file, subtasks of the inserted project are hidden by default. Inserted project subtasks can be quickly displayed or hidden by using the outline symbols next to the inserted tasks.

View subtasks

In this exercise, you display the subtasks of an inserted project file.

1   Click the plus sign (+) outline symbol next to task 4, Relocation Plan.

The subtasks of the Relocation Plan summary task are displayed.

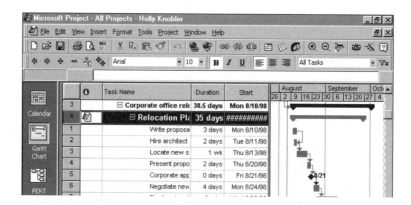

2   Click the minus sign (-) outline symbol next to task 4, Relocation Plan.

The subtasks of the Relocation Plan summary task are hidden.

3   On the Standard toolbar, click Save and then click OK to all..

4   Close the file.

Using a Resource Pool

When working with several different projects, the projects might be using some or all of the same resources. When this occurs, there can be cross-project overallocations that are not identified until the overlapping tasks are underway. To help eliminate resource conflicts across multiple projects, resources can be coordinated using a *resource pool*. A resource pool is a set of resources that is available for assignment to a project. A resource pool can be used by one project exclusively or shared by several projects. When resources are shared from a common pool, scheduling conflicts for a resource can be identified immediately. A resource sheet is a resource pool whether it is used by one project or multiple projects.

A resource pool can be created in two different ways: 1) A new project file can be created that contains only resource information and no tasks, or 2) An existing project file can be designated as the pool. In either case, other projects can be directed to use the resource pool for resource assignments. As changes are made to resource assignments in the projects sharing the pool, the pool needs to be updated. By updating the pool, the latest information is available to those sharing the resources from the pool.

When the resource pool or project files sharing the resource pool are opened, a dialog box with several open options appears. For example, when the resource pool is opened and at least one project file is sharing the pool, the Open Resource Pool dialog box appears. The options are to open the pool read-only, open the pool read-write, or open the pool and all project files sharing the pool. Opening the pool read-only allows others to work with the pool file. Opening the pool as read-write locks out others from opening the pool. Once a pool is established, it should be opened only read-write to update resource names, costs, and calendar information. Similar options are displayed in the Open Resource Pool Information dialog box when a project file sharing the pool is opened.

For a demonstration of how to share a resource pool, refer to page xxviii in the Installing and Using the Practice Files section.

Because the resource pool file does not contain tasks, you are not prompted to save the file with or without a baseline.

When any changes are made to a project file sharing a resource pool, the pool should be updated with those changes. Changes are updated by pointing to Resources on the Tools menu, and then clicking Update Resource Pool. When saving a file or closing a file, you are prompted to update the pool if you haven't already done so. When working in a project file sharing the pool, the resource information can be updated in the file from the pool by pointing to Resources on the Tools menu, and then clicking Refresh Resource Pool.

Share a resource pool

In this exercise, you create a sharing link between an independent resource pool file and a project file.

1   From the Project SBS Practice folder, open the Pool file.

2   Save the file as Resource Pool in the Project SBS Practice folder.

Resource Sheet

3 From the Project SBS Practice folder, open the Relocation Move file.

4 On the View Bar, click the down arrow until the Resource Sheet icon is displayed, and then click the Resource Sheet icon.

The Resource Sheet for the Relocation Move file is blank. No resources have been entered in this file.

5 On the Tools menu, point to Resources, and then click Share Resources.

The Share Resources dialog box appears.

6 Click the Use Resources From down arrow, and then click Resource Pool.

7 In the On Conflict With Calendar Or Resource Information area, be sure that the Pool Takes Precedence option is selected.

8 Click OK.

The resource list from the pool is displayed on the resource sheet for the Relocation Move file.

9 Save the file without a baseline.

Verify pool links

When a resource pool is being shared among multiple projects, it can be help-ful to know what project files are currently using the pool. In this exercise, you go to the resource pool and verify the link to the Relocation Plan file.

1 On the Window menu, click Resource Pool.

The Resource Pool file is displayed.

2 On the Tools menu, point to Resources, and click Share Resources.

The Share Resources dialog box appears with some changes from its previous form. The Relocation Move file is displayed in the Sharing Links box.

3   Click Cancel.

4   Save and close the Resource Pool file.

5   Save the Relocation Move file without a baseline, and then close the file.

Resolving Resource Overallocation in a Resource Pool

After a resource pool has been shared and the resource assignments are made in the individual project files, the resource pool should be checked for overallocations. Resolving overallocations with resources shared in a pool is similar to resolving overallocations when the resources are used on only a single project. When opening the resource pool or a project file sharing the pool to resolve overallocations, the Open Resource Pool And All Other Shared Files To See All Tasks In All Projects Sharing The Same Pool option should be selected. This option makes all tasks and assignments active when using the Resource Allocation view.

One Step Further: Cross-linking Projects

Dependencies, lead time, and lag time are discussed further in Lesson 5, "Establishing Task Dependencies."

When tasks are dependent upon one another across projects, they can be linked just like tasks within a single project. Tasks within a consolidated project or tasks between separate projects can be linked. Linked tasks between projects can have any of the four dependency types, as well as lead time and lag time. When a link is established between tasks in projects, a new task that represents the link to the other project task is automatically established in both project files. If any changes are made to either file, the Links Between Projects dialog box on the Tools menu can be used to accept the changes or delete the link.

Create a cross-project link

In this exercise, you establish a link between tasks in the consolidated All Projects file.

1   From the Project SBS Practice folder, open the All Projects file.

2   Click the plus sign (+) outline symbol next to task 4, Relocation Plan.

The subtasks of the Relocation Plan summary task are displayed.

3   Click the plus sign (+) outline symbol next to task 5, Relocation Remodel.

The subtasks of the Relocation Model summary task are displayed.

4   Be sure that the Gantt bars for task 8, Select subcontractors, in the Relocation Plan phase and task 1, Demolition of existing space, in the Relocation Remodel phase are visible.

231

5 Place the mouse pointer over the center of the Gantt bar for task 8, Select subcontractor.

The pointer changes to a four-headed arrow.

6 Click and hold down the mouse button and drag down and over the middle of the Gantt bar for task 1, Demolition of existing space. Release the mouse button.

A Finish-To-Start dependency is established between the tasks in the two projects.

7 On the Standard toolbar, click the Save button.

A message to save the Relocation Remodel file is displayed.

Save button

8 Click Yes To All.

Changes to the All Project file and each of the inserted project files are saved. The Planning Wizard dialog box appears.

9 Be sure that the Save Relocation Remodel Without A Baseline option is selected, and then click OK To All.

All files are saved without a baseline.

10 Close the All Projects file.

Display the cross-link tasks

In this exercise, you open the individual project files to view the cross-links.

A ScreenTip displays the link information.

1 From the Project SBS Practice folder, open the Relocation Plan file.

Task 9, Demolition of existing space, is added to the file. The task is dimmed to indicate that it is a cross-project link. Your screen should look similar to the following illustration.

Cross-
project —
link

2 From the Project SBS Practice folder, open the Relocation Remodel file.

Task 1, Select subcontractors, is added to the file.

Finish the lesson

1   To continue to the next lesson, close all open files.

2   If you are finished using Project for now, on the File menu, click Exit.

Lesson Summary

To	Do this
Insert project files	On the Insert menu, click Project. In the Insert Project dialog box, select the appropriate file, and then click Insert.
Share a resource pool	Open the resource pool file. Open the project file that will share the pool. Be sure that the sharing file is displayed. On the Tools menu, point to Resources, and then click Sharing Resources. Click the Sharing Resources From down arrow, and then click the resource pool file name. Click the appropriate pool options, and click OK.

For online information about	On the Help menu, click Contents And Index, click the Index tab, and then type
Inserting project files	**insert projects** *or* **consolidate projects**
Sharing a resource pool	**resource pools** *or* **pool**

Customizing the Project Environment

Estimated time
25 min.

In this lesson you will learn how to:

- Change the display of information in the Gantt Chart.
- Format Gantt bars.
- Create text boxes on the Gantt Chart.
- Create a custom toolbar.

In Microsoft Project 98, you can make creating and managing a project schedule more efficient by customizing the look of Project. In the Gantt Chart view, you can customize the Gantt bars by changing the information that is displayed or by changing the color to make the bars stand out. New Gantt bars can also be created to display information that is not displayed by any predefined Gantt bar. Custom toolbars can be created to improve efficiency by displaying frequently used toolbar buttons, menus, and menu commands.

In this lesson, as you've worked on the corporate office relocation project, you've become very comfortable with Project and want to customize the Gantt Chart and Project environment. Before you present the project progress at the management review meeting, you make changes to the Gantt Chart view to emphasize specific information.

Start the lesson

1 Start Microsoft Project.

2 From the Project SBS Practice folder, open the Format file.

3 Save the file as Customizing Project in the Project SBS Practice folder.

Customizing the Gantt Chart

There are many elements to each view in Project. Each of these elements, such as font, color, pattern, or display, can be customized by changing the view settings. The Gantt Chart, along with views such as the Calendar and Usage views, can be manipulated to emphasize a task, a group of tasks, a period of time, or a specific area of importance.

Changes in color primarily affect the online viewing of the schedule, unless it is printed in color, or color slides or projection systems are used to communicate the information.

In the following exercise, you change the color of the nonworking time and a Gantt bar on the Gantt Chart to emphasize the information. In addition, you create a new bar style to display slack time in the project and add a text box to point out when the slack time should be used.

Change the color of the timescale

In this exercise, you change the color of the time scale so that nonworking periods are emphasized.

1 On the Format menu, click Timescale, and then click the Nonworking Time tab.

The Timescale dialog box appears. The Nonworking Time tab is selected.

Changing the color of the non-working bands only affects the current file.

2 Click the Color down arrow, and then click the fourth color in the list, bright green.

A preview of the color change is displayed in the dialog box.

3 Click OK.

The change is made to the Gantt Chart.

> **TIP** The appearance of Link Lines can also be changed. On the Format menu, click Layout. The settings for link style, date format, line width, rounding, splits, and drawings can be changed.

Change the font

In this exercise, you change the font used in the field for the main summary task.

1 Click in the Task Name field for task 1, Corporate Relocation.

To change the formatting of all text in a column, click the appropriate column heading. To change the format for an entire table, click the Select All button.

2 On the Formatting toolbar, click the Font down arrow, and then click Times New Roman.

3 On the Formatting toolbar, click the Font Size down arrow, and then click 12.

The font changes to Times New Roman, and the font size changes to 12 pt.

4 Save the file.

TIP To preview formatting changes to the font, font size, font style, and color before they are applied, use the Font dialog box. On the Format menu, click Font. Select the appropriate formats, and click OK.

Formatting the Gantt Bars

If a specific task has special requirements or project implications, you can call attention to that task by formatting the associated Gantt bar separately from other bars of a similar type. The Gantt bar can be changed by adding text to the left, right, top, bottom, or inside of a Gantt bar. The type, color, pattern, and shape of the start, middle, and end of a Gantt bar can also be changed. Individual bar formatting overrides category formatting.

To call attention to all tasks of a certain type, the format of the Gantt bars that represent that type of task can be changed using bar styles. Bar styles can be used to change predefined Gantt bars or to create new Gantt bars. For example, you can create a new Gantt bar to show available slack or to call attention to delayed tasks.

In addition to changing individual Gantt bar formats and bar styles for categories of tasks, the GanttChartWizard can quickly and easily format the Gantt Chart display. The GanttChartWizard can create custom settings, and it can format the critical path, baseline information, and status information.

Format a Gantt bar

In this exercise, you change the color of a single Gantt bar.

1 Place the mouse pointer over the Gantt bar for task 5, Locate new site.

The pointer changes to a four-headed arrow.

You can also select the task, and then, on the Format menu, click Bar.

2 Double-click the Gantt bar for task 5, Locate new site.

The Format Bar dialog box appears. The Bar Shape tab is selected.

3 In the Middle Bar area, click the Color down arrow, and then click the seventh color in the list, bright pink.

4 Click OK.

The Gantt bar color is changed to bright pink. The progress bar is still black.

NOTE On a progressed Gantt bar, depending where you double-click the Gantt bar or the progress line, that area will be changed. To change the Gantt bar, be sure the mouse pointer is a four-headed arrow. To change the progress bar, be sure the mouse pointer is a left-pointing arrow.

Create a bar style

In this exercise, you create a bar style to display Slack Time.

1 Press F5, type **29**, and press ENTER.

The Gantt Chart scrolls to task 29, Moving.

2 On the Format menu, click Bar Styles.

The Bar Styles dialog box appears.

3 Scroll down, and select the first blank field in the Name column.

4 Type **Slack Time**, and then press TAB.

The Bar tab is active.

5 In the Middle Bar area, click the Shape down arrow, and then click the fifth shape in the list.

6 In the Middle Bar area, click the Color down arrow, and then click the 13th color in the list, purple.

7 Click in the Show For Tasks field, click the down arrow, and then click Not Started.

Only those tasks that have not started have a Slack Time bar.

8 Click in the From field, click the down arrow, and then click Early Start.

9 Click in the To field, click the down arrow, and then click Finish.

Name	Appearance	Show For ... Tasks	Row	From	To
Rolled Up Milestone	◇	Milestone,Rolled Up,Not Summ.	1	Start	Start
Rolled Up Progress	▬▬▬	Normal,Rolled Up,Not Summary	1	Actual Start	Complete Through
Split	....	Split	1	Start	Finish
External Tasks	▬▬▬	External Tasks	1	Start	Finish
Project Summary	▼▬▬▼	Project Summary	1	Start	Finish
Slack Time	▬▬▬	Not Started	1	Early Start	Late Finish

Bar Styles

Cut Row | Paste Row | Insert Row

Late Finish

Text | Bars

Start shape — Shape: — Type: — Color:

Middle bar — Shape: — Pattern: — Color:

End shape — Shape: — Type: — Color:

10 Click OK.

The new bar style, Slack Time, is displayed for tasks that have not started and have total slack. Your screen should look similar to the following
illustration.

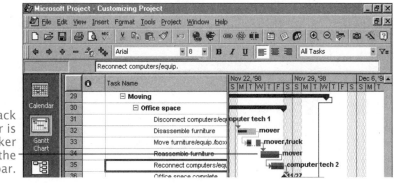

The slack
time bar is
the darker
half of the
taskbar.

11 Save the file.

Creating Text Boxes on the Gantt Chart

Notes can be saved for both tasks and resources to document additional information. These notes can be viewed only in the Notes box on the Task Information dialog box, the Resource Information dialog box, or in the Notes field. Occasionally, it would be useful to have additional information displayed directly on the Gantt Chart to quickly identify important points. For example, you need notes about tasks to be visible to the audience during a presentation. Using the drawing tools on the Drawing toolbar, you can draw text boxes on the Gantt Chart.

Create a text box

In this exercise, you draw a text box on the Gantt Chart to add information about the slack time bars.

Text Box

1 Right-click a toolbar, and then click Drawing.

The Drawing toolbar is displayed under the Formatting toolbar.

2 On the Drawing toolbar, click the Text Box button.

The pointer changes to a crosshair.

3 To the left of the Gantt bars for tasks 34, 35, and 36, drag to create a 1-inch by 1-inch box.

4 Type **Slack time to be used if server room tasks slip.**, and then click outside the text box.

5 On the Drawing toolbar, click the Arrow button.

6 Drag the crosshair from the right side of the text box to the left of the Gantt bar for task 35.

7 Click anywhere in the Gantt Chart.

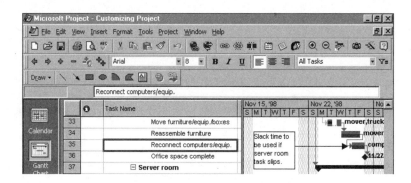

8 Right-click a toolbar, and then click Drawing.

The Drawing toolbar is hidden.

9 Save the file.

 TIP Text boxes can be resized. To resize a text box, click the text box to select it. Place the mouse pointer over a sizing handle and drag to the appropriate size.

Creating Custom Toolbars, Menus, and Commands

Toolbar buttons are used to provide quick access to menu commands and procedures. Custom toolbars can be created to streamline the work environment by organizing the most frequently used buttons and menu commands on a single toolbar.

When a custom toolbar is created, Project saves it in the global template. Any other project files that are opened on the computer using the global template have access to the new toolbar. Toolbars can also be saved with specialized templates so that the toolbar is only available to the project file created from that template.

In the following exercises, you create a custom toolbar. The toolbar displays two buttons you use to open frequently used dialog boxes. You also add the Tools menu, which has commands that you use on a regular basis, and a single command to open the Project Information dialog box.

NOTE If a custom button is created and placed on a built-in toolbar, resetting the built-in toolbar to its original appearance deletes the custom button.

Create a custom toolbar

In this exercise, you create a custom toolbar that includes the toolbar buttons and the menu commands you use most often.

1   On the View menu, point to Toolbars, and then click Customize.

The Customize dialog box appears. The Toolbars tab is selected.

2   Click New.

The New Toolbar dialog box appears.

3   In the Toolbar Name dialog box, type **Mine**, and click OK.

The new toolbar name is added to the Toolbars list. A blank toolbar is displayed on the screen.

When you drag a button onto a toolbar, an I-beam is displayed to indicate where the button will be placed.

4   Drag the Mine toolbar to the left below the Customize dialog box.

TIP If you create a custom toolbar and then later decide it is not needed, the toolbar can be deleted. On the View menu, point to Toolbars, and then click Customize. On the Customize dialog box, click the Toolbars tab. Click the appropriate toolbar name, and then click Delete. Toolbars can also be deleted from the Organizer.

Place buttons on a toolbar

For a demonstration of how to place buttons on a toolbar, refer to page xxviii in the Installing and Using the Practice Files Section.

In this exercise, you place several frequently used buttons on the custom toolbar.

1   Click the Commands tab.

All menu commands and buttons are accessible from the Commands tab.

2   In the Categories box, click Tools.

The buttons and commands in the Tools category are displayed.

Organizer
The Organizer is discussed further in Lesson 13, "Customizing Tables, Views, and Reports."

3   In the Commands box, scroll until the Organizer button is displayed, and then drag the Organizer button onto the toolbar.

The Organizer button is displayed on the toolbar.

4   In the Categories box, click Project, and then, in the Commands box, drag the Tasks/Resource Notes button onto the toolbar.

Place a menu and a command on a toolbar

In this exercise, you place a frequently used command and menu on the custom toolbar.

1 In the Categories box, click All Commands.

2 In the Commands box, scroll until the ProjectSummaryInfo command is displayed, and then drag the ProjectSummaryInfo command onto the toolbar.

3 In the Categories box, click Built-In Menus.

4 In the Commands box, scroll until the Tools command is displayed, and then drag the Tools command onto the toolbar.

5 Click Close.

Your custom toolbar should look similar to the following illustration.

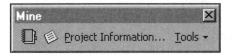

Use a custom toolbar

In this exercise, you use the buttons, command, and menu on the custom toolbar.

1 On the Mine toolbar, place the pointer over the Organizer button.

A ScreenTip is displayed with the button name. This is the same as with built-in toolbars.

2 On the Mine toolbar, click the Organizer button.

The Organizer dialog box appears.

3 Click Cancel.

4 On the Mine toolbar, click the Tools menu.

The Tools menu is displayed.

5 Press ESC.

6 On the Mine toolbar, click the Project Information command.
The Project Information dialog box appears.

7 Click Cancel.

8 Save the file.

TIP A toolbar can be placed on the bottom, side, or workspace of the screen. To move a toolbar to a new location, drag it by clicking a blank area between buttons or by clicking the title bar if it is not docked under the Menu bar.

One Step Further: Customizing a Button

A button on a toolbar can be customized by changing its function or image. The button image can be changed by editing or replacing the existing image without altering the functionality. If the functionality and the image are to be customized, the function should be changed before the image is changed so that no changes are lost when a command or macro is assigned to the button.

The Button Editor is used to edit the image of any toolbar button. A 16-color palette is provided in the Button Editor. An Erase selection, which applies the background color to the grid area that is selected, is also provided. The image can be moved within a grid, the grid can be cleared, and the changes can be accepted or cancelled. When a color is selected in the color palette, the color is applied by clicking a cell in the grid or dragging over multiple cells.

Customize a button

In this exercise, you change the appearance of a button by using the Button Editor.

1 Be sure that the Mine toolbar is displayed.

2 On the View menu, point to Toolbars, and then click Customize.

3 Be sure that the Commands tab is selected.

You can also right-click a toolbar, and then click Mine.

4 On the Mine toolbar, click the Organizer button.

While the Customize dialog box is open, the button command is not activated when clicked.

5 In the Customize dialog box, click Modify Selection, and then click Edit Button Image.

The Button Editor dialog box appears. The Organizer button image is displayed in the Picture box.

6 In the Colors area, click the first color in the fourth row, dark blue.

7 Click the individual light gray squares in the picture box to create a circle.

243

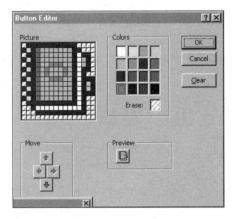

8 Click OK, and then click Close.

The changes to the button image are displayed.

9 Save the file.

Finish the lesson

1 On the Mine toolbar, click the Close button.

A Close button is displayed to the right of the title bar on a toolbar that is not docked below the Menu bar. The Mine toolbar is hidden.

2 To continue to another lesson, on the File menu, click Close.

3 If you are finished using Project for now, on the File menu, click Exit.

Lesson Summary

To	Do this
Change the color of the non-working bands in the Gantt Chart	On the Gantt Chart, double-click a gray nonworking band. In the Timescale dialog box, be sure that the Nonworking Time tab is selected. Click the Color down arrow, and then click a color. Click OK.
Change text, font, and font size	Select the appropriate text or column heading. On the Formatting toolbar, click the Font down arrow, and then click a font. On the Formatting toolbar, click the Font Size down arrow, and then click a font size.

To	Do this
Change the color of a Gantt bar	Double-click a Gantt bar. In the Format Bar dialog box, be sure that the Bar Shape tab is selected. In the Middle Bar area, click the Color down arrow, and click a color. Click OK.
Create a bar style	On the Format menu, click Bar Styles. In the Bar Styles dialog box, click the first empty field in the Name column. Type a name for the new bar. Click in the Appearance field. On the Bars tab, select the appropriate shape and color. Click in the Show For Tasks field, click the down arrow, and then click the appropriate field that the bar is to represent. Click in the From field, click the down arrow, and then click the appropriate start field for the bar. Click in the To field, click the down arrow, and then click the appropriate to field for the bar. Click OK.
Create text boxes	Right-click a toolbar, and then click Drawing. On the Drawing toolbar, click the Text Box button. Drag the crosshair pointer to create a text box of the appropriate size. Type the appropriate text, and then click outside the text box.

To	Do this
Create a custom toolbar	On the View menu, point to Toolbars, and then click Customize. In the Customize dialog box, on the Toolbars tab, click New. Type a name for thenew toolbar, and click OK. Drag the new toolbar away from the Customize dialog box. Click the Commands tab. In the Categories box, click the appropriate category. In the Commands box, drag the appropriate button, command, or menu to the new toolbar. Continue until all appropriate buttons, commands, and menus are added to the toolbar. Click Close.

For online information about	On the Help menu, click Contents And Index, click the Index tab, and then type
Customizing the Gantt Chart	**Gantt Chart** *or* **timescale** *or* **fonts**
Formatting Gantt bars	**Gantt bars**
Create custom bar styles	**custom Gantt bars**
Creating text boxes	**Drawing toolbar** *or* **drawing tools**
Creating custom toolbars	**customize toolbars** *or* **toolbars**

Part

5

Review &
Practice

Estimated time
25 min.

You will review and practice how to:

- Consolidate projects by inserting project files.
- Share a resource pool with project files.
- Customize the Gantt Chart view.
- Create a custom toolbar.

Before you complete this book, you can practice the skills you learned in Part 5 by working through this Review & Practice section. You will insert project files into another project file, share a resource pool, customize the Gantt Chart, and create a custom toolbar.

Scenario

The shareholders meeting project has been broken into three separate files, each representing a phase of the project. Each phase has been assigned to an assistant with you as the overall manager. The Accounting department has recently provided you with a list of resources that are available for assignment on each phase of the project.

247

Step 1: *Consolidate Projects*

As the manager of the shareholders meeting project and several other projects, you want an overall view of the projects under your direction. You also want to view the subtasks of each project when necessary. To accomplish this, you insert the phases of the shareholders meeting project into an existing project file that tracks all the projects under your control.

1 Open the Review5 file in the Project SBS Practice folder, and then save the file as Overall Projects without a baseline in the Project SBS Practice folder.

2 Open the Planning file in the Project SBS Practice folder, and then save the file as Preliminary Plan without a baseline in the Project SBS Practice folder. Close the file.

3 Open the Letter file in the Project SBS Practice folder, and then save the file as Notification Letter without a baseline in the Project SBS Practice folder. Close the file.

4 Open the Details file in the Project SBS Practice folder, and then save the file as Meeting Details without a baseline in the Project SBS Practice folder. Close the file.

5 Insert the Meeting Details, Notification Letter, and Preliminary Plan files under task 3, Shareholders Meeting.

6 Indent task 4, Preliminary Plan, task 5, Notification Letter, and task 6, Meeting Details, under task 3, Shareholders Meeting.

7 Link task 4, task 5, and task 6, in a finish-to-start relationship.

8 Display the subtasks for each summary task.

9 Hide the subtasks for each summary task.

10 Save the files without a baseline, and then close the files.

For more information about	See
Inserting project files	Lesson 14

Step 2: *Share a Resource Pool*

The resource list provided by the Accounting department has been turned into a resource pool file. Each phase of the shareholders project will share the pool. You start by sharing the pool with the Preliminary Plan phase file.

1 Open the Meetpool file in the Project SBS Practice folder, and then save the file as Meeting Resource Pool in the Project SBS Practice folder.

2 Open the Preliminary Planning file.

3   Share the Meeting Resource Pool resources with the Preliminary Plan project.

4   Verify the shared link in the Meeting Resource Pool file.

5   Save the Meeting Resource Pool file, and then close the file.

6   Save the Preliminary Planning file without a baseline, and then close the file.

For more information about	See
Sharing a resource pool	Lesson 14

Step 3:   *Customize the Gantt Chart*

To make a meeting on the Notification Letter phase of the shareholders meeting project more interesting, you make some changes to the Gantt Chart. You change the display of the nonworking time on the project and the font for the task names. You also change the color of the Gantt bar on the Approve letter task to emphasize it as a critical element of the project.

1   Open the Notification Letter file.

2   Change the color of the nonworking time on the Gantt Chart to teal.

3   Change the font and font size for the task names to Times New Roman 10 pt.

4   Change the color of the Gantt bar for task 4, Approve letter, to hot pink.

5   Save the file without a baseline.

For more information about	See
Changing the nonworking time bands	Lesson 15
Changing the font and font size	Lesson 15
Changing the color of a Gantt bar	Lesson 15

Step 4:   *Create a Custom Toolbar*

As you've been working with Project, you've noticed that there are several features that you use frequently that are not on the Standard or Formatting toolbar. You create a custom toolbar so you can quickly use those features.

1   Create a custom toolbar named My Work.

2   In the Insert category, add the Insert Recurring Task button.

3 In the Project category, add the Sort By button.

4 In the Tracking category, add the Update Tasks button.

5 In the All Commands category, add the Change Working Time command.

6 Use the buttons and commands on the My Work toolbar, closing each dialog box after viewing.

7 Hide the My Work toolbar.

8 Save the file without a baseline.

For more information about	See
Creating a custom toolbar	Lesson 15
Adding buttons and commands to a toolbar	Lesson 15

Finish the Review & Practice

1 On the View menu, point to Toolbars, and then click Customize.

The Customize dialog box appears.

2 On the Toolbars tab, click My Work, and then click Delete.

A message asking if you want to delete the toolbar is displayed.

3 Click OK, and then, on the Customize dialog box, click Close.

4 Close the Notification Letter file.

5 If you are finished using Project for now, on the File menu, click Exit.

Appendixes

If You Are New to Windows 95, Windows NT, or Microsoft Project 98

If you're new to Microsoft Windows 95, Microsoft Windows NT version 4.0, or to Microsoft Project 98, this appendix will show you all the basics you need to get started. You'll get an overview of Windows 95 and Windows NT features, and you'll learn how to use online Help to answer your questions and find out more about using these operating systems. You'll also get an introduction to Microsoft Project 98.

If You Are New to Windows 95 or Windows NT

Windows 95 and Windows NT are easy-to-use computer environments that help you handle the daily work that you perform with your computer. You can use either Windows 95 or Windows NT to run Microsoft Project—the explanations in this appendix apply to both operating systems. The way you use Windows 95, Windows NT, and programs designed for these operating systems is similar. The programs have a common look, and you use the same kinds of controls to tell them what to do. In this section, you'll learn how to use the basic program controls. If you're already familiar with Windows 95 or Windows NT, skip to the "What is Microsoft Project 98?" section.

Start Windows 95 or Windows NT

Starting Windows 95 or Windows NT is as easy as turning on your computer.

1   If your computer isn't on, turn it on now.

In Windows 95, you will also be prompted for a username and password if your computer is configured for user profiles.

2 If you are using Windows NT, press CTRL+ALT+DEL to display a dialog box asking for your username and password. If you are using Windows 95, you will see this dialog box if your computer is connected to a network.

3 Type your username and password in the appropriate boxes, and then click OK.

If you don't know your username or password, contact your system administrator for assistance.

☒

Close

4 If you see the Welcome dialog box, click the Close button.

Your screen should look similar to the following illustration.

My Computer   Desktop

My Computer

Network Neighborhood

Recycle Bin

My Briefcase

Set Up The Microsoft Network

Start   10:50 AM

Start button   Taskbar   Mouse pointer

Using the Mouse

Although you can use the keyboard for most actions, many of these actions are easier to do by using a mouse. The mouse controls a pointer on the screen, as shown in the previous illustration. You move the pointer by sliding the mouse over a flat surface in the direction you want the pointer to move. If you run out of room to move the mouse, lift the mouse up, and then put it down in a more comfortable location.

You'll use five basic mouse actions throughout this book.

When you are directed to	Do this
Point to an item	Move the mouse to place the pointer on the item.
Click an item	Point to the item on your screen, and quickly press and release the left mouse button.
Right-click an item	Point to the item on your screen, and then quickly press and release the right mouse button. Clicking the right mouse button displays a shortcut menu from which you can choose from a list of commands that apply to that item.
Double-click an item	Point to the item, and then quickly press and release the left mouse button twice.
Drag an item	Point to an item, and then hold down the left mouse button as you move the pointer.

IMPORTANT In this book, we assume that your mouse is set up so that the left button is the primary button and the right button is the secondary button. If your mouse is configured the opposite way, for left-handed use, use the right button when we tell you to use the left, and vice versa.

Using Window Controls

All programs designed for use on computers that have Windows 95 or Windows NT installed have common controls that you use to scroll, size, move, and close a window.

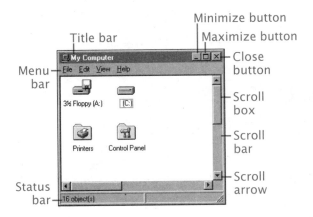

To	Do this	Button
Move, or *scroll*, vertically or horizontally through the contents of a window that extends beyond the screen	Click a scroll bar or scroll arrow, or drag the scroll box. The previous illustration identifies these controls.	
Enlarge a window to fill the screen	Click the Maximize button, or double-click the window's title bar.	
Restore a window to its previous size	Click the Restore button, or double-click the window title bar. When a window is maximized, the Maximize button changes to the Restore button.	
Reduce a window to a button on the taskbar	Click the Minimize button. To display a minimized window, click its button on the taskbar.	
Move a window	Drag the window title bar.	
Close a window	Click the Close button.	

Using Menus

Just like a restaurant menu, a program menu provides a list of options from which you can choose. On program menus, these options are called *commands*. To select a menu or a menu command, you click the item you want.

NOTE You can also use the keyboard to make menu selections. Press ALT to activate the menu bar, and press the key that corresponds to the highlighted or underlined letter of the menu name. Then, press the key that corresponds to the highlighted or underlined letter of the command name.

Open and make selections from a menu

In the following exercise, you'll open and make selections from a menu.

1 On the Desktop, double-click the My Computer icon.

   The My Computer window opens.

You can also press ALT+E to open the Edit menu.

2 In the My Computer window, click Edit on the menu bar.

   The Edit menu is displayed. Some commands are dimmed; this means that they aren't available.

Command is not available.

Shortcut
key

Command is available.

3 Click the Edit menu name to close the menu.

The menu closes.

*On a menu, a
check mark
indicates that
multiple items
in this group of
commands can
be selected at
one time. A
bullet mark
indicates that
only one item in
this group can
be selected at
one time.*

4 Click View on the menu bar to open the View menu.

5 On the View menu, click Toolbar.

The View menu closes, and a toolbar is displayed below the menu bar.

Toolbar

6 On the View menu, click List.

The items in the My Computer window now appear in a list, rather
than as icons.

7 On the toolbar, click the Large Icons button.

Clicking a button on a toolbar is a quick way to select a command.

Large Icons

8 On the View menu, point to Arrange Icons.

A cascading menu is displayed listing additional menu choices. When
a right-pointing arrow appears after a command name, it indicates
that additional commands are available.

9 Click anywhere outside the menu to close it.

10 On the menu bar, click View, and then click Toolbar again.

The View menu closes, and the toolbar is now hidden.

11 In the upper-right corner of the My Computer window, click the Close button to close the window.

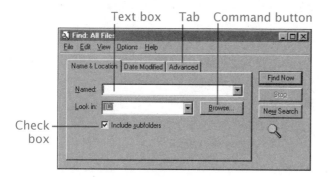

Close

> **TIP** If you do a lot of typing, you might want to learn the key combinations for commands you use frequently. Pressing the key combination is a quick way to perform a command by using the keyboard. If a key combination is available for a command, it will be listed to the right of the command name on the menu. For example, CTRL+C is listed on the Edit menu as the key combination for the Copy command.

Using Dialog Boxes

When you choose a command name that is followed by an ellipsis (...), a dialog box will appear so that you can provide more information about how the command should be carried out. Dialog boxes have standard features, as shown in the following illustration.

Text box   Tab   Command button

Check box

To move around in a dialog box, you click the item you want. You can also use the keyboard to select the item by holding down ALT as you press the underlined letter. Or, you can press TAB to move between items.

Display the Taskbar Properties dialog box

Some dialog boxes provide several categories of options displayed on separate tabs. You click the top of an obscured tab to make it visible.

1 On the taskbar, click the Start button.

The Start menu opens.

2 On the Start menu, point to Settings, and then click Taskbar.

3 In the Taskbar Properties dialog box, click the Start Menu Programs tab.

On this tab, you can customize the list of programs that is displayed on your Start menu.

Click here. When you click a check box
that is selected, you turn the option off.

4 Click the Taskbar Options tab, and then click to select the Show Small Icons In Start Menu check box.

When a check box is selected, it displays a check mark.

5 Click the check box a couple of times, and watch how the display in the dialog box changes.

Clicking any check box or option button turns the option off or on.

6 Click the Cancel button in the dialog box.

This closes the dialog box without changing any settings.

Getting Help with Windows 95 or Windows NT

When you're at work and you want to find more information about how to do a project, you might ask a co-worker or consult a reference book. To find out more about functions and features in Windows 95 or Windows NT, you can use the online Help system. For example, when you need information about how to print, the Help system is one of the most efficient ways to learn. The Windows 95 or Windows NT Help system is available from the Start menu. After the Help system opens, you can choose the type of help you want from the Help Topics dialog box.

To find instructions about broad categories, you can look on the Contents tab. Or, you can search the Help index to find information about specific topics. The Help information is short and concise, so you can get the exact information you need quickly. There are also shortcut icons in many Help topics that you can use to go directly to the task you want.

Viewing Help Contents

The Contents tab is organized like a book's table of contents. As you choose top-level topics, called *chapters*, you see a list of more detailed subtopics from which to choose. Many of these chapters have Tips and Tricks sections to help you work more efficiently as well as Troubleshooting sections to help you resolve problems.

Find Help about general categories

Suppose you want to learn more about using Calculator, a program that comes with Windows 95 and Windows NT. In this exercise, you'll look up information in the online Help system.

1   Click Start. On the Start menu, click Help.

    The Help Topics: Windows Help dialog box appears.

2   If necessary, click the Contents tab to make it active.

3   Double-click "Introducing Windows" or "Introducing Windows NT."

    A set of subtopics is displayed.

4   Double-click "Using Windows Accessories."

5   Double-click "For General Use."

6 Double-click "Calculator: For Making Calculations."

A Help topic window opens.

7 Read the Help information, and then click the Close button to close the
Help window.

Finding Help About Specific Topics

You can find specific Help topics by using the Index tab or the Find tab. The
Index tab is organized like a book's index. Keywords for topics are organized
alphabetically. You can either scroll through the list of keywords or type the
keyword you want to find. You can then select from one or more topic choices.

With the Find tab, you can also enter a keyword. The main difference is that
you get a list of all Help topics in which that keyword appears, not just the
topics that begin with that word.

Find Help about specific topics by using the Help index

In this exercise, you use the Help index to learn how to change the background
pattern of your Desktop.

1 Click Start, and on the Start menu, click Help.

The Help Topics dialog box appears.

2 Click the Index tab to make it active.

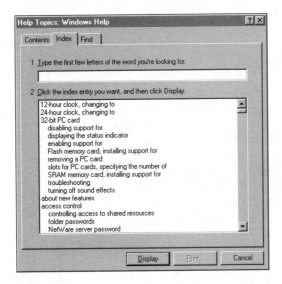

3 In the Type The First Few Letters Of The Word You're Looking For box,
type **display**

A list of display-related topics is displayed.

4 Click the topic named "background pictures or patterns, changing," and then click Display.

The Topics Found dialog box appears.

5 Be sure that the topic named "Changing the background of your desktop" is selected, and then click Display.

6 Read the Help topic.

7 Click the shortcut icon in step 1 of the Help topic.

Shortcut

The Display Properties dialog box appears. If you want, you can immediately perform the task you are looking up in Help.

8 Click the Close button on the Display Properties dialog box.

Close

9 Click the Close button on the Windows Help window.

> **NOTE** You can print any Help topic, if you have a printer installed on your computer. Click the Options button in the upper-left corner of any Help topic window, click Print Topic, and click OK. To continue searching for additional topics, you can click the Help Topics button in any open Help topic window.

Find Help about specific topics by using the Find tab

In this exercise, you use the Find tab to learn how to change your printer's settings.

1 Click Start, and then click Help to display the Help Topics dialog box.

2 Click the Find tab to make it active.

```
┌─────────────────────────────────────────────────┐
│ Help Topics: Windows Help                  ? X   │
├─────────────────────────────────────────────────┤
│ Contents │ Index │ Find │                        │
│                                                   │
│ 1 Type the word(s) you want to find              │
│ ┌─────────────────────────────┬─┐  ┌──────────┐ │
│ │                             │▼│  │  Clear   │ │
│ └─────────────────────────────┴─┘  └──────────┘ │
│ 2 Select some matching words to narrow your search  ┌──────────┐ │
│ ┌───────────────────────────────┬─┐ │ Options... │ │
│ │ a                             │▲│ └──────────┘ │
│ │ A                             │ │ ┌──────────┐ │
│ │ able                          │ │ │Find Similar..│ │
│ │ about                         │ │ └──────────┘ │
│ │ above                         │ │ ┌──────────┐ │
│ │ accept                        │▼│ │ Find Now │ │
│ │ access                        │ │ └──────────┘ │
│ └───────────────────────────────┴─┘ ┌──────────┐ │
│                                      │ Rebuild... │ │
│ 3 Click a topic, then click Display  └──────────┘ │
│ ┌─────────────────────────────────────────────┬─┐ │
│ │ Accessories: Playing Windows games          │▲│ │
│ │ Accessories: Using a parallel or serial cable to connect to a computer │ │
│ │ Accessories: Using Backup to back up your files │ │
│ │ Accessories: Using Briefcase to keep documents up-to-date │ │
│ │ Accessories: Using Calculator to make calculations │ │
│ │ Accessories: Using CD Player to play compact discs │ │
│ │ Accessories: Using Dial-Up Networking to connect to a computer or network │▼│ │
│ └─────────────────────────────────────────────┴─┘ │
│ ┌──────────────────┐ ┌─────────────────────────┐ │
│ │ 351 Topics Found │ │ All words, Begin, Auto, Pause │ │
│ └──────────────────┘ └─────────────────────────┘ │
│         ┌─────────┐ ┌────────┐ ┌────────┐         │
│         │ Display │ │ Print.. │ │ Cancel │         │
│         └─────────┘ └────────┘ └────────┘         │
└─────────────────────────────────────────────────┘
```

3   If you see a wizard, click Next, and then click Finish to complete and close the wizard.

The wizard creates a search index for your Help files. This might take a few minutes. The next time you use Find, you won't have to wait for the list to be created.

The Find tab is displayed.

4   In the text box, type **print**

All topics that have to do with printing are displayed in the list box at the bottom of the tab.

5   In step 3 of the Help dialog box, click the "Changing printer settings" topic, and then click Display.

The Help topic is displayed.

6   Read the Help topic, and then click the Close button on the Windows Help window.

Find Help in a dialog box

Almost every dialog box includes a question mark Help button in the upper-right corner of its window. When you click this button and then click any dialog box control, a Help window that explains what the control is and how to use it appears. In this exercise, you'll get help for a dialog box control.

1   Click Start, and then click Run.

The Run dialog box appears.

Help

2   Click the Help button.

The mouse pointer changes to an arrow with a question mark.

3   Click the Open text box.

A Help window providing information about how to use the Open text box appears.

4   Click anywhere on the Desktop, or press ESC, to close the Help window.

The mouse pointer returns to its previous shape.

5   In the Run dialog box, click Cancel.

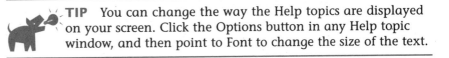

TIP You can change the way the Help topics are displayed on your screen. Click the Options button in any Help topic window, and then point to Font to change the size of the text.

What is Microsoft Project 98?

Microsoft Project 98 is a powerful and flexible project management program that helps you to efficiently plan, manage, and communicate a project schedule and project information. With Project, you can simplify the process of scheduling and tracking activities within a project. Project can help to quickly plan a project by organizing a task list and setting realistic time frames. Project maintains information about resources and task assignments to accurately schedule tasks when resources are available. Keeping track of a project budget is enhanced by resource and task costing. The many views, tables, and reports in Project make the process of disseminating information easier and more informative.

With Project, you can keep project information up-to-date in one location so decisions can be made based on accurate data. Project can also be used to create what-if scenarios to anticipate the effects of events on a project and to distribute information to everyone involved in a project.

Quit Windows 95 or Windows NT

1   If you are finished using Windows 95 or Windows NT, close any open windows by clicking the Close button in each window.

2   Click Start, and then click Shut Down.

The Shut Down Windows dialog box appears.

3   Click Yes.

A message indicating that it is now safe to turn off your computer is displayed.

 ∠WARNING   To avoid loss of data or damage to your operating system, always quit Windows 95 or Windows NT by using the Shut Down command on the Start menu before you turn off your computer.

Using Workgroup Features

In this lesson you will learn how to:

- Set up a workgroup.
- Send task assignment requests.
- Accept or decline task assignment requests.
- Request task status reports.
- Submit task status reports.
- Send task updates.
- Respond to task updates.

In this appendix section, you learn the basics of setting up, administering, and working as a member of a *workgroup* using your current Project files and appropriate e-mail addresses.

Setting Up a Workgroup

Communication is one of the essential elements to completing a successful project. In Project, the responsibility of communicating and coordinating schedule details with the project team members can be accomplished by setting up a workgroup. A workgroup is a group of people composed of a *workgroup manager* and *workgroup members* who are working on the same project. By using e-mail, an *intranet*, or the *World Wide Web*, the process of communicating information among the workgroup is made faster and easier.

For more infor-
mation on how
to setup
Workgroup Fea-
tures, consult
the Microsoft
Project User
Guide or
Microsoft
Project Help.

The first step in setting up a workgroup is to ensure that each workgroup member can communicate across the workgroup. Each member can communicate through e-mail, an intranet, or the Web. The requirements for each communication method are listed below.

- The workgroup manager must have Project installed on his or her computer for any communication method.

- If the workgroup is using e-mail as their communication method, they must be using an *MAPI-compliant*, 32-bit e-mail system. If the workgroup member does not have Project installed on his or her computer, Wgsetup.exe must be run on the computer. This enables the workgroup member's e-mail to receive and send workgroup messages.

- If the workgroup is using an intranet, each team member, including the workgroup manager, must have a *Web browser* to access the *TeamInbox*. They must also have access to the network and Web server.

- If all or some of the workgroup will be using the World Wide Web, they must have a Web browser to access the TeamInbox, an *Internet* connection and address, and access to the Web server.

When using an intranet or the Web as the communication method, a *WebInbox* and a TeamInbox is established to receive and track workgroup messages. Using a Web browser, workgroup members log on to the TeamInbox to receive and respond to workgroup messages. The workgroup manager then opens the WebInbox in Project to receive workgroup member responses.

Configure Project for a workgroup

In this exercise, the workgroup manager's computer is configured for the workgroup.

1 On the Tools menu, click Options, and then click the Workgroup tab.

2 Click the Default Workgroup Messaging For Resources down arrow, and then click the appropriate messaging method.

   For e-mail, skip to step 5. For an intranet or the Web, go to step 3.

3 In the Web Server URL (For Resource) box, type the URL for the Web server that is servicing the workgroup, plus the folder name where the workgroup messages are placed and tracked.

4 In the Web Server Root (For Manager) box, type the path to where the Web server software resides, plus the folder name where the workgroup messages are placed and tracked.

5 Select the Notify When New Web Messages Arrive check box so you are notified when a new workgroup message arrives from the Web.

6 Select the Send Hyperlink In E-Mail Note check box to have a hyperlink to the TeamInbox added to e-mail messages.

7 Click Set As Default to have the settings apply to all project files.

8 Click OK.

If Web or E-Mail And Web was selected as the communications method, a message indicating that it needs to copy files to the Web server is displayed.

If the workgroup is using e-mail as the communications method and the resource's e-mail address is different than the resource's name in Project, an e-mail address must be entered for each resource. An e-mail address can be added in the Resource Information dialog box. On the General tab, type the e-mail address in the Email box. If the e-mail address is outside the organization, be sure to include the entire address.

Managing a Workgroup

Once a workgroup is established, the workgroup manager can assign tasks to the workgroup members, request status reports, and send task updates. The workgroup members can accept or decline task assignments, submit status reports, respond to a task update, route a project file, and send notes on tasks.

The Workgroup toolbar provides tools for exchanging information with others in a workgroup. The Workgroup toolbar is described in the following table.

Button	Name	Description
	Team Assign	Notifies a resource using e-mail, an intranet, or the World Wide Web that the workgroup manager wants to assign the resource to a task.
	TeamUpdate	Notifies resources using e-mail, an intranet, or the World Wide Web about changes in their assigned tasks.
	TeamStatus	Requests the current status of tasks from the resources assigned to the tasks using e-mail, an intranet, or the World Wide Web.
	WebInbox	Opens the WebInbox.
	Set Reminder	Sets reminders in Microsoft Outlook for the selected tasks.

Button	Name	Description
	Send To Mail Recipient	Sends an e-mail message to project participants.
	Send To Routing Recipient	Adds to or changes the mail routing slip for the current project file.
	Send To Exchange Folder	Sends a copy of the project file to an Exchange-based folder that you specify when prompted.
	Insert Project	Inserts a project file into your currently displayed file.
	Open From Database	Opens a file that was saved to a Microsoft Access database or another database.
	Save To Database As	Saves a file to a Microsoft Access data base or another database.

Display the Workgroup toolbar

In this exercise, you display the Workgroup toolbar.

1   Right-click anywhere in the toolbar area.

    A shortcut menu is displayed.

2   Click Workgroup.

    The Workgroup toolbar is displayed under the Formatting toolbar.

Assigning and Accepting Tasks

TeamAssign messages notify a resource via e-mail, an intranet, or the World Wide Web that the workgroup manager wants to assign them to a task. Workgroup members can then respond to the workgroup manager by accepting or declining the proposed assignment. TeamAssign is accessed by clicking the TeamAssign button on the Workgroup toolbar or pointing to Workgroup on the Tools menu, and then clicking TeamAssign.

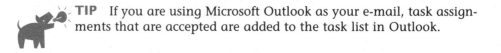

TIP   If you are using Microsoft Outlook as your e-mail, task assignments that are accepted are added to the task list in Outlook.

Assign tasks to resources

In this exercise, the workgroup manager notifies a resource of a proposed assignment.

1 Open a current Project file.

2 Select the task or tasks to be assigned.

If only one task or no tasks are selected, the Workgroup Mail dialog box appears. All tasks or only the selected task option can be selected.

3 On the Workgroup toolbar, click the TeamAssign button.

The TeamAssign dialog box appears.

TeamAssign				? X
Send	Cancel			

To:

Subject: |TeamAssign

Date: Tue 9/2/97

Please reply to this message and let me know if the task assignments listed below are acceptable.
Thank you.

To:	Task Name	Work	Start	Finish
	Demolition of existing space	3d	Tue 10/6/98	Thu 10/8/98
	Frame interior walls	4d	Fri 10/9/98	Wed 10/14/98
	Install electrical	6.5d	Thu 10/15/98	Fri 10/23/98
	Install voice and data lines	3d	Fri 10/23/98	Wed 10/28/98

Resources already assigned to a task that have not confirmed their assignment are listed automatically in the To field for the task.

4 In the Subject box, type a subject if other than TeamAssign.

5 In the message area, type an appropriate message.

Assign Resources

6 Click the Assign Resources button.

The Resource Assignment dialog box appears.

7 Click a resource.

If e-mail is being used for the workgroup, click address, and select the e-mail address for the resource. The address can also be typed directly into the To field.

8 Click Assign.

9 Repeat steps 3-7 for each task in the TeamAssign dialog box.

10 Click Send.

NOTE When a workgroup manager requests a resource for a task, an envelope icon with a question mark is displayed in the indicators field. The icon signifies that the resource assignment request has not yet been updated with a response from the resource.

Accept a task assignment request

In this exercise, the workgroup member accepts a task assignment from the workgroup manager using e-mail.

1 Open the TeamAssign message.

2 Click Reply.

The TeamAssign dialog box appears.

Type No in the Accept field to decline a task assignment request.

3 In the message area, type an appropriate return message.

4 In the Accept field, type Yes.

The request will be accepted.

5 In the Comments field, type any applicable information.

6 Click Send.

A task assignment request response is sent to the workgroup manager.

NOTE If a workgroup member is using an intranet or the Web to communicate, open the TeamInbox, and then open the TeamAssign message. To accept a task assignment request, select the Accept check box. To decline a task assignment request, clear the Accept check box.

Requesting and Submitting Status Reports

Once a project is underway, TeamStatus messages can be used to monitor the project. Using TeamStatus messages, the responses can be automatically incorporated into the schedule. This automates the process of gathering and entering status information, thus saving time.

NOTE In Project, the workgroup manager can automatically incorporate responses to TeamAssign and TeamStatus messages into the schedule. In the WebInbox or e-mail program, open the response, and then click Update Project.

Request a status report

In this exercise, the workgroup manager requests a status report.

1   Open a current Project file.
2   Select the task or tasks status information for which the status report is being requested.
3   On the Workgroup toolbar, click the TeamStatus button.

Team Status

    The TeamStatus dialog box appears.
4   In the Subject box, type a subject if other than TeamStatus.
5   In the message area, type an appropriate message.
6   Click Send.

 WARNING   If the workgroup manager is using e-mail to update the schedule, do not automatically update resource usage in the project file based on the percent complete of each task. Automatically updating by percentages will delete the information entered by the resource in the status request message that was incorporated into the schedule.

Submit a status report

In this exercise, a workgroup member submits a response to a status report request using e-mail.

1   Open the TeamStatus message.
2   In the appropriate fields, enter the actual work performed on each task for each period. (For example, overtime hours in the Overtime field.) If an overtime field is not available, enter then hours in the Comments field.
3   In the Remaining Work field, type an estimate of the amount of time remaining to complete the task.
4   In the Message box, type an appropriate message.
5   In the Comments field, type any applicable information.
6   Click Send.

 NOTE   If a workgroup member is using an intranet or the Web to communicate, open the TeamInbox, and then open the TeamStatus message.

Sending and Receiving Task Updates

A TeamUpdate message is used to indicate changes to the workgroup that the workgroup manager has already made to the schedule. When workgroup members respond, changes are not rejected in the same way tasks are declined. However, replies to the workgroup manager can communicate any concerns or issues regarding the TeamUpdate.

Send a task update

In this exercise, the workgroup manager sends a task update request using e-mail.

1 On the Workgroup toolbar, click the TeamUpdate button.
2 In the Subject box, type a subject for the update.
3 In the message area, type an appropriate message.
4 Click Send.

Reply to a task update request

In this exercise, a workgroup member sends a reply to a task update request using e-mail.

1 Open the TeamUpdate message.
2 Review the changes to the schedule in the message text.
3 Click Reply.
4 In the message box, type an appropriate reply message.

Additional comments can be added to the Comments field.

4 Click Send.

 NOTE If a workgroup member is using an intranet or the Web to communicate, open the TeamInbox, and then open the TeamUpdate message.

Finish the appendix lesson

1 Right-click anywhere in the toolbar area, and then click Workgroup.
The Workgroup toolbar is hidden.
2 To continue to another lesson, on the File menu, click Close.
3 If you are finished using Project for now, on the File menu, click Exit.

Appendix Summary

To	Do This	Button
Display the Workgroup toolbar	Right-click anywhere in the toolbar area, and then click Workgroup.	
Assign a task to a resource using TeamAssign	For the workgroup manager, select the task or tasks to be assigned. On the Workgroup toolbar, click the Team Assign button. In the Subject box, type a subject. In the message area, type an appropriate message. Click the Assign Resources button. Click a resource, and then click Assign. Repeat for any additional resource assignments for the selected tasks. Click Send.	
Accept or decline a resource assignment request	For the workgroup member, open the TeamAssign message. Click Reply. In the message area, type an appropriate return message. In the Accept field, type Yes to accept and No to decline. Click Send.	
Request a status report	For the workgroup manager, select the task or tasks for which you'd like a status report. On the Workgroup toolbar, click the TeamStatus button. In the Subject box, type subject. In the message area, type an appropriate message. Click Send.	
Submit a status report	For the workgroup member, open the TeamStatus message. In the appropriate fields, enter the actual work information. In the Remaining Word field, enter the remaining work estimates. In the Message box, type an appropriate message. Click Send.	

To	Do This	Button
Send a task update	For the workgroup manager, on the Workgroup toolbar, click the TeamUpdate button. In the Subject box, type the appropriate subject. In the message area, type an appropriate message. Click Send.	
Respond to a task update	For the workgroup member, open the TeamUpdate message. Review the changes to the schedule in the message text. Click Reply. In the message box, type an appropriate reply message. Click Send.	

For online information about	On the Help menu, click Contents And Index, click the Index tab, and then type
Setting up a workgroup	**workgroup requirements**
Assigning tasks	**workgroup tasks**
Accepting or declining task assignments	**workgroup tasks**
Requesting a status report	**status updates** *or* **TeamStatus message**
Submitting a status report	**status updates** *or* **TeamStatus message**
Sending a task update	**TeamUpdate message**
Responding to task updates	**TeamUpdate message**

Using PERT Charts

In this appendix you will learn how to:

- View a PERT Chart for a project.
- Add a task in PERT Chart view.
- Change the layout and format of the PERT Chart view.
- Display the Task PERT view.

In this appendix, you learn the basics of the *PERT Chart* view. You display the PERT Chart view and identify the different elements within the view. You add a new task to the PERT chart, create a new dependency, and assign a resource to the new task. You change the layout and format of the view to display the information you need. You also display the *Task PERT* view in a combination view.

Start the lesson

1 Start Microsoft Project.
2 From the Project SBS Practice folder, open the PERT file.
3 Save the file as PERT Chart without a baseline in the Project SBS Practice folder.

Understanding a PERT Chart

The PERT Chart, which stands for Program Evaluation and Review Techniques, is a graphical view of the dependencies between tasks in a project schedule. A PERT Chart represents each task in the project as a box, called a *node*. In the node, up to five fields of information can be viewed. The default node fields are: task name, task ID number, scheduled duration, scheduled start date, and scheduled finish date. Each field can be changed to display the desired information. The line connecting the nodes, called a task link, reflects the task dependencies.

The border around each node indicates whether the node is a summary task, a subtask, or a milestone, and whether the task is on the critical path. By default, nodes on the critical path have a thick red or patterned border, non critical nodes have a thin black border, summary tasks have a shadow box border, and milestone tasks have a double or frame border. The following are examples of the different borders for the four task types.

Locate new site	
5	1w
Mon 9/18/00	Mon 9/25/00

Task

Corporate approval	
8	0d
Wed 10/4/00	Wed 10/4/00

Summary task

Planning	
2	32.38d
Mon 9/11/00	Wed 10/25/0

Milestone task

Move Warehouse	
1	7.5d
Mon 2/19/96	Wed 2/28/96

Subproject

Viewing the PERT Chart

The PERT Chart provides an overall view of a project. Any changes made to the PERT Chart are reflected in the other views in Project. The PERT Chart for a project can be viewed by clicking PERT Chart on the View menu. The scroll bars, or the Go To command, are used to move around in the PERT Chart. A node or a field in a node is selected when it is clicked. The magnification of the view can be changed to focus on the overall project or to focus on details of a task node.

View the PERT Chart

In this exercise, you display a project schedule in PERT Chart view.

1 On the View menu, click PERT Chart.

The PERT Chart view is displayed.

2 Use the scroll bar arrows to move through the PERT Chart, looking for the various node types.

Change the view magnification

In this exercise, you zoom out in the PERT Chart view to display more task nodes.

1 Press SHIFT+HOME, and then press CTRL+HOME.

The first task node is selected.

Zoom Out

2 On the Standard toolbar, click the Zoom Out button twice.

The magnification of the view changes.

Zoom In

3 On the Standard toolbar, click the Zoom In twice.

277

Adding and Deleting Nodes

A new task node can be added by using the mouse to drag across a blank area of the PERT Chart. The ID of the new task will be one greater than the currently selected task. All subsequent tasks are automatically renumbered, just as in Gantt Chart view. The New Task command, on the Insert menu, can also be used to add new nodes. When the New Task command is used, a new node is added to the right of the selected node. The Layout Now command, on the Format menu, is used to align new nodes with existing nodes.

Once a new node is created, there are two ways that task information can be entered. You can type directly in the node fields, or you can double-click a node to open the Task Information dialog box.

To delete a task node, select the node to be deleted, and then press DELETE or, on the Edit menu, click Delete Task. If a summary task node is deleted, all subtask nodes of that summary task are deleted.

Add a new task

In this exercise, you add a new task to the PERT Chart.

1 Press F5, type **5**, and press ENTER.

The node for task 5, Locate new site is selected.

2 In an empty area above task 5, drag to create a rectangle.

A new node is created. The size of the node is automatically formatted to that of the other nodes. The task name area is selected.

3 Type **Present proposal**, and press ENTER.

The task name is entered.

The field displaying 1 day is the duration field.

4 Click the duration field, type **2**, and press ENTER.

A task duration of two days is entered.

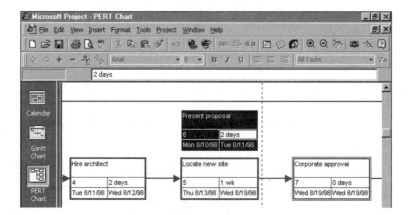

5 Save the file without a baseline.

Adding and Deleting Dependencies

A dependency is created between task nodes by dragging from the predecessor task to the successor task. A default, finish-to-start dependency is created with no lead or lag time. To change the dependency or add lead or lag time, double-click the line between the nodes to open the Task Dependency dialog box. A dependency can also be deleted from the Task Dependency dialog box.

If a new task node is added using the New Task command, a link should automatically be created based on the selected task. By default, the Autolink Inserted Or Moved Tasks check box is selected on the schedule tab in the Options dialog box.

Create a dependency between nodes

In this exercise, you create a dependency between the new task node and an existing task node.

1 Place the mouse pointer over the node for task 5, Locate new site.

The pointer changes to a plus sign.

2 Drag over the node for task 6, Present proposal.

The pointer changes to a link of chain while dragging between nodes. A finish-to-start dependency is created between task 5 and task 6.

3 Drag to create a dependency between task 6, Present proposal, and task 7, Corporate approval.

A finish-to start dependency is created between task 6 and 7.

Delete a dependency between nodes

In this exercise, you delete the dependency between two nodes.

1 Double-click the task link between the nodes for task 5, Locate new site, and task 7, Corporate approval.

The Task Dependency dialog box appears.

2 Click Delete.

The dependency is deleted.

3 Save the file without a baseline.

Changing the PERT Chart Layout and Format

There are many changes you can make to the layout and format of a PERT Chart to meet the required needs of an individual or project. Several of the layout and format changes are aligning new task nodes, changing the display of task links, formatting the node text, changing the style and color of node borders, and changing the information contained in any one of the node field boxes.

Align a new node

In this exercise, you align the new node with the existing nodes.

Zoom Out

1　On the Standard toolbar, click the Zoom Out button.

2　On the Format menu, click Layout Now.

　　The PERT Chart displays the first task in the project.

3　Press F5, type **6**, and press ENTER.

　　The new node is now aligned with the existing nodes based on the dependencies.

Change the layout options

In this exercise, you change the way the lines connecting the nodes are displayed.

1　On the Format menu, click Layout.

　　The Layout dialog box appears.

2　In the Links area, click the second option.

　　The second option displays the lines at right angles.

3　Click OK.

4　Press F5, type **22**, and press ENTER.

　　The view scrolls to display the task node for task 22, Install carpet: office space. The lines connecting the nodes are at right angles.

5　Save the file without a baseline.

Change the fields displayed

In this exercise, you replace the node field scheduled finish date with the resource initials field.

Zoom In

1　On the Standard toolbar, click the Zoom In button.

2　Double-click a blank area on the PERT Chart.

　　The Box Styles dialog box appears. The Boxes tab is selected.

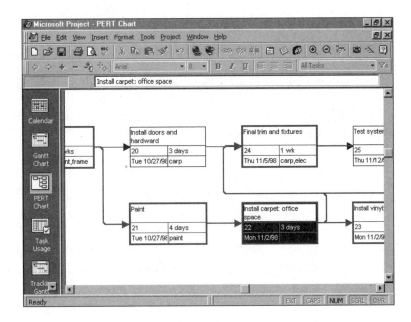

3 Click the 5 Finish down arrow, and then click Resource Initials.

4 Click OK.

The resource initials field is formatted for each node. The field is blank for task 22.

5 Save the file without a baseline.

Assigning Resources

Resources can be assigned to a task node by using the Assign Resource dialog box, or by typing the resource name or initials in a node field. To type the resource into a node, a field must first be made available for that information.

Assign a resource

In this exercise, you assign a resource to a task using the task node. The task node field was changed in the previous exercise.

1 Be sure that the node for task 22, Install carpet: office space, is selected.

2 Click in the lower-right field of the node for task 22.

3 Type **fc**, and press ENTER.

The resource initials are entered into the node field and the resource is assigned to the task.

4 Save the file without a baseline.

Using the Task PERT Chart

The Task PERT view is a more specific version of the PERT Chart, which shows the immediate predecessor and successor tasks of the selected task node. The Task PERT view displays dependency types and lead and lag time next to the task link lines. By viewing the PERT Chart and the Task PERT view together, the project can be viewed as a whole and as individual task dependencies. The Task PERT view is especially useful when used for troubleshooting or solving problems related to dependencies.

View task dependencies in detail

In this exercise, you use the Task PERT Chart to view task dependencies.

1 Double-click the split bar in the lower-right corner of the view.

The Task Form view is displayed in the bottom pane.

2 Click in the bottom pane to make it active.

3 On the View Bar, click the down arrow until the More Views icon is displayed, and then click the More Views icon.

The More Views dialog box appears.

4 In the View box, click Task PERT, and then click Apply.

The Task Pert view is displayed in the bottom pane.

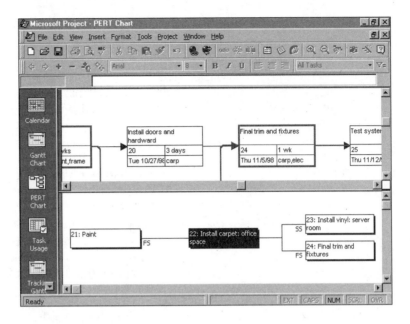

5 Click different nodes in the top pane to display the task dependencies in the bottom pane.

6 Double-click the split bar in the lower-right corner of the top pane.

The view returns to a single view of the PERT Chart.

7 Save the file without a baseline.

Finish the appendix

➤ If you are finished using Project, on the File menu, click Exit.

Appendix Summary

To	Do this
View the PERT Chart for a project schedule	Open the project file. On the View menu, click PERT Chart.
Add a new node	Select the node for the task that the new task should follow. On a blank area of the PERT Chart, drag to create a rectangle. Type the task name, and press ENTER. Click in the duration field for the task node, type the duration, and press ENTER.

To	Do this	Button
Create a dependency between task nodes	Place the mouse pointer over the predecessor node. Drag over the successor node.	
Align new nodes with existing node.	On the Format menu, click Layout Now.	
Change the fields displayed in the nodes on the PERT Chart	Double-click a blank area on the PERT Chart. Click the down arrow of the field being replaced. Select the appropriate field name of the new field. Click OK.	
Assign a resource to a task node	Change a node field to either resource name or resource initials. Click in the node field, type the appropriate resource information, and press ENTER. *or* Select the task node the resource is being assigned to. On the Standard toolbar, click the Assign Resources button. In the Assign Resources dialog box, click the resource to be assigned, and then click Assign. Click Close.	
Display the Task PERT view	Double-click the split bar. Click in the bottom pane to make it active. On the View Bar, click the down arrow until the More Views icon is displayed and then click the More Views icon. In the Views box, click Task PERT, and then click Apply.	

For online information about	On the Help menu, click Contents And Index, click the Index tab, and then type
Using the PERT Chart	**PERT Chart**
Adding and deleting nodes	**PERT Chart** *or* **PERT boxes**
Adding and deleting dependencies	**PERT Chart** *or* **PERT boxes**
Changing the PERT Chart layout and format	**PERT Chart** *or* **PERT boxes**
Viewing the Task PERT	**Task PERT view** *or* **PERT Chart**

Take productivity in stride.

Microsoft Press® *Step by Step* books provide quick and easy self-paced training that will help you learn to use the powerful word processor, spreadsheet, database, desktop information manager, and presentation applications of Microsoft Office 97, both individually and together. Prepared by the professional trainers at Catapult, Inc., and Perspection, Inc., these books present easy-to-follow lessons with clear objectives, real-world business examples, and numerous screen shots and illustrations. Each book contains approximately eight hours of instruction. Put Microsoft's Office 97 applications to work today, *Step by Step*.

Microsoft® Excel 97 Step by Step
U.S.A. $29.95 ($39.95 Canada)
ISBN 1-57231-314-5

Microsoft® Word 97 Step by Step
U.S.A. $29.95 ($39.95 Canada)
ISBN 1-57231-313-7

Microsoft® PowerPoint® 97
  Step by Step
U.S.A. $29.95 ($39.95 Canada)
ISBN 1-57231-315-3

Microsoft® Outlook™ 97 Step by Step
U.S.A. $29.99 ($39.99 Canada)
ISBN 1-57231-382-X

Microsoft® Access 97 Step by Step
U.S.A. $29.95 ($39.95 Canada)
ISBN 1-57231-316-1

Microsoft® Office 97 Integration
  Step by Step
U.S.A. $29.95 ($39.95 Canada)
ISBN 1-57231-317-X

Microsoft ·*Press*

Keep things **running** smoothly

around the **Office.**

These are *the* answer books for business users of Microsoft Office 97 applications. They are packed with everything from quick, clear instructions for new users to comprehensive answers for power users. The Microsoft Press® *Running* series features authoritative handbooks you'll keep by your computer and use every day.

Running Microsoft® Excel 97
Mark Dodge, Chris Kinata, and Craig Stinson
U.S.A. $39.95   ($54.95 Canada)
ISBN 1-57231-321-8

Running Microsoft® Word 97
Russell Borland
U.S.A. $39.95   ($53.95 Canada)
ISBN 1-57231-320-X

Running Microsoft® PowerPoint® 97
Stephen W. Sagman
U.S.A. $29.95   ($39.95 Canada)
ISBN 1-57231-324-2

Running Microsoft® Access 97
John L. Viescas
U.S.A. $39.95   ($54.95 Canada)
ISBN 1-57231-323-4

Running Microsoft® Office 97
Michael Halvorson and Michael Young
U.S.A. $39.95   ($53.95 Canada)
ISBN 1-57231-322-6

IMPORTANT—READ CAREFULLY BEFORE OPENING SOFTWARE PACKET(S). By opening the sealed packet(s) containing the software, you indicate your acceptance of the following Microsoft License Agreement.

MICROSOFT LICENSE AGREEMENT

Book Companion CD-ROM

This is a legal agreement between you (either an individual or an entity) and Microsoft Corporation. By opening the sealed software packet(s) you are agreeing to be bound by the terms of this agreement. If you do not agree to the terms of this agreement, promptly return the unopened software packet(s) and any accompanying written materials to the place you obtained them for a full refund.

MICROSOFT SOFTWARE LICENSE

1. GRANT OF LICENSE. Microsoft grants to you the right to use one copy of the Microsoft software program included with this book (the "SOFTWARE") on a single terminal connected to a single computer. The SOFTWARE is in "use" on a computer when it is loaded into the temporary memory (i.e., RAM) or installed into the permanent memory (e.g., hard disk, CD-ROM, or other storage device) of that computer. You may not network the SOFTWARE or otherwise use it on more than one computer or computer terminal at the same time. For the files and material referenced in this book which may be obtained from the Internet, Microsoft grants to you the right to use the materials in connection with the book. If you are a member of a corporation or business, you may reproduce the materials and distribute them within your business for internal business purposes in connection with the book. You may not reproduce the materials for further distribution.

2. COPYRIGHT. The SOFTWARE is owned by Microsoft or its suppliers and is protected by United States copyright laws and international treaty provisions. Therefore, you must treat the SOFTWARE like any other copyrighted material (e.g., a book or musical recording) except that you may either (a) make one copy of the SOFTWARE solely for backup or archival purposes, or (b) transfer the SOFTWARE to a single hard disk provided you keep the original solely for backup or archival purposes. You may not copy the written materials accompanying the SOFTWARE.

3. OTHER RESTRICTIONS. You may not rent or lease the SOFTWARE, but you may transfer the SOFTWARE and accompanying written materials on a permanent basis provided you retain no copies and the recipient agrees to the terms of this Agreement. You may not reverse engineer, decompile, or disassemble the SOFTWARE. If the SOFTWARE is an update or has been updated, any transfer must include the most recent update and all prior versions.

4. DUAL MEDIA SOFTWARE. If the SOFTWARE package contains more than one kind of disk (3.5", 5.25", and CD-ROM), then you may use only the disks appropriate for your single-user computer. You may not use the other disks on another computer or loan, rent, lease, or transfer them to another user except as part of the permanent transfer (as provided above) of all SOFTWARE and written materials.

5. SAMPLE CODE. If the SOFTWARE includes Sample Code, then Microsoft grants you a royalty-free right to reproduce and distribute the sample code of the SOFTWARE provided that you: (a) distribute the sample code only in conjunction with and as a part of your software product; (b) do not use Microsoft's or its authors' names, logos, or trademarks to market your software product; (c) include the copyright notice that appears on the SOFTWARE on your product label and as a part of the sign-on message for your software product; and (d) agree to indemnify, hold harmless, and defend Microsoft and its authors from and against any claims or lawsuits, including attorneys' fees, that arise or result from the use or distribution of your software product.

DISCLAIMER OF WARRANTY

The SOFTWARE (including instructions for its use) is provided "AS IS" WITHOUT WARRANTY OF ANY KIND. MICROSOFT FURTHER DISCLAIMS ALL IMPLIED WARRANTIES INCLUDING WITHOUT LIMITATION ANY IMPLIED WARRANTIES OF MERCHANTABILITY OR OF FITNESS FOR A PARTICULAR PURPOSE. THE ENTIRE RISK ARISING OUT OF THE USE OR PERFORMANCE OF THE SOFTWARE AND DOCUMENTATION REMAINS WITH YOU.

IN NO EVENT SHALL MICROSOFT, ITS AUTHORS, OR ANYONE ELSE INVOLVED IN THE CREATION, PRODUCTION, OR DELIVERY OF THE SOFTWARE BE LIABLE FOR ANY DAMAGES WHATSOEVER (INCLUDING, WITHOUT LIMITATION, DAMAGES FOR LOSS OF BUSINESS PROFITS, BUSINESS INTERRUPTION, LOSS OF BUSINESS INFORMATION, OR OTHER PECUNIARY LOSS) ARISING OUT OF THE USE OF OR INABILITY TO USE THE SOFTWARE OR DOCUMENTATION, EVEN IF MICROSOFT HAS BEEN ADVISED OF THE POSSIBILITY OF SUCH DAMAGES. BECAUSE SOME STATES/COUNTRIES DO NOT ALLOW THE EXCLUSION OR LIMITATION OF LIABILITY FOR CONSEQUENTIAL OR INCIDENTAL DAMAGES, THE ABOVE LIMITATION MAY NOT APPLY TO YOU.

U.S. GOVERNMENT RESTRICTED RIGHTS

The SOFTWARE and documentation are provided with RESTRICTED RIGHTS. Use, duplication, or disclosure by the Government is subject to restrictions as set forth in subparagraph (c)(1)(ii) of The Rights in Technical Data and Computer Software clause at DFARS 252.227-7013 or subparagraphs (c)(1) and (2) of the Commercial Computer Software — Restricted Rights 48 CFR 52.227-19, as applicable. Manufacturer is Microsoft Corporation, One Microsoft Way, Redmond, WA 98052-6399.

If you acquired this product in the United States, this Agreement is governed by the laws of the State of Washington.

Should you have any questions concerning this Agreement, or if you desire to contact Microsoft Press for any reason, please write: Microsoft Press, One Microsoft Way, Redmond, WA 98052-6399.

The
Microsoft® Project
Step by Step CD-ROM

The enclosed CD-ROM contains timesaving, ready-to-use practice files that complement the lessons in this book. To use the CD, you'll need Microsoft Project 98 and either the Windows 95 or the Windows NT version 4 operating system.

Before you begin the *Step by Step* lessons, read the "Installing and Using the Practice Files" section of this book. There you'll find detailed information about the contents of the CD and easy instructions telling you how to install the files on your computer's hard disk.

Please take a few moments to read the License Agreement on the previous page before using the enclosed CD.